The Politics
of Structural Adjustment
in Nigeria

The Politics of
Structural Adjustment
in Nigeria

EDITED BY

Adebayo O. Olukoshi

James Currey
LONDON

Heinemann Educational Books Nigeria Plc
IBADAN

Heinemann
PORTSMOUTH (N.H.)

James Currey is an imprint of Boydell & Brewer Ltd
PO Box 9, Woodbridge, Suffolk IP12 3DF, UK
and of Boydell & Brewer Inc.
668 Mount Hope Ave, Rochester, NY 14620-2731, USA
www.jamescurrey.com
www.boydellandbrewer.com

Heinemann
A division of Reed Elsevier Inc.
361 Hanover Street
Portsmouth, NH 03801-3912
USA

Heineman Educational Books Nigeria Plc
PMB 5205 Ibadan

ISBN 978–0–85255–130–1 (James Currey cloth)
ISBN 978–0–85255–131–8 (James Currey paper)

ISBN 978–0–435–08072–3 (Heinemann)

ISBN 978–978–129–504–1 (Heinemann Nigeria)

Transferred to digital printing

Typeset in 10/11 pt Plantin by Colset Private Limited, Singapore

This publication is printed on acid-free paper

To the memory of
Mahmud M. Tukur
Teacher · Patriot · Activist

1944 · 1988

Contents

Preface
& Acknowledgements

In the last quarter of 1988, during visits to Lagos by Yusuf Bangura and Bjorn Beckman, I discussed with them the idea of a book project which I had been thinking about and which I thought could, fruitfully, be undertaken by those of us who were, one way or another, directly or indirectly, associated with the political economy programme of Ahmadu Bello University, Zaria. This programme was introduced in the 1970s against the background of the dominance in Nigerian political and wider social science circles of American behaviouralist analyses and it was meant to provide students and teachers alike with a viable alternative approach to understanding Nigerian, African and global social, political and economic problems. Within a short period of its establishment, the Zaria political economy programme became very popular and was widely acclaimed while behaviouralism went into retreat. By the end of the 1980s, not only had the political economy approach become the leading methodological framework in the Department of Political Science, where the programme was primarily based, it also became the hallmark of the University's Faculty of Arts and Social Sciences (FASS). The output of the individual scholars who helped to develop the programme was quite impressive with subjects such as class formation, the state, the National Question, the Agrarian Question, the multinational corporations, development and underdevelopment, imperialism, colonialism and neo-colonialism, Nigerian government and politics, national integration, the military and foreign policy, among others, featuring prominently in the seminar papers produced by the teaching staff.

Yet, for all the acclaim which the Zaria political economy programme won for itself, no collective work had, as of 1988, been produced by the students and staff associated with it. While in the early years of the programme such a collective work was neither pressing nor called for, it seemed to me that by the mid-1980s this had become absolutely necessary for two important reasons. First, in the course of the 1980s, and especially after 1986 when the Nigerian state embraced the adjustment programme of the International Monetary Fund (IMF) and the World Bank, a systematic campaign was mounted by government officials and the World Bank against the teaching of political economy courses in Nigerian universities with the Zaria programme particularly targeted as 'irrelevant' and 'subversive'. Embarking on a collective book project seemed to me to be one of various ways of responding to this campaign and of demonstrating the continuing relevance of the political economy method to a holistic understanding of Nigeria's contemporary problems. This book project, at a second level, would help to maintain the bond of scholarly interaction that had been a hallmark of the Zaria programme and which the departure of some of its prime movers appeared, temporarily at least, to threaten as the politics of intolerance and witch-hunting engulfed FASS. It was in this context that I raised the idea of the book project with Bangura and Beckman in the hope that at least some of those associated with the Zaria programme would be able to contribute; structural adjustment seemed to be the natural subject to focus on not only because it was in 1988 and still remains today the most fiercely debated subject in Nigeria, but also because its introduction in July 1986 represented a major attempt to shift the basis of accumulation in the country away from the post-colonial state-led pattern towards a market-based alternative. Moreover, some of the diverse issues associated with and thrown up by structural adjustment fell within the on-going research interests of many of the potential contributors to the book.

After a period of consultation with other likely project participants, it was agreed that structural adjustment should form the focus of our collective effort; an attempt should be made after the completion of the initial project to develop a new one, this time focusing on the question of democracy. In March 1989, some of those who indicated a willingness to participate in the SAP project convened in Oxford at a seminar hosted by St Peter's College, partly to discuss the proposed book. A larger, more focused meeting was held in October 1989, also at St Peter's College, where each participant presented a synopsis of the arguments that were to be developed into chapters for the book. This meeting also agreed on the outline of the book and the modalities for conducting peer criticism and assessment. What we have presented here, under the broad title *The Politics of Structural Adjustment in Nigeria*, is the final revised version of the papers written by those who participated in the Oxford seminar of October 1989. Our concern in the book has been to carry out an assessment of selected aspects of the adjustment programme whilst simultaneously pointing to some of the diverse political issues arising from the implementation of the policy package.

It would have been difficult to hold the October 1989 Oxford meeting were it not for a grant made available to us by the Swedish Agency for Research Co-operation (SAREC) to help meet basic travel, accommodation and organizational costs. We would like to place on record our thanks to SAREC for its kind generosity. Thanks too are due to the authorities of St Peter's College, particularly Gavin Williams, who kindly agreed to host the seminar and to provide some secretarial support. I would also like to acknowledge with gratitude the generosity of the Director of the United Nations Research Institute for Social Development (UNRISD) for granting us the permission to use in this book the paper by Bangura and Beckman which he originally commissioned them to write for a conference held in April 1989, in Kingston, Jamaica, on *Economic Crisis and Third World Countries: Impact and Response*.

Finally, I would like to thank the various contributors to this book not only for making this collaborative effort possible but also for their extremely helpful support at various stages of the preparation of the manuscript for publication. But for their commitment and selflessness, this book would not have been produced in its present form. I can only look forward with enthusiasm to further collaboration with them as we strive to make our own contribution to an understanding of the problems facing Nigeria and the ways in which they could be tackled to the benefit of the people.

Adebayo Olukoshi

Contributors

YUSUF BANGURA obtained his doctorate from the London School of Economics. He taught for a year at the University of Dalhousie, Canada, before joining the Department of Political Science, Ahmadu Bello University, Zaria, where he lectured from 1980 to 1988. From November 1988 to the end of October 1989, he was a guest researcher with the Department of Political Science, University of Stockholm, under the Swedish Institute Fellowship Programme. He is presently working with the United Nations Research Institute for Social Development (UNRISD) in Geneva as a co-ordinator of the Institute's research programme on structural adjustment. His main research interest is crisis, adjustment and politics in Nigeria and he is both widely published and acknowledged as a leading scholar in the field. He is an overseas editor of the *Review of African Political Economy*.

BJORN BECKMAN holds a doctorate from the University of Uppsala, Sweden. He taught at the Department of Political Science, Ahmadu Bello University, Zaria, from 1978 to 1987. For two of those years (1985–7) he was Reader in Political Science. He has published widely on Ghanaian and Nigerian peasant politics and is currently studying Nigerian textile workers in collaboration with Gunilla Andrae of Stockholm University, whilst simultaneously studying the politics of Third World structural adjustment. He is widely published and is an overseas editor of the *Review of African Political Economy*, to which he contributes frequently. He is currently Reader at the University of Stockholm, with a research affiliation to Bayero University, Kano.

AKIN FADAHUNSI is a statistician and economist trained in Poland and the Soviet Union. He has a long-standing association with CODESRIA, under whose auspices he has carried out extensive studies on industrialization and technological development in Nigeria. He has also published extensively on issues of economic policy and planning in Nigeria. Akin Fadahunsi has been a research fellow at the Centre for Social and Economic Research (CSER), Ahmadu Bello University, Zaria, where he once served as Director and is currently Professor.

JIBRIN IBRAHIM lectured for several years at the Department of Political Science, Ahmadu Bello University, Zaria, before obtaining a study leave to research for his doctorate on Nigerian party politics at the University of Bordeaux. He has published widely in English and French on the democratic struggle in Nigeria. He has also been an active member and executive of the Nigerian Political Science Association. Jibrin Ibrahim is currently co-ordinating a project involving scholars and activists on the quest for a democratic social and political order in Nigeria.

ATTAHIRU JEGA wrote his doctorate at the Northwestern University, Illinois, on the politics of irrigation in Nigeria. He has been lecturing at the Bayero University, Kano for several years and has published widely on various aspects of the contemporary political economy of Nigeria. As the National President of the Academic Staff Union of Universities (ASUU), he has been watching closely the politics of structural adjustment from the perspective of Nigeria's professional associations and has commented widely on this issue. He is currently a senior lecturer.

ABDUL RAUFU MUSTAPHA was for several years a lecturer at the Department of Political Science, Ahmadu Bello University, Zaria, before proceeding to Britain, on study leave, to do his doctoral work. He obtained his doctorate from Oxford University on the basis of a thesis on politics and class formation in a northern Nigerian village. He is widely published and has been active in the *Review of African Political Economy,* for which he is presently an overseas editor based in Zaria. In addition to his teaching responsibilities, he is involved in a number of projects on structural adjustment and agrarian change.

ADEBAYO OLUKOSHI obtained his doctorate from the University of Leeds, where he worked on a thesis on multinational corporations and industrialization in Nigeria. Since 1987, he has been on the research staff of the Nigerian Institute of International Affairs, where he is currently a senior fellow. He has been involved in research on the politics of structural adjustment in Nigeria, Ghana and Sierra Leone and has published widely on this subject. He is editor of the *Nigerian Forum,* a publication of the Nigerian Institute of International Affairs.

SHEHU YAHAYA, after obtaining his Bachelor and Masters degrees at Ahmadu Bello University, taught Economics for several years at Bayero University, Kano, before proceeding to the University of Sussex, where he did his doctoral work on the privatization of public enterprises in Nigeria. He is an active member of the Nigerian Economic Society. He is presently a senior lecturer at Bayero University and Head of the Department of Economics. He is, with Attahiru Jega, co-ordinating a study on the economy and politics of Kano since colonial times.

List
of Abbreviations

ABU	– Ahmadu Bello University
AFRC	– Armed Forces Ruling Council
ASUU	– Academic Staff Union of Universities
AUT	– Association of University Teachers
CBN	– Central Bank of Nigeria
CDHR	– Committee for the Defence of Human Rights
CFA	– Communauté Financière Africaine
CKD	– Completely Knocked Down (Parts)
CLO	– Civil Liberties Organization
CODESRIA	– Council for the Development of Social and Economic Research in Africa
DAS	– Dutch Auction System
DFRRI	– Directorate of Food, Roads and Rural Infrastructure
ECA	– Economic Commission for Africa
EFF	– Extended Fund Facility
ESS	– Elongated Salary Structure
FAO	– Food and Agriculture Organization
FEM	– Foreign Exchange Market
FOB	– Free on Board
FOS	– Federal Office of Statistics
GDP	– Gross Domestic Product
GNP	– Gross National Product
IAP	– Industrial Arbitration Panel
IFEM	– Inter-bank Foreign Exchange Market
IMF	– International Monetary Fund
IRDP	– Integrated Rural Development Project
ISI	– Import-Substitution Industrialization
KSIP	– Kano State Investment and Properties Ltd
LDCs	– Less Developed Countries
MAN	– Manufacturers' Association of Nigeria
MD	– Managing Director
NADC	– National Association of Democratic Students
NANS	– National Association of Nigerian Students

NARD	– National Association of Resident Doctors
NBA	– Nigerian Bar Association
NBCI	– Nigerian Bank for Commerce and Industry
NDE	– National Directorate of Employment
NEC	– National Electoral Commission
NEPB	– Nigerian Enterprises Promotion Board
NEPD	– Nigerian Enterprises Promotion Decree
NICs	– Newly Industrialized Countries
NIDB	– Nigerian Industrial Development Bank
NLC	– Nigerian Labour Congress
NMA	– Nigerian Medical Association
NNIL	– Northern Nigeria Investments Ltd
NNSC	– Nigerian National Supply Company
NPN	– National Party of Nigeria
NRC	– National Republican Convention
NSE	– Nigerian Society of Engineers
NSO	– National Security Organization
NTA	– Nigerian Television Authority
NUC	– National Universities Commission
NUJ	– Nigerian Union of Journalists
NUT	– Nigerian Union of Teachers
OAU	– Organization of African Unity
OFN	– Operation Feed the Nation
OPEC	– Organization of Petroleum Exporting Countries
PAC	– Presidential Advisory Commission
PEs	– Public Enterprises
PPP	– Purchasing Power Parity
PSN	– Pharmaceutical Society of Nigeria
PTP	– Political Transition Programme
RBDA	– River Basin Development Authority
SAP	– Structural Adjustment Programme
SDP	– Social Democratic Party
SEC	– Securities and Exchange Commission
SFEM	– Second-tier Foreign Exchange Market
SOEs	– State-owned Enterprises
SSAUTHRIA	– Senior Staff Association of Universities, Teaching Hospitals, Research Institutes and Associated Institutions
SSS	– State Security Service
TCPC	– Technical Committee on Privatization and Commercialization
UAC	– United Africa Company
UBA	– United Bank for Africa
UI	– University of Ibadan
UK	– United Kingdom
UNIBEN	– University of Benin
UNILAG	– University of Lagos
UNRISD	– United Nations Research Institute for Social Development
US	– United States
USAID	– United States Agency for International Development

1

General Introduction: From Crisis to Adjustment in Nigeria

I. Introduction

The period since the beginning of the 1980s in Nigeria has been marked by a steadily deepening economic crisis which has had adverse, far-reaching consequences for various sectors of the economy and the living standards of most Nigerians. Prior to the onset of the crisis, the Nigerian economy enjoyed almost a decade of unprecedented revenue boom arising from the petroleum price increases of the 1970s. As a major exporter of crude petroleum, upon which it came, from the early 1970s onwards, to depend for an increasing proportion of its foreign exchange earnings, Nigeria was a key beneficiary of the two so-called oil shocks of the 1970s. From less than $4 a barrel in 1973, the price of the country's light grade crude oil rose in the world market to about $42 in 1980 in the context of an increasing daily output for export (Olukoshi, 1991a: 5). Revenue accruing to the state rose from N4.733 billion in 1975 to N7.00 billion in 1977 and some N9.825 billion in 1981 (Olukoshi, 1990). It was precisely because of this oil revenue boom that Nigeria was shielded from the effects of the world capitalist recession of the 1970s, whose adverse consequences were refracted into most, mainly non-oil exporting, African countries. Indeed, while most African states suffered economic stagnation and decline, Nigeria enjoyed what seemed at the time as an unstoppable economic boom, evidenced by a growing industrial sector and output, a rising per capita national income, a respectable payments position, external reserves sufficient to cover the import needs of the economy for several months, an increased inflow of foreign investments and a massive building and infra-structural development programme, among other indicators.

In the early 1980s, the Nigerian economic boom came to an abrupt end and a deep-seated crisis set in, rapidly engulfing industry, agriculture, the country's payments position, domestic price levels and the general living conditions of the majority of the people. Some scholars have argued that it is the most severe economic crisis to have been experienced by the Nigerian state since its creation at the beginning of the twentieth century as a specific Anglo-colonial project (Bangura, 1982: 1). It is the crisis that provides the immediate domestic context for the adoption by the Nigerian state of an orthodox programme of structural adjustment sponsored by the International Monetary Fund (IMF) and the World Bank. Since its introduction in 1986, structural adjustment, as the various chapters in this book attempt to show,

1

has become part and parcel of the dynamics of the country's economic crisis, exacerbating existing pre-adjustment problems whilst creating new ones specific to its own internal contradictions. Whether it be in the agricultural sector (see Chapter 7), or in industry (Chapter 4), or with regard to employment, inflation and economic growth (Chapter 3), the Nigerian experience suggests that structural adjustment has tended to complicate the country's economic crisis, a fact which partly underlies the intense and increasingly politically-specific contestation of the programme by workers (see Chapter 5), urban-based professional groups, including students (Chapter 6), and even sections of the ruling class, particularly those represented by the Manufacturers' Association of Nigeria (MAN).

Our purpose in this chapter is to provide a broad introductory framework for this book, the chief concern of which is to offer an assessment of selected aspects of the adjustment programme of the Nigerian state and pinpoint some relevant issues of politics, be they the contestation of the programme by diverse social forces whose livelihood it touches upon directly, the political context within which the reforms are being implemented, the political repercussions that have accompanied the implementation of the programme, or the democracy question, among others, thrown up by the adjustment process. In providing the broad introductory context for subsequent analyses in this book, we begin by offering a short account of the origins of the crisis and the initial dimensions it took prior to the introduction of structural adjustment in 1986. We also attempt to summarize some of the leading non-official and official explanations that were tabled to explain the crisis. The attempts by the governments of Alhaji Shehu Shagari (1979–83) and General Muhammadu Buhari (1983–5) to contain the deepening crisis are discussed briefly. Thereafter, we examine the process by which the Babangida regime introduced the adjustment programme. We outline the objectives of the programme and its contestation by various social groups in the country. We conclude the chapter with some remarks on the organizational structure of the book and a summary of the key issues raised in the various contributions. On the basis of these issues, we argue that the stalemate that characterizes much of the contemporary African conjuncture can only be resolved if the aspirations of the majority of the people form a central part of a new social contract for Africa's political and economic development.

II. Origins and Dimensions of the Nigerian Economic Crisis

The roots of the Nigerian economic crisis could be traced to the lopsided character of the post-colonial developmental path followed by the state. The foundations of this path to development began to be laid from about 1945 when the state, under late colonialism, sought, in alliance primarily with foreign capital, to promote import-substitution industrialization using peasant surpluses to finance the importation of the inputs necessary for the growth and expansion of manufacturing activities. This model was carried over, on an extended scale, into the post-colonial period. Up to the end of the 1960s, agricultural surpluses emanating primarily from peasant cash crop production continued to provide the foreign exchange for sustaining manufacturing activities. The rise of the oil economy in the 1970s led to the use of petrodollars for financing the import needs of industry in a context of growing oil exports and declining agricultural output. As the post-colonial import-substitution industrialization process developed, it became clear that its sustainability depended on the ability of the state to earn sufficient foreign exchange to meet its needs, namely, raw materials, spare parts and machinery. These needs grew as the manufacturing sector expanded; the emergence of a class of indigenous Nigerian manufacturers operating in competition and collaboration with foreign corporate and Levantine capital did not alter this basic character of industry as the indigenous bourgeoisie was itself heavily externally-oriented in its operations.[1]

The strong dependence of the Nigerian import-substitution industrial sector on external inputs had several implications. First, the level of local value added was very low in spite of the massive growth in manufacturing activities in the country. Second, and related to the first point, is the fact that very few forward and backward linkages were established in the economy as a result of local manufacturing activities; industry articulated with agriculture and mining through the external sector and not locally. Partly as a result of the absence of local linkages, there was a marked concentration, at the third level, of industries in the light manufacturing, consumer goods department, the intermediate and capital goods sub-sector being virtually non-existent. These contradictions in the post-colonial development strategy did not seem to matter for as long as the state was able to provide the foreign exchange necessary for meeting the needs of industry; once there was a shortfall in its ability to do so, a crisis of immense proportions was bound to unfold in the economy. This was precisely what happened in the early 1980s when the world market price for oil, a commodity on which Nigeria had come to depend for more than 90 per cent of its foreign exchange earnings, collapsed, creating an instant revenue shortfall for the state with severe repercussions for an economy that, at about that time, required on average about $1 billion worth of imports monthly for its smooth functioning.[2] The collapse of the world oil market therefore served to accentuate sharply the contradictions that underlay the post-colonial development model in a context where the agricultural sector was in decay, its problems compounded by a mixture of relative neglect and misdirected, essentially anti-peasant and pro-absentee, large-scale farmer policies. These points are elaborated upon in some depth in Chapters 4 and 7. Suffice it to note here that the contradictions in the post-colonial industrial and agricultural development strategy combined with structural, inter- and intra-sectoral imbalances to underline the fragility of the Nigerian economy and its acute vulnerability to a volatile external environment.

The collapse of the world oil market which resulted in Nigeria's oil earnings falling dramatically from a peak of N10.1 billion in 1979 to about N5.161 billion in 1982 immediately triggered a major crisis in industry and the rest of the economy (Olukoshi, 1991b: 30–1). At the level of industry, many firms either suspended production or scaled down capacity utilization drastically because of the inability of the state to continue to meet their foreign exchange needs. It is generally reckoned that about 50 per cent of the total number of manufacturing establishments operating in Nigeria stopped production for some time with adverse consequences for workers who were retrenched in their thousands (Olukoshi, 1990). An inflationary spiral also took hold in the economy as there emerged an acute shortage of consumer goods and imported food items like rice. The widespread shortfall of consumer goods was the result of both the collapse of many of the factories that produce such commodities and the decline of the import capacity of the state. Having enjoyed a favourable payments position for much of the 1970s, the state began to suffer serious deficits in its external payments from 1982 onwards. Unable to sustain its expenditure at its pre-crisis levels, the state also started to run huge deficits in its budget whilst at the same time embarking on foreign borrowing from private and official international sources to sustain some of its spending programmes. This borrowing spree was to lay the basis for the country's debt crisis which has served to compound the problems afflicting the wider economy (Olukoshi, 1990). As part of measures adopted in the public sector to cope with the crisis, many workers employed in the civil and public service and in parastatal organizations were laid off. Internal public debts also rose astronomically from N4.6 billion in 1979 to N22.2 billion in 1983. National output fell by 8 per cent in 1983 and a further 5.5 per cent in 1984. Inflation, put officially at 23 per cent in 1983, rose to 40 per cent in 1984. The country's external reserve, which was put at $8.50 billion at the end of May 1981, could not, by 1984, support up to two months of import, even at the diminished level of the period (Okongwu, 1987: 3). Social services, including the educational sector, suffered severe neglect and decline while infrastructural facilities went into decay. The living and working conditions of many Nigerians deteriorated sharply as the crisis deepened. Let us now proceed to discuss some of the explanations that have been tabled to explain the crisis.

III. Official and Non-Official Explanations of the Crisis

The national debate that accompanied the onset of the crisis in the economy in 1982 brought to the fore several official and non-official explanations of the causes of the problem. At the official level, the main argument tabled by state officials was that the crisis was caused not by domestic factors but by the international oil market glut, which was beyond the control of the government. This line of reasoning was taken up by several orthodox economists who, in addition to the oil glut, pointed to the recession in the world market as an added source of the crisis. Nigeria, they argued, would have to wait for a turnaround in the world economy and the oil market in order for it to return to the path of economic expansion.[3]

Against the official and orthodox economic explanation of the crisis, Nigerian nationalists have focused their critique on the prevalence of fraud and mismanagement during the Second Republic (1979–83). They argue that the wholesale looting of the economy by civilian politicians and the managerial ineptitude of the Shagari regime were central to the onset of the crisis. Matters were not helped by the permeation of Nigerian society by indiscipline. This nationalist position is modified and extended by radical commentators who, in explaining the roots of the crisis, insist on the specific role of contractors, consultants and middlemen and their ruinous activities. These radical commentators emphasize the central role which the commercial strata came to assume in the Nigerian economy and the way in which their patron–client networks contributed to the country's economic decline.[4]

When these explanations of the Nigerian crisis are carefully considered, it will be clear that, although they point to problems that are relevant, they fail to locate the central contradictions that *generated* crisis within the domestic system of accumulation and the way in which these contradictions made possible the easy refraction of the crisis of global capitalism into the country. Thus while those who emphasize the world oil market glut are right to the extent that there was indeed a glut created by excessive oil supply, they miss the point when they claim that the glut created the crisis. What the collapse of the world oil market did was to expose in sharp relief the contradictions that characterized the post-colonial Nigerian pattern of accumulation and reinforce the problems which they posed for the country's capitalist development process. This same basic argument could be extended to the claim that the world recession caused the Nigerian crisis; the recession merely served to expose the fragility of a domestic economy characterized by acute structural imbalances. Regarding the view that corruption and mismanagement were the central factors that triggered the crisis, what the advocates of this position ignore is the fact that there are objective factors embedded in the Nigerian economy and the pattern of accumulation promoted by the state which were bound, sooner or later, to lead to a crisis; mismanagement and fraud could only have helped to hasten the onset of the crisis and compound it. Likewise, the roots of the crisis cannot be limited to the activities of the commercial strata; the problems besetting the Nigerian economy are closely tied to contradictions built into the post-colonial production process and it is erroneous to attempt to treat problems manifesting themselves at the level of circulation independent of the sphere of production.[5] How did the Shagari and Buhari administrations attempt to manage the economic crisis from 1982 to 1985? This is the question to which we now turn our attention.

IV. The Crisis Management Policies of the Shagari and Buhari Administrations

From a position of initially denying the existence of a serious crisis in the Nigerian economy, the civilian government of Alhaji Shehu Shagari eventually admitted its existence and severity with the promulgation in April 1982 of the Economic Stabiliza-tion (Temporary Provisions) Act. The essence of the Act was to reduce government expenditure and curtail imports. In this regard, import duties were imposed where they were hitherto non-existent or increased where they were already in force. All unused import licences were recalled for review, business travel allowances were cut from N3,000 to N2,500 and compulsory advance deposits were required from importers of a variety of food items, industrial raw materials, capital goods and spare parts. The April 1982 measures were widened in January 1983 with the introduction of further import restrictions, an increase in tariff charges on a host of consumer and non-consumer goods, the closure of private jetties and the restriction of external borrowing by state governments, among other steps (Onoh, 1983: chapter 6).

The austerity measures introduced by the Shagari government have been strongly criticized for their failure to address the structural deficiencies in the Nigerian economy (Olukoshi, 1991b). Precisely because of this, the rapidly dwindling fortunes of the world oil market and the inability of the regime to apply its crisis management policies rigorously and consistently, the country's economic problems continued to deepen. This reinforced the problems of instability, indiscipline and repression that charac-terized the politics of the Second Republic. The continuing deterioration of the economy also paved the way for the demise of civilian rule and the re-emergence of military dictatorship. The regime of General Muhammadu Buhari which replaced the discredited administration of Alhaji Shagari sought to enforce much more rigor-ously the austerity measures which it inherited from its predecessor and to widen their scope. Thus, a renewed push was made to reduce the import profile of the economy. All imports placed on open licence by the deposed government shortly after its inauguration in 1979 were placed under specific licence by the Buhari regime. Foreign travel allowances were slashed further from N500 to N100 while business travel allowances were suspended. A major retrenchment exercise was carried out in the public sector in which thousands of workers lost their jobs. The government also placed an embargo on the recruitment of new employees in the civil service whilst imposing a generalized wage freeze. Public expenditure was further curtailed, new projects were frozen, state governments were completely prohibited from raising external loans, excise duties were extended from 68 commodities to cover a total of 400 items, the colours of the five, ten and twenty naira notes were swapped to check the activities of the parallel market and reduce the amount of money in circulation, and bank interest rates were raised, among other steps. Negotiations were also opened with various local manufacturing groups on the question of domestic sourcing of raw materials. Some incentive measures were introduced to encourage manufacturers to look inward for their inputs (Olukoshi, 1991b).

One of the factors that underlay the Buhari regime's crisis management policies was its conviction that fraud and indiscipline were central to the economic problems of Nigeria and that all steps would have to be taken to eliminate these ills. Spurred by a self-righteous conviction, the regime proceeded to unleash severe attacks on civil liberties and human rights and in doing so alienated various social groups. A rash of decrees was passed aimed at curtailing the freedom of the press, permitting preventive detention, preventing workers from seeking redress for retrenchment, forbidding demonstrations and public processions, authorizing the indefinite detention of Second Republic politicians and ousting the jurisdiction of the judiciary in several matters of civil interest. Thus, although the Buhari regime took very strong nationalist positions in its negotiations with the IMF for an Extended Fund Facility (EFF) loan of up to $2.5 billion, for which the Shagari administration had applied in 1982, it was unable to carry the majority of Nigerians along with it because many people felt alienated by its repressive and authoritarian political practices. While agreeing, like its predecessors, with the Fund on the need for fundamental reforms in the Nigerian economy, the Buhari regime was unwilling to accept the recommendations of the IMF for the devaluation of the naira, the across-the-board privatization of public enterprises, the liberalization of trade and the withdrawal of the petroleum subsidy. In the view of the regime, these measures were inappropriate for tackling Nigeria's economic problems. Like the Shagari regime, the government of General Buhari placed great emphasis on state regulations, insisting that to abandon the economy to market forces as the IMF recommended would merely complicate matters. Not surprisingly, a stalemate developed in the negotiations between the Fund and the Buhari regime (Olukoshi, 1991b).

One consequence of the stalemate was the tightening of the boycott of Nigeria by Western banks and export credit guarantee agencies. The leading financial institutions insisted that the government had to obtain a clean bill of health from the IMF before the country's debt, put at about $20 billion in 1984, could be rescheduled and fresh capital injections authorized. The IMF would issue such a bill of health only if its adjustment recommendations were adopted wholesale. In the face of this, the problems of the Nigerian economy worsened, with inflation rising still further, infrastructural facilities deteriorating, more workers losing their jobs, the payments problem persisting, the industrial sector suffering more setbacks and the agricultural sector stagnating. In a bid to mitigate the worst effects of cross-conditionality, the Buhari regime adopted a two-pronged strategy. At one level, it significantly stepped up the servicing of the country's external debt, devoting a staggering 44 per cent of the total foreign exchange earnings accruing to the state in 1985 to that purpose. It was a strategy calculated to win the confidence of international financiers and gain their support for the regime's economic recovery programme. It did not work; the Western financial boycott of Nigeria continued with intensity. If anything, the high debt service ratio which the regime maintained brought into sharp focus the relationship between debt management and economic development, thereby triggering further domestic opposition to the government, not least amongst students, workers, medical doctors, university lecturers and school teachers. The linkage between the Buhari administration's crisis management strategy and the increasing militancy of Nigerian professional associations in the period just before the adoption of structural adjustment is discussed extensively in Chapter 6.

The second approach adopted by the government of General Buhari in its bid to mitigate the effects of cross-conditionality on the economy was the introduction of the policy of counter-trade, whereby Nigeria's crude oil was bartered for raw materials, spare parts, machinery and consumer goods from Brazil, the Soviet Union, Italy and a number of other countries. Through this strategy, it was hoped that some inputs would be made available to sustain essential industries while the acute shortage of consumer goods would also be eased. The scale of the counter-trade deals was, however, too small relative to the magnitude of the country's economic problems and the management of the scheme was fraught with too many difficulties for it to make a significant impact. The Nigerian economy therefore continued to deteriorate, reinforcing the intolerance and authoritarianism of the regime and eventually paving the way for its overthrow in a palace *coup* staged by General Ibrahim Babangida, the Chief of Army Staff, on 27 August 1985. The *coup* marked the beginning of a new phase in the management of the national economic crisis at a time when, as Jega and Ibrahim show in Chapters 6 and 8 respectively, various groups had started to establish a politically significant link between their interests and the policies of the state. It was a development which structural adjustment was to push forward.

V. The March to Structural Adjustment

General Babangida assumed office in August 1985 on a platform that promised to break the deadlock that had developed in the negotiations between its predecessors and the IMF over the conditions which the Fund attached to the Nigerian application for an EFF loan. In order to assess more closely the attitude of Nigerians to the Fund and its conditionality, the government decided to call a national debate on the IMF and the role, if any, which it should play in the management of the national economic crisis. The decision to declare the debate was taken as part of wider confidence-building measures such as the abrogation of Decree no. 4 which was promulgated in 1984 to limit the freedom of the press and prevent criticism of public officials, the unbanning of associations such as the Nigerian Medical Association (NMA) and the National Association of Resident Doctors (NARD) that had been proscribed by the Buhari regime, the declaration by the government of its intention to respect human rights, and the public disgrace of the National Security Organization (NSO), among other moves (Olukoshi, 1991b: especially chapter 4).

While the national debate on the IMF was in progress, the government decided to declare a state of national economic emergency to last for fifteen months from 1 October 1985. Under the emergency, a general pay cut for both civilian and military personnel was introduced ranging from 2 per cent to 20 per cent of their annual wages and income. This decision was bitterly contested by workers' unions, who criticized it as much for the failure of the government to seek their opinion as for the further hardship which it imposed on working people (see Chapter 5). Union opposition to the income levy was only marginally assuaged by the promise made by the government to refund the deducted monies to junior workers at the end of the emergency period.

If it was the expectation of the regime that it would be able, through the national debate, to carry Nigerians along in its quest for an accommodation of some sort with the IMF, it could not have made a greater error. Having been compelled by the existing internal groundswell of opposition to the Fund to concede the national debate, the government was confronted with widespread opposition to any role for the organization in the quest for national economic recovery. Workers, market women, students, religious leaders and associations, youth organizations, professional groups, including university lecturers, as well as roadside mechanics, the Manufacturers' Association of Nigeria (MAN) and even elements of the armed forces such as the men of the 82nd Airborne Battalion openly voiced their opposition to the Fund and its conditionality clauses. It was a genuinely popular debate in which a clear majority of participants took a stand against the IMF and thereby compelled the government to announce on 12 December 1985 that it had, in accordance with the wishes of the people, taken a decision to reject the loan (Olukoshi, 1991b).

In interpreting the outcome of the debate, however, the government claimed that Nigerians, while rejecting the IMF loan outright, had also simultaneously declared themselves willing to make whatever sacrifices were necessary to put the economy on the path of recovery and growth. General Babangida claimed that in practical terms this meant that Nigerians were willing to design an adjustment programme of their own, no less rigorous than the IMF's, but implemented by them at their own pace. The earliest hint of what this supposedly 'home-grown' adjustment programme would entail emerged when the 1986 budget proposals were announced. In that budget, a host of policy measures, akin to the IMF's standard prescriptions, was outlined and implemented. For instance, the petroleum subsidy was reduced by 80 per cent while the Nigerian National Supply Company (NNSC) was disbanded. Non-statutory transfers to all economic and quasi-economic parastatals were reduced by 50 per cent. In the framework of a promise to institute a comprehensive adjustment programme, the government committed itself to the privatization/commercialization of public enterprises, the liberalization of trade and the exchange system, and the reduction of administrative controls in the economy (Olukoshi, 1991b).

On 27 June 1986 the commitment to market reforms contained in the 1986 budget was carried forward with the launching of the Structural Adjustment Programme, which, all the protestations of the regime to the contrary notwithstanding, bore the imprint of the IMF. At the centre of the adjustment programme was a commitment by the government to devalue the naira. This goal was achieved through the introduction in September 1986 of a second-tier foreign exchange market (SFEM) where the naira was allowed to depreciate drastically. This depreciation continued even after the merger of the first- and second-tier markets, as Fadahunsi shows in Chapter 3. Side by side with the devaluation of the naira, the government began to implement its programme of subsidy removal, including the petroleum 'subsidy'; the privatization and commercialization of public enterprises; trade liberalization first through an interim tariff structure and then through a revised, more comprehensive version expected to last several years; the deregulation of prices and interest rates; the removal of administrative controls, particularly in the area of foreign exchange transactions, profit repatriation and foreign investment inflow; the reduction of public expenditure; and the imposition of a credit and liquidity squeeze. One immediate consequence of the adjustment policies was the abolition of the import licensing system that had been the basis for the allocation of foreign exchange in the 1970s and which was much abused during the Second Republic.

With the commencement of the implementation of the above-mentioned policies, Nigeria finally joined the league of Third World states that have been implementing the orthodox adjustment programmes of the IMF and the World Bank. The process by which the state adopted the programme was a long and tortuous one which entailed the overthrow of two regimes, an attempted *coup* against General Babangida's government less than two months after it came to power and a national debate on the IMF. And even after the state adopted the adjustment package, it had to forego the IMF loan and instead arranged for support from the World Bank such that, in time, the latter came to play in Nigeria the open monitoring role which the Fund normally reserves for itself. Thus, although the adoption of structural adjustment represented a significant turning-point in the management of the Nigerian economic crisis, entailing as it does a commitment by the government to replace the post-colonial state-led pattern of development with a market-based one, the Babangida administration has constantly had to contend with articulate and organized opposition to its policies with consequences for the implementation of the reforms.

Since 1986, when the implementation of structural adjustment began in earnest in Nigeria, a whole host of questions has arisen centring on the appropriateness or otherwise of the market as a mechanism for development and for economic recovery. Can an economy adjust better under a system of state regulations or under the market? What has the attempt to push market reforms meant for various sectors of the economy such as agriculture, industry, the services and the parastatals? What have the reforms meant for the various social forces whose activities give life to these sectors? These and many other questions have been posed by the decision of the state to adopt structural adjustment and are closely addressed in the subsequent chapters of this book. Suffice it to note at this point that because the market ideology is still heavily contested by various social forces, not least the vested interests that had developed around the import-licensing system, the contract-content of public expenditures, the regulated interest rates and tariff regimes, the subsidy system and exchange controls (Bangura, 1989), the responses of these social forces to the decision of the state to adopt structural adjustment form a central aspect of the politics of the market reform process in Nigeria. This is reinforced, as this book attempts to bring out, by the fact that the adjustment programme has undermined the living standards of most Nigerians and posed major livelihood challenges for others in the context of a reform process in which there appear to be more losers than winners (Beckman, 1990; Olukoshi, 1991a).

VI. The Politics of Transition to Civilian Rule

The introduction and implementation of the structural adjustment went hand in hand with the articulation and subsequent inauguration of major reforms in the political system. As with the IMF loan, the government of General Babangida decided in 1986 to ask Nigerians to debate the country's political future. For this purpose, a Political Bureau was established to co-ordinate the debate and synthesize the views expressed by Nigerians. The Bureau reported, *inter alia*, that Nigerians had expressed a preference for a socialist ideology and a two-party system of political competition. The government, whilst enthusiastically embracing the two-party idea, not surprisingly rejected the Bureau's recommendation of a socialist ideology. A whole host of First and Second Republic politicians, described as the 'old breed', were banned from participating in the politics of the Third Republic for varying lengths of time. Strong emphasis was placed on the need for 'newbreed' politicians to emerge. As part of the process of encouraging the 'newbreed', the government invited them to form political parties in readiness for the commencement of the transition to civilian rule. Thirteen of the over fifty parties that were formed sought recognition as one of the two parties that the military regime said it would permit to contest elections. In the end, none of them was registered as the government claimed that they were all unable to fulfil its unnecessarily and unreasonably stiff requirements, including a demand that the parties state their attitude to structural adjustment. The government then proceeded to create two political parties which it named the National Republican

Convention (NRC) and the Social Democratic Party (SDP) and, after writing their constitutions and manifestos as well as providing them with offices, invited 'newbreed' politicians to join them. The NRC was supposed to be a little to the right; the SDP a little to the left (Olukoshi, 1991a). The remarkable zeal with which the regime has sought to narrow the space for political competition and its refusal to allow the market freely to determine party formation and political participation not only contrasts sharply with its commitment to economic liberalization but also forms an important part of what Ibrahim describes in Chapter 8 as the 'sapping of democracy'.

To be sure, the over-regimented programme of transition to civil rule has been contested by various groups, not least the 'old breed' politicians who have sought to develop countervailing methods of overcoming the restrictions placed on them by the military regime. Various social groups such as the Nigeria Labour Congress (NLC) and the National Association of Nigerian Students (NANS) have also challenged the arbitrariness with which the government has attempted to handle the administration of the transition process. The politics of the transition have generally fed into and are reinforced by the politics of the market reform process and both have combined to produce, at the level of civil society, a growing struggle for popular democracy and, at the level of the state, an increasing disposition towards intolerance, authoritarianism and repression. Thus, for example, trade union opposition to structural adjustment has served as a factor influencing the leadership of the NLC to seek an active political role for the labour movement. This development has, in turn, caused alarm in government circles and the response of the regime has been to seek to repress the NLC and harass its militants, a development which has pushed the labour organization to seek to construct alliances with other groups for the purpose of defending broadly defined democratic rights. As with the adjustment programme, therefore, several questions have been brought to the fore by the political reforms which the military government has sought to push through. For example, can the political programme, inter-laced as it is with the objectives of structural adjustment as captured by the regime's declared commitment to consolidate the adjustment process at every stage of the transition of civilian rule in 1992, accommodate the contradictions thrown up by the market reforms? Are questions of structural adjustment tied closely to the question of political power? What prospect does the political transition programme hold for democracy (Bangura, 1989)? These are issues which are raised in this book, particularly in Chapter 8.

VII. Continued Contestation

Against the background of all the foregoing, it can be argued that neither the heavily manipulated political transition programme nor the very limited record of achievement under structural adjustment appears capable of guaranteeing the future of market reforms in Nigeria. Even as the march towards 1992 progresses, unsteadily, the contestation of the adjustment programme continues to gather pace. Not only are local manufacturing groups calling for the reflation of the economy through a significant increase in consumer purchasing power, a lowering of interest rates and the expansion of credit and liquidity, they are joined in this campaign by workers and professionals who insist that the naira is, at an exchange rate of N10 to $1, heavily undervalued and should be reviewed upwards. Workers have also been persistent in their demand for an upward review of wages and salaries in line with the inflationary consequences of devaluation on real income. Together with some of their employers, they have exposed cases of dumping arising from the trade liberalization component of the adjustment package. The privatization programme, after a very slow start, continues to be plagued by regionalist and ethnic problems, as very clearly dramatized in late February and early March 1991 by the conflict over the Cocoa Industries Limited, a company of the O'dua group of Yoruba-speaking states sold to a northern Nigerian Hausa businessman. The transaction was later revoked with the approval of the federal government against the background of vociferous protests from the Ooni of Ife, spiritual head of the Yorubas, and a section of the Yoruba bourgeoisie (*Newswatch*, 11 February 1991: 26-8; 4 March 1991: 30-1; 15 April 1991: 26-35). In the mean time, workers, as represented by the NLC, continue to campaign against the sale of public assets to the propertied few and for the return of these assets to public ownership, this time under an autonomous, purposeful and efficient management. In several instances, the state has had to give way to the critics of its programme with consequences for the pace, and content, of its reforms. This contestation is bound to continue beyond 1992 and its remains to be seen how the 'newbreed' politicians of the Third Republic will handle it.

The quest for alternatives to structural adjustment has been a key part of the politics of the forces that have been in the frontline of opposition to the market reform programme. These forces, made up mostly of unionists, academics, lawyers and other professionals, have sought to canvass opinion in support of alternative economic management programmes that run directly counter to the adjustment policies of the state. Where the state, for example, opted for price and exchange deregulation, the NLC, the Academic Staff Union of Universities (ASUU) and the Ife Socialist Collective have presented the case for controls in the context of a fundamentally transformed state system.[6] At the heart of the alternatives is a fundamental distrust of the market as an agency for a fair and equitable system of development. The search for alternatives fed, in 1990, into the struggle for the assertion of democratic rights to create a movement bringing together two normally disparate groups, the one made up of radical lawyers, doctors, academics, students and unionists, the other made up of retired senior civil servants from the Gowon days, in a bid to convene a national conference to discuss a whole host of national, political, economic and social problems afflicting contemporary Nigeria.[7] It was the clearest indication of the depth of scepticism that continues to afflict the political and economic policies of the Babangida regime and which underlies, at least partially, the legitimation problems facing the state as it attempts to push through its reform programmes. Although the government prevented the conference from convening, the issues which it raised remain quite central to Nigeria's current political and economic direction and its future stability and growth.

VIII. An Outline of the Chapters

Apart from this chapter, which has focused on some introductory issues, the book is made up of seven other chapters covering diverse aspects of the adjustment programme of the Nigerian state. Chapter 2 focuses on the state/market debate using the privatization programme of the government as its reference point. In the chapter, Shehu Yahaya traces the wider global and specific local contexts of the Nigerian state's privatization programme. He also undertakes a detailed review of the various stages of the march to privatization in Nigeria and the arguments that have been advanced in the literature for and against that policy option by various theoretical schools. Using the experience of the Kano manufacturing sector, Yahaya attempts to assess the validity of the arguments, official and non-official, that have been tabled to justify privatization in Nigeria. He compares the performance of state-owned and private manufacturing establishments in Kano, Nigeria's second industrial centre, and finds that no significant relationships exist between the mode of ownership of the sample firms and their financial or economic profitability. This finding, according to Yahaya, suggests that there is no basis for concluding, *a priori*, that public enterprises in Nigeria have been an unmitigated disaster thus justifying their privatization. The private enterprises covered in the survey did not achieve higher factor productivity, labour productivity or capacity utilization than the publicly-owned ones. The challenge which Shehu Yahaya sees his findings as posing for policy is that because arbitrary privatization could be counter-productive, it would be necessary to recognize the constructive role which effective and efficient public ownership of enterprises could play in the performance of certain crucial functions, such as the promotion of a more integrated pattern of development.

Chapter 3 focuses on the implications which the drastic devaluation of the naira since September 1986 has had for employment, inflation, growth and development in Nigeria. In the chapter, Akin Fadahunsi traces the history of Nigeria's exchange rate management from 1962 to 1986 as a necessary background to a discussion of the devaluation experience from September 1986 onwards. He underlines the point that the hallmark of the attempt to manage the exchange rate of the naira after the introduction of structural adjustment is the effective abandonment of administrative and legal controls and the embrace of the philosophy of liberalization and deregulation. The consequence has been the rapid movement of the naira from a position of overvaluation to drastic undervaluation at a time when the national economy is in deep crisis and therefore can ill-afford such a radical exercise. The repercussions of the undervaluation which the naira has been suffering since September 1986 have manifested themselves in the sharp fall in the living standards of the majority of Nigerians; a fall in per capita income from $778 in 1985 to $108 in 1989; a sharp increase in the level of unemployment and underemployment (in spite of the establishment by the government of job-creation schemes); a massive flight of capital from the economy as speculators and bona fide businessmen take full advantage of deregulation; a series of multiple increases in price levels in the context of the rapidly falling exchange rate of the naira; a worsening of the host of problems facing the industrial sector, including the persistence of low capacity utilization in a context of collapsing consumer purchasing power; and the deepening of the agrarian crisis as the full effects of devaluation and subsidy removal translate into heavily increased costs for the rural community. For Fadahunsi, what Nigeria needs to do quickly before the economy suffers far-reaching damage is the revaluation of the naira upwards using the system of purchasing power parity (PPP) to stabilize it at around N2.5–3.5 to the dollar. Nigeria cannot afford to operate a floating exchange rate, not least because of the acute instability associated with it; a controlled flexible rate that permits a rate of fluctuation of about 15 per cent will have to be pursued side by side with a programme of far-reaching political and economic restructuring.

Chapter 4 examines the impact of the adjustment programme on industry in Nigeria. It traces the origins of the country's industrial crisis to contradictions and distortions in the import-substitution model which was followed in the period up to the end of the 1970s. These contradictions, according to Olukoshi, remained hidden for as long as the state was able to earn sufficient foreign exchange to meet the import needs of industry. That ability was undermined in the early 1980s, however, when the collapse of the world oil market resulted in a sharp decline in the revenue base of the state. The structural adjustment programme has, however, created varying degrees of difficulties for the different sub-sectors of industry with the result that employment levels, capacity utilization and sales turnover have remained dismally poor. This fact, according to Olukoshi, has forced various manufacturing groups to campaign against several of its key components. Particularly criticized by the manufacturers are the government's tariff structure, which they claim has encouraged dumping; the continuing free fall of the naira and the instability associated with this; the deregulation of interest rates, which has meant that the cost of borrowing has risen astronomically; and the liquidity and credit policy of the government, which has made the reflation of the economy difficult. The chapter also considers the impact of adjustment measures on small-scale industry and touches on the debate as to whether or not Nigeria is undergoing a process of de-industrialization.

The fifth chapter of this book examines the arguments that have been made by the authors of structural adjustment policies and their intellectual supporters against the African worker. Using the experience of Nigerian workers, Bangura and Beckman examine their ideological and policy basis and present the viewpoint of the workers. They defend the right of workers to act in their own self-interest, as does every other social group, and show how in Nigeria workers have resisted various aspects of the adjustment programme that touch on their livelihood. The struggle between Nigerian workers and the state over the removal of the 'oil subsidy' is one dimension of the politics of structural adjustment which this chapter examines. Workers' strategies at the workplace in the face of adjustment and the way these feed into national strategies of the Nigeria Labour Congress are also analysed. In addition, the attempt by the Nigerian labour movement to construct alliances with other groups adversely affected by structural adjustment is considered. This section of the chapter discusses from the workers' perspective some of the issues in alliance politics which Jega covers in Chapter 6 from the professionals' viewpoint. Bangura and Beckman conclude their analysis with the way in which the aspiration of Nigerian workers and the leadership which they may offer could form the basis for broadly-based strategies of national reconstruction. In doing this, they insist that the capacity of the state to undertake socio-economic reforms depends on its ability to come to terms with various social forces in the field, including workers.

Resistance to structural adjustment by Nigerian workers has developed side by side with resistance by Nigerian professionals and their associations. In Chapter 6, Attahiru Jega shows how, first with the intensification of the Nigerian economic crisis, and then with the exacerbation of that crisis by the structural adjustment programme, Nigerian professional associations have been compelled to abandon their culture of political aloofness and narrow professional concerns as an increasing number of their members, particularly the younger ones, face deprivation. This has led many of the associations to take on a militant role in the struggle against structural adjustment and in support of political democratization. Jega illustrates this development with a detailed study of academics and lawyers but their experience can also be generalized to include medical doctors, students, nurses and other professionals. The increasing militancy of Nigerian professionals has elicited campaigns of intimidation, divide and rule, co-optation and even proscription from the state but this has not turned the tide against the development of a more activist community of professionals and the wider national struggle for democracy.

The main plank on which the Nigerian government and some officials of the IMF and the World Bank have sought to justify structural adjustment is by arguing that it is meant to redress the decades of injustices suffered by the rural poor who had been neglected by post-colonial development programmes. In Chapter 7, Abdul Raufu

Mustapha considers this issue in his assessment of the implications of structural adjustment for agrarian change in Nigeria. Locating the problematic of Nigerian agrarian development in the relative neglect of the agricultural sector in the post-colonial period, the promotion of wasteful expenditure on schemes of dubious value and the attempt to sidestep the peasantry in favour of 'progressive farmers', Mustapha argues that a key point of departure for the resolution of the Agrarian Question is the far-reaching restructuring of the state itself in order to enhance its allocative efficiency. This restructuring is something which the adjustment programme of the IMF and the World Bank has proved incapable of doing as various aspects of the agrarian crisis such as the problem of food security for Nigerians and the persistence of rural poverty remain unresolved in spite of several years of market reforms. Neither has the market managed to tackle effectively the problem of state failure in Nigeria as corruption has plagued the new bureaucracy established to renew the drive towards rural development. What all of this suggests, according to Mustapha, is that there is still a strong need for an effective developmental state which is able to address the twin issues of economic rationality and political accountability. In this, it cannot be simply assumed that where the state has failed, developmental needs will be served by turning to the fabled market.

The contestation by various social groups of the adverse effects on their interests of the market reforms of the state and the way in which this has translated into a political struggle between an increasingly repressive state and a traditionally active civil society is the object of analysis in Chapter 8. In this chapter, Jibrin Ibrahim focuses on the transitional programme of the military regime which is meant to usher Nigeria into the Third Republic in October 1992, and shows how, in the context of structural adjustment, it has been aimed at narrowing the space for democratic organization and popular participation in the struggle for the improvement of living standards.

Attacks that the state has launched against the mass media, students, trade and professional unions as well as civil liberties are documented and analysed in the context of the quest by the military to shrink the national political space. The heavily regimented transition programme, intermittently amended by the government to suit its shifting whims and caprices, appears set, according to Ibrahim, to launch Nigeria on the path of pro-forma democracy. This is bound to be reinforced by the decision taken by the Armed Forces Ruling Council in April 1990 to dispense with the secret ballot and impose on Nigerians an open ballot queuing system similar to that which Moi practised for two years in Kenya (*Newswatch*, 15 April 1991: 6; 18 February 1991: 8–13). Ibrahim notes, however, that the movement for democracy, manifested through the activities of professional associations and a host of human and civil rights groups, is gathering momentum against all odds.

The centrality of politics to structural adjustment is now widely recognized by supporters and opponents of the programme in the Third World and beyond. The chief proponents of adjustment, in seeking to push the programme, attempt to discredit the opposition and to co-opt its platform. Those forces in the frontline of the struggle against the programme assert the legitimacy of their case and attempt to compel the state to come to terms with them (Beckman, 1990). It is therefore little wonder that so much conflict and contestation accompanies the attempt to implement market reforms. In the view of the contributors of this book, it is inconceivable that the stalemate that characterizes the present Nigerian and wider African conjuncture can be effectively overcome without coming to terms seriously with the aspirations of the majority of the people as captured by the demands for better living conditions which they believe the market cannot offer, at least not in isolation. What the contributors to this book have sought in different ways to underline is that these aspirations will have to be given a central place in the search for a non-repressive, democratic social arrangement in support of economic and political reforms.

Notes

1. See Chapter 4 below for further details.
2. Ibid.
3. For a discussion and critique of these explanations, see Bangura, 1982, 1989: 4–5, 1991.
4. Ibid.
5. Ibid.
6. Some of these alternatives were tabled during the Nigerian national debate on the IMF in 1985. More recently, in 1989, there was an attempt to convene a national conference on alternatives to SAP but this was brutally repressed by the government. Ironically, it was the government that had earlier challenged its critics to present alternatives to the adjustment programme.
7. The retired civil servants wing of the national conference movement was led by Philip Asiodu, one of the 'super' permanent secretaries of the Gowon era, while the radical wing was led by Alao Aka-Bashorun. Aka-Bashorun and his colleagues have set up a national conference secretariat in the hope that it will still be possible for them to convene a conference before October 1992.

References

Y. Bangura (1982), 'The Payments Crisis of the Nigerian State' (mimeo). Zaria.
—— (1989), *Crisis, Adjustment and Politics in Nigeria*, AKUT, 38.
—— (1991), 'Overcoming Some Basic Misconceptions of the Nigerian Economic Crisis', in Olukoshi (1991b).
B. Beckman (1990). 'Empowerment or Repression? The World Bank and the Politics of African Adjustment' (mimeo).
C.S.P. Okongwu (1987), *A Review and Appraisal of the Structural Adjustment Programme July 1986 to July 1987.* Lagos: Government Printer.
A. Olukoshi (ed.) (1990), *Nigerian External Debt Crisis.* Lagos and Oxford: Malthouse.
A. Olukoshi (1991a), 'Dimensions of the Politics of Structural Adjustment with Nigerian Examples', *Sociology of Development Discussion Paper No. 5.* University of Uppsala.
—— (ed.) (1991b), *Crisis and Adjustment in the Nigerian Economy.* Lagos: JAD Publishers.
J.K. Onoh (1983), *The Nigerian Oil Economy.* London: Croom Helm.

SHEHU YAHAYA

State versus Market: The Privatization Programme of the Nigerian State

I. Introduction

Since the beginning of the 1980s, there has been a decisive swing in the dominant intellectual attitudes and development strategy away from state initiative, ownership and control in the direction of the market mechanism, private ownership and the rolling back of the spheres of state action, especially in relation to industrial investments. This swing has been primarily generated by a number of factors: the perceived success of the Newly Industrialized Countries (NICs) amidst a deepening economic crisis in those Less Developed Countries (LDCs) which apparently placed greater reliance on the state than on the market; the ascent to power of conservative regimes in the key Western industrialized countries, a development which has encouraged the flourishing of right-wing economic doctrines and ideologies; and the deep and extensive macro-economic and social crises facing LDCs. These crises have generally been blamed on mismanagement, inefficiency and the wrong economic policies pursued by most developing countries. In particular, the extensive regulation of trade policies as part of the import-substitution industrialization (ISI) strategy and public ownership of enterprises have been emphasized as causes of distortions, slow or negative growth, and the multiplication of inefficient structures. The correction of these distortionary policies has therefore been at the heart of conditionality clauses which are attached to loans for the LDCs from the International Monetary Fund (IMF), the World Bank, the United States Agency for International Development (USAID) and bilateral donors in the industrialized countries. During the 1980s, not surprisingly, there was an extensive divestiture of state holdings and other forms of privatization in a large number of developing countries. However, it is argued in this chapter that neither a rigorous theoretical analysis, nor a world-wide survey of the performance of public enterprises, would warrant the view that these enterprises have been an unmitigated failure. Similarly, evidence obtained on the performance of public enterprises in Kano, Nigeria's second industrial and commercial centre after Lagos, and presented in this chapter, does not support this view either. We proceed in the second section to analyse the background to the privatization programme of the Nigerian state, examining the provisions of the privatization decree of the government. In the third section, the theoretical issues surrounding the controversy over the state and state intervention, from both the neo-classical/liberal and radical/Marxist frameworks, are examined. In the fourth section, a brief discussion of the national debate on privatization in Nigeria is undertaken while an empirical study of manufacturing enterprises in Kano is conducted in Section Five. The final section draws the implications of the discussions.

II. Background to Privatization in Nigeria

Apart from the parliamentary discussions and debates between political parties conducted between 1959 and 1963 during the First Republic,[1] the first serious attempt to re-examine the role of the state in the economy in terms of its ownership of enterprises and parastatals came in 1981 when the government of Alhaji Shehu Shagari appointed a Presidential Commission on Parastatals to study the matter. The Commission submitted its report in October 1981 against the background of the decline in the country's oil revenue from its peak in 1980. The report of the Commission painted a picture of low returns, low or negative profits, lack of cost effectiveness, and insufficient attention to financial records by parastatals. It recommended an increased role for the private sector, especially in non-sensitive or non-security-related parastatals (The Presidential Commission on Parastatals, 1981).

Before the government could issue a formal response to the report, the country's economic fortunes started to decline rapidly as the effects of the sharp fall in oil incomes and world recession began to be felt. Internationally, the Gross National Product (GNP) of the industrialized countries fell by 0.3 per cent in 1982, and that of the oil-exporting countries by 4.3 per cent in 1981 and by another 4.7 per cent in 1982. In Nigeria, the production of crude oil fell by 2.056 million barrels a day in 1980 to 1.434 million in 1981 and to 1.229 million in 1982. Total federally collected revenue fell from N15,234 million in 1980 to N12,180.1 million in 1981, and further to N11,067 million in 1982. Although agricultural production rose by 3.4 per cent between 1980 and 1981, industrial output fell by 7.9 per cent. Exports of goods and services fell from N13,295 million in 1980 to N9,604 million in 1981 and further to N7,427 million in 1982; external reserves fell by more than 50 per cent in 1982. Payments arrears on imports rose to N2.2 billion. The Gross Domestic Product (GNP) fell by 5.9 per cent in 1981 (at 1977/8 prices) and by a further 3.4 per cent in 1982 (CBN, 1981, 1982, 1983).

In a bid to contain the growing crisis in the country's economy, the government of Alhaji Shagari introduced an economic stabilization programme in April 1982 with a view, primarily to reducing internal and external deficits through demand management. Although the situation of the industrialized countries and especially Nigeria's trading partners improved slightly, with modest increases in output and decline in inflationary pressure, the domestic situation in Nigeria merely deteriorated further. GDP fell by a further 4.4 per cent, inflation rose by 23.2 per cent and industrial output fell by a record 11.9 per cent. Although the import restrictive measures succeeded in cutting imports by 23 per cent, because crude oil exports declined by 14.7 per cent to N7.3 billion, the trade deficit was still at N2.1 billion. External reserves fell by another 15 per cent to N885.2 billion, barely enough for a month's imports at the prevailing rate (CBN, 1984).

It was against this background that the government approached the IMF for an extended fund facility of between N1.9 and N2.4 billion. The IMF insisted on the fulfilment of a number of conditionalities in order for the loan to be granted. These included a curb on government spending; privatization and commercialization of parastatals; rationalization of tariff structures, which would involve considerable trade liberalization and a vigorous export promotion drive involving non-oil products; the introduction of sales taxes; an increased share for the private sector in credit issues; the phasing-out of subsidies and quantitative import restrictions; and a reduction in budget deficits and a more widespread use of efficiency criteria for determining projects (Bangura, 1987). No concrete agreements were reached with the IMF before the Shagari government was overthrown in a military *coup* on 31 December 1983. However, the new military regime which came into power accepted and implemented some of the contradictory demand policies recommended by the IMF.

In relation to the parastatals, a Study Group on Statutory Corporations and State-owned Enterprises and Public Utilities was set up in August 1984 with the mandate to examine the causes of the inefficiency of state-owned enterprises (SOEs), the desirability and methodology of privatization, possible methods for reviewing the management structure of the enterprises and ways in which cost recovery measures could be realized (The Report of the Commission, 1984: chapter 2, 1). Most of the members of the Study Group recommended the adoption of selective privatization of parastatals, with between 55 and 70 per cent in favour of the private sector enabling greater efficiency in resource use, provided that this did not extend to areas which might be injurious to the 'national interest' (The Report of the Commission, 1984: 51–2).[2]

The government, while accepting the arguments of the Group, nevertheless rejected privatization as a general solution, and instead opted for commercializing the enterprises (Adamolekun and Laleye, 1986). Counter-trade was also explored as a way of relieving immediate scarcity of vital imports, and of escaping the credit squeeze that had, by 1984, been imposed by international financiers on Nigeria in the face of the country's worsening crisis. The military government, however, refused to devalue the currency, and mapped out plans for the repayment of external debt, which in 1984 consumed 44 per cent of export earnings. Moreover, the regime took far-reaching steps to suppress domestic dissension to its policies. It inaugurated the 'War Against Indiscipline' to combat various forms of inefficiency, lack of dedication to service, lateness to and absenteeism from work, corruption, embezzlement and other related problems.

While it received some support for its nationalist stance against devaluation, which stand had led to the breakdown of negotiations with the IMF, the military regime, because of its high-handedness, provoked widespread opposition from a cross-section of pressure groups, which it sought to suppress as part of its crisis management strategy. It alienated the media by enacting a decree that sought to prevent the press from criticizing the government and its functionaries; the media barons by starving them of newsprint; the unions and intellectuals by freezing wages, arresting union leaders and reducing expenditure on health and education; the south by its apparently northern bias; and the senior army officers by its proposals for asset and wealth investigation. In general, it lost whatever political constituency and initial popularity it had gained after coming to power in 1983. Only a tiny cabal of traders involved in the counter-trade scheme and a small section of the bureaucracy and petty bourgeoisie who perceived the regime as tough and capable of imposing discipline on national life continued to support the government. Its overthrow in August 1985 did not therefore come as a surprise.

The new government, after launching a national debate on the IMF, announced a Structural Adjustment Programme (SAP) in July 1986 which contained most of the IMF conditionalities, although it conceded to public opinion by not taking the IMF loan itself. SAP, which, officially, was to last two years, had as its main objectives the restructuring and diversification of the economy; the achievement of balance of payments and fiscal viability; non-inflationary growth; reducing the breadth of the public sector and improving the opportunities of the private sector; reducing the value of the naira and rationalizing the tariff structure; a general liberalization of the economy aimed at derestricting market forces; establishing more appropriate prices for public sector goods and petroleum; rationalization and privatization of SOEs; and generally stimulating domestic production (Phillips, 1987). Wages were also to be frozen during the SAP period. The programme was obviously enunciated within a perspective that endorsed the free market as the framework for a major restructuring of the Nigerian economy.

In the new year budget of 1988, the government issued a list of SOEs, categorized according to whether they would be privatized or commercialized, fully or partially. On 5 July 1988, the government proceeded to promulgate the privatization and commercialization decree no. 25 of 1988 which, like the 1988 budget, categorized all state-owned enterprises and parastatals into four main groups, according to whether they were to be fully or partly privatized, or fully or partly commercialized. Those slated for full privatization included 13 insurance companies in which the federal government had between 25 per cent and 49 per cent shareholding, 10 medium- to large-scale manufacturing firms, 2 hotels, 4 companies in the transportation sub-sector and 15 agricultural and agro-allied firms. The total value of shares which the government expected to sell in these firms was estimated at about N150 million. Enterprises billed for partial privatization were made up of 27 commercial and merchant banks, 23 major manufacturing firms spanning cement production, truck and car assembly plants, fertilizer factories, newsprint and paper mills, engineering and electricity components plants. They also included three steel rolling mills, newspapers, oil companies, shipping and airline companies, etc. The total value of government holdings in these firms was put at over N2.1 billion. Towards the end of 1989, the four commercial vehicle assembly plants in the country were added to the list of firms to be privatized. About 10 major SOEs were to be fully commercialized, and 14 others to be partially commercialized (Federal Government of Nigeria, *Official Gazette*, vol. 75, no. 42, 6 July 1988; CBN, *Bullion*, 1988: 23–4). A Technical Committee on Privatization and Commercialization (TCPC) was set up to oversee and implement the exercise. It was further explained that enterprises which were in a good financial position should be sold or commercialized as appropriate. Those earmarked for privatization but which were not commercially attractive would be given financial injections in the form of debt cancellation or increased user charges; parastatals with very low equity/debt ratios would be revived with the injection of more equity or the conversion of some of their loans to equity; those with inadequate accounts would have their accounts prepared for five consecutive years in order to enable proper share valuation; those that appeared unrescuable would be dismantled, and their assets sold (Falae, 1988). In selling shares, inter regional, inter-personal and inter-state distribution effects would be considered. Specifically, according to the decree, associations and interest groups like state investment agencies, trade unions, universities, women, friendly and community associations would all be encouraged to buy shares.

By the end of 1989, the TCPC had arranged for the sale of 16 firms, including the Nigerian Flour Mills, 2 petroleum firms and 13 insurance companies. The sales were organized through the Nigerian stock exchange. As we shall attempt to show later, the pattern which the sale of public enterprises has taken contradicts the purported objectives of the privatization/commercialization programme. Before we consider the arguments on privatization in the specific context of Nigeria, let us first of all review the current theoretical debate on the state and the market.

III. The Theoretical Debate on Privatization

The Neo-Classical and Liberal Approaches
The earliest arguments for state intervention within the neo-classical and liberal frameworks were closely linked with the views held by various scholars on the conditions necessary for import-substitution industrialization in the Third World and the obstacles posed for it by the international division of labour, as evidenced by the works of R. Prebisch, H. Singer, G. Mydral, and a host of other scholars. Their arguments in support of state interventionism were premised on various platforms within the neo-classical and liberal economic traditions. The Rosenstein–Rodan model, for example, premises its support for state interventionism on the need for a wide range of complementary activities in order to achieve rapid industrial growth.[3] Hirschman also pointed out the substantial benefits that could be derived from forward, and especially backward, linkages, if concrete action is taken by the state (Hirschman, 1968). Nurske, Prebisch, Singer and other structuralists all joined the debate in favour of state intervention, and against the unfettered market mechanism.

By the end of the 1960s and early 1970s, however, most developing countries following the state-interventionist framework of accumulation began to undergo economic crises whilst the NICs, presented as the models of Third World market capitalism, were enjoying a boom and were generally doing much better. A number of critiques against the ISI model and state intervention thereby emerged.

Reasserting the Case for the Market
One set of criticisms against ISI centred on various kinds of protection against trade, engendered by state intervention, which induced inefficient, oligopolistic structures of production, thereby undermining consumer welfare, without delivering the technological developments and learning effects it had promised. This was then contrasted with the success of the NICs in achieving rapid rates of output and export growth through liberal and more efficient policies. The critics argue further that state policies on wages, interest rates and prices encouraged inappropriate production techniques and drove interest rates close to zero; these combined to generate unwarranted levels of capital-intensity in production, and discouraged exports (Krueger et al., 1981–3).

Another view, advocated by Lal, Little and others, while recognizing the reality of market failure, contends that the attempt by the state to intervene in order to correct this has produced bureaucratic failure of such dimensions as to be greater than the market failure it had set out to correct. Furthermore, attempts to use planning and modelling techniques to correct the bureaucratic failure have merely compounded the problem by magnifying the smaller effects of mistakes committed by individual economic agents at the micro-level to a higher, more pervasive national macro-level. Besides, such intervention incurs further costs on acquisition and processing of information, implementation of decisions, etc., which would have been avoided if the market had been allowed sway (Lal, 1983; Little, 1982). Due to these factors, the case for the market is reasserted, not because market failure is not recognized, but because the alternative to the market would produce inferior outcomes.

The literature on public choice theory on the other hand suggests that the state consists of a coalition of different groups, sometimes acting in concert to promote common interests at the expense of the rest of society, and sometimes breaking into component parts, pursuing competing interests.[4] In this case, the idea of a monolithic state, acting to maximize social welfare in a general sense, is no more than a myth.[5]

The Rosenstein–Rodan argument as a justification for government intervention is also challenged by Little on the grounds that it does not apply to open economies.[6] Hirschman's linkages, when administratively promoted, are said by him to contribute to inappropriately capital-intensive methods of production. In general, many ISI and interventionist policies are dismissed as emerging more out of nationalist fervour and an uncritical copying of Soviet models.

There have also been cruder arguments against state intervention, mainly arising out of the ideological impact of the ascension of powerful conservative regimes in the US, UK and to a lesser extent in other parts of Europe. Referred to as the 'New Right', the political and ideological partisans of these regimes argue that state intervention, especially in the form of public enterprises, is responsible for economic decay, especially in countries like the UK, and re-emphasize the philosophical heritage of Adam Smith and J.S. Mill as the more useful models of economic and social organization (Wiltshire, 1987).

The implications of these arguments are to call for divestiture or privatization of public enterprises, and a general review of the scope for state intervention. While the more intellectually serious arguments for the unfettering of the market would be in favour of a range of policies, from changes in ownership to various forms of reform, de-control and liberalization, the more overtly ideological approaches argue for a more comprehensive and far-reaching reduction in income tax and welfare programmes, wholesale privatization in all sectors, restriction or elimination of union power as a restraint on the operation of the market mechanism, and the promotion of widespread share-ownership in society.

Lastly, especially in the context of the UK, arguments for privatization have often challenged the notion that state intervention and extensive public ownership imply a more equitable inter-personal income and wealth distribution. Instead, it is argued that privatization offers an important avenue for widespread share-ownership, 'popular capitalism', which will enable a wide range of ordinary workers to own shares (Wiltshire, 1987).

The Dirigiste Response

The responses to the arguments against state intervention and in favour of the market have been quite varied. The view championed by the 'New Right' has been generally dismissed as an unserious argument. This is because within the liberal tradition, since the time of Karl Polanyi, it has been recognized that there is nothing natural, inevitable or spontaneous about *laissez-faire*ism or the unfettered market mechanism. Even during earlier, more competitive stages of capitalism, measures like social legislation, factory laws, unemployment insurance, trade unions and other measures were introduced to protect workers from the effects of *laissez-faire*ism; land laws and agrarian tariffs have conditioned the exploitation of resources; and central banking and management of the monetary system have been developed to guide the use of money. 'The road to the free market was opened and kept open by an enormous increase in centrally organised and controlled interventionism' (Polanyi, 1944: 140, cited in Mjoset and Bohlin, 1985). Any trumpeted calls for a reversion to some previous *laissez-faire* ideal models cannot therefore, at the intellectual level, be regarded as serious.

Others have argued, as a direct response to the anti-dirigistes, that there is still a case for ISI and state intervention. One line of argument is that, even for the NICs, the state has played a crucial role in their strategy, and that the avowed success of their export promotion strategies was possible only because of the tremendous effects of a previous, and in many instances co-existing, import-substitution strategy,[7] and because of strategic and geo-political factors. Besides, the results of a number of empirical studies on public enterprises in several countries have also cast serious doubt on the assertion that they have been uniformly inefficient and ineffective (Gantt and Dutto, 1968; Tyler, 1979; Trebat, 1983; Killick, 1983; Kirkpatrick et al., 1984; Saulniers, 1985, etc.).

Secondly, to ensure that the decisions taken under the free market today will bring about an inter-temporally efficient allocation of investments, a perfect futures market and perfect foresight must be assumed. But these assumptions clearly do not apply in the real world. In LDCs, where information is especially inadequate, institutional arrangements are poor and long-term extrapolation especially unreliable, even hazardous, the decision of private economic agents may be very short-sighted, hence providing a case for government to stimulate investments in sectors important to the future, since it is likely to have more resources to acquire information than have private agents. Even if such information is distributed, rather than used to make direct investments, there is still the problem of political and social instability which causes private agents to avoid long-gestating investments, no matter how much it will enhance social welfare.[8] Hence there is a clear case for the state in LDCs to undertake socially desirable, long-gestating projects, especially those associated with techno-logical innovations, and which are critical to development.

The Hirschman linkages argument also still retains considerable validity. This is because objections to it on the basis that it generates capital-intensity are not founded on any theoretical premise, so it is a matter for empirical validation.

Another ground on which state intervention is justified in economic theory is the existence of externalities, in which private firms cause, for example, pollution, or create externalities through staff training, but which do not appear in the firms' books. Here again, it is often objected that the proper policy measure is not state intervention in production, but a system of taxes and subsidies.

The 'discovery' by the public choice theorists that the state consists of different interest groups may be somewhat new to neo-classical economics, but is no more than a shallow and partial abstraction from the Marxist theoretical framework, and does not make an unambiguous case for the market. It reminds us that the state may not be acting in the interests of a common weal, but the market also acts to produce outcomes that are certainly not representative of 'common' welfare.

In general, it is frequently argued that whenever LDCs are confronted with the problems of monopoly and oligopoly, which cause distortions and reduce welfare, the types of interventions called for are taxes, price regulation, administrative control; when the problem is one of externalities, then taxes and subsidies are called for. In broad terms, government policy, working through the price system, can usually correct for these distortions, and this approach is more effective than direct state intervention in production. The problem, however, is that all these administrative measures are also likely to suffer from inefficiencies and lapses. For example, it is well known that a substantial proportion of income tax in LDCs is never collected. Subsidy schemes for fertilizers, irrigation equipment and farm implements, fuel, etc. have encountered enormous problems and incurred substantial costs due to inefficient implementation, corruption and smuggling. So, although state intervention in produc-tion requires additional costs of acquisition of information and processing, and may generate managerial and operational inefficiencies, it is also true that systems of taxes, incentives, subsidies, etc. would also entail administrative costs and are also threatened by inefficiency and mismanagement. To put it another way, the arguments for taxes and subsidies, in essence, merely advocate the substitution of some forms of state intervention for others. Which of the two is more costly and inefficient, and which will result in greater loss to consumer welfare, cannot, it seems, be settled on an *a priori* basis. Intuitively, states which possess a capacity to implement the market strategies effectively would also be able to intervene and operate public enterprises more effectively.

Secondly, the notion that the public sector is inherently more inefficient, which is tied up with the property rights argument, cannot withstand a close examination. This is because of the well-known managerial utility functions which arose in the context of the separation between ownership and control in the modern private enterprise, extensively discussed by Berle and Means and Galbraith for example, and which indicated that management in private enterprises could pursue goals different from the objectives of shareholders. Furthermore the takeover (or liquidation) threat, which is supposed to motivate managers in the private sector, does not unambiguously apply.[9] Besides these, the case for state intervention in macro-economic policy issues like investment, unemployment, inflation, money supply and the credit system, etc. have never been substantially dented by the advocates of the market mechanism.[10]

The Radical and Marxist Approach
The starting-point for radical and Marxist analyses is that the state serves the interests of dominant classes, and is a crucial agent for private accumulation, especially in the underdeveloped countries. Much of the debate concerns itself with arguments on the particular patterns of class formation; the existence of the bourgeoisie and its sub-categories, namely, the comprador, national, commercial, managerial, etc.; and which fractions have a greater grip on the state. Other important issues are the particular role and significance of international capital, whether the state is 'soft', underdeveloped or overdeveloped, and the organization, strength, struggles and impacts of the dominated classes.

Those who have focused on the 'soft' or underdeveloped state in Africa argue that it lacks autonomy and is dominated by particularistic interest groups rooted in ethnic and regional constituencies, who plunder it for personal accumulation, thus rendering it ineffective and inefficient in pursuing genuine developmental goals (Booth, 1987; Joseph, 1983).

Others contend that the state is primarily controlled by an alliance of the domestic comprador bourgeoisie and foreign capital; they explicitly or implicitly attribute the weaknesses of the state to the weakness or absence of a domestic national bourgeoisie. This is again used to explain the corruption, inefficiency and mismanagement that has become pervasive in so many African countries (Williams, 1976; Forrest, 1982; Osoba, 1978; Usman, 1984; Turner, 1980).

A critique of this approach instead emphasizes the facilitating role of the state in the emergence and consolidation of the bourgeoisie in Africa through trade policies, direct investment in manufacturing and infrastructure, allocation of foreign exchange, licences, credit and other facilities, and a general expansion of the state sector (Sender and Smith, 1986).

A similar position is taken by Beckman, who argues that the state, as a 'transnational project', is in fact busily promoting capitalist development, its actions determined not only by the relative impact of various fractions of the domestic bourgeoisie and international capital, but also influenced by the struggles of various segments of the oppressed classes (Beckman, 1981, 1982, 1983).

Specifically referring to state institutions like parastatals, Sobhan argues that the extent of state intervention and its effectiveness is largely determined by the circumstances of the transition to independence and the relative strengths of the national, comprador, international and petty bourgeoisie, as well as that of the masses (Sobhan, 1979).

Collins, on the other hand, seeks to explain the state and state action in West Africa as an outcome not only of class forces but also of complex combinations of ethnic, regional and sectional factors (Collins, 1977).

Most of the discussion and debate within the radical and Marxist tradition has been principally concerned with developing a clear and coherent theoretical and analytical framework for understanding the state and its intervention, its dimensions, its success or failure; much less attention has been devoted to addressing the contemporary debate of the state and the market in the context of Africa. This is partly because, even when the inefficiency, mismanagement and ineffectiveness of state institutions are discussed, there is a tendency to argue that only a revolutionary transformation of the state can solve the problem (Toyo, 1984); or simply to shrug it off on the grounds that the private sector in these countries is no better (Dahiru, 1987). But the real and immediate alternative facing most of these countries is between various kinds of state intervention and various forms of the market mechanism, rather than between capitalism and socialism. Alternatively, it is argued either directly or indirectly that both the public and private enterprises in capitalist societies are instruments through which private accumulation is facilitated anyway. Even if public enterprises are inefficient and corrupt, and fail to carry out their objectives, it may only mean that various kinds of contractors, consultants, suppliers and bureaucrats will benefit from such inefficiency, and enhance their own private accumulation (Beckman, 1989). So either way, accumulation goes on, especially if such private appropriation or misappropriation results in increased private investment. But this approach ignores the basic premise that public enterprises, at least theoretically, fulfil important functions for capitalism at particular moments in its development which cannot be performed by private capital.[11] These functions are similar to those discussed in the context of the neo-classical model, i.e. the establishment of infrastructure, generating linkages, technological development and research, inducing appropriate technologies, educating and training the work-force, and the provision of certain aspects of social welfare so as to try to ensure system stability. These functions are required in the interests of capital in general, and yet cannot be provided, except by accident, by private capital. Thus the appropriation of the resources of public enterprises by private agents, even if invested, will not substitute for these functions. An appraisal of the performance of the state, especially of state enterprises, whatever else it includes, should therefore take into account measures which will test its capacity to perform these functions. A re-evaluation of the frontiers of state intervention *vis-à-vis* the market should hence be based on the outcome of such analyses.

Following the above logic, we arrive at the peculiar position in which the criteria that are required for an empirical assessment of the performance of state enterprises, using both the neo-classical and radical frameworks, are similar. The necessity for conducting a concrete analysis of specific forms of state intervention in specified settings is similarly derived from both premises. Any policies for large-scale privatization as being implemented in Nigeria must be based on an exhaustive study which can demonstrate the unambiguously poor performance of state enterprises.

In conducting such an examination of state intervention, I have selected state investments in the manufacturing sector in Kano, Nigeria, partly because manufacturing is the sector where the arguments for the relinquishment of state intervention have been most powerfully advanced, and partly due to convenience. Before discussing the case study I shall first briefly review the privatization debate in Nigeria.

IV. The Argument for Privatization in Nigeria

It must be remembered that the initial impetus for state ownership in the 1960s and 1970s was concerned with both pragmatism and ideology. It was attributable to nationalism; the prevalent wisdom in development economics at the time which favoured import-substituting industrialization; the phenomenal expansion of the resources available to the state from oil exports; the weakness of the private sector which corresponded to the relatively low level of development of capitalism; and the need to attain certain welfare objectives. In articulating arguments for privatization, the supporters of the programme in Nigeria have sought either to question the initial wisdom of state intervention, or to argue that, regardless of the initial motives for intervention, a review of SOEs has been necessitated by their unacceptably poor level of performance.

Perhaps the most influential argument for privatization during the recent debate in Nigeria was the one put forward by the first Chief of General Staff in the Babangida administration, Ebitu Ukiwe. According to him, privatization has been made necessary by the abysmally low return on physical capital invested on parastatals. He stated that of the N23.2 billion invested in parastatals up to that period, the returns from equity amounted to a paltry N933.7 million, equivalent to 4 per cent. He noted that the poverty of these returns spoke for itself, and therefore privatization and commercialization were necessary in order to foster greater efficiency.[12]

It has similarly been argued that private enterprises are inherently more efficient, hence even if SOEs were made to improve, it would still pay greater dividends if they were privatized; that in many cases, state investment was really due to the weakness of private capital, and that since the private sector is now much stronger, obstacles to further progress in its path should be lifted; similarly, many areas reserved exclusively for the state as 'strategic' or 'commanding' are no longer so, and should therefore be opened to the private sector; enterprises established to make contributions to national coffers, but which suffered perennial losses, have lost the right to remain in government hands. SOEs operating side by side with the private sector, but doing demonstrably less well, should be privatized; in general, fiscal difficulties provide a basis for stopping the subsidization of SOEs (The Report of the Commission, 1984: 47–9).

The Managing Director of the Nigerian Industrial Development Bank (NIDB), the most important state-owned industrial investment company, has also argued that:

> Operationally, most of the PEs in Nigeria are grossly inefficient and are much behind in meeting the purpose for which they were established. Financially, they are most unprofitable. They have maintained a consistent record of increasing losses, year after year, and have depended on government subsidy for survival. . . . Why is NEPA not in a position to meet cost, whereas its counterparts in Britain (the British Electricity Generating Board) and some Third World countries, which are equally public enterprises, have been very profitable? (Abdulkadir, 1987)

Another argument also accepts the inherent superiority of the market mechanism and perceives state intervention as simply one of ground-breaking and pioneering. Once this is done, the private sector should be allowed to take over and operate these areas more productively and more efficiently, while the state moves into other new frontiers (Falae, 1988: 7).

On the strength of these arguments, the total privatization of SOEs in the manufacturing and services sector is advocated, except in sub-sectors beyond the financial capability or willingness of the private sector, or in security-sensitive areas.

It can be seen that most of the arguments that have been advanced to support privatization tend to focus on the financial losses of SOEs and the basic ideological contention that production of goods and services is mainly the proper province of the private sector, which is inherently more able to operate it effectively. But these kinds of arguments provide a very feeble justification for privatization.

Firstly, the low return on equity invested in SOEs conceals some of the facts. The N23.2 billion investment cited is actually made up of N11.43 billion in equity investment, N10.42 billion in direct government loans and N1.4 billion in loans guaranteed by the government. The third component should therefore not be counted as part of government investment. Secondly, these figures represent total equity investments and loans over time, so they were obviously not all made right at the beginning. Thirdly, investments in manufacturing and finance sectors, in which commercial rates of return are expected, are bunched together with investments in capital-intensive industries which are uncompleted or are in their first few years of operation (like the steel industry or the petrochemical plants for example), and with sectors which are not, and have never been, expected to generate surplus but were rather to serve welfare and research purposes (like the various research institutes, water supply, procurement and distribution agencies, etc.). This is obviously a very muddled approach, and cannot be expected to provide a useful guide to the performance of SOEs.

More generally, based on the arguments presented earlier, the incurrence of financial losses cannot by itself provide a wholesale justification for privatization. Moreover, from the list of firms being privatized, it can be seen that many of them are not the archetypal loss-making SOEs, but have actually been making profits and contributing, by way of taxes and dividends, to government funds. NIDB, from which the government is shedding at least 30 per cent of its shareholding, earned a profit of N4.7 million on a turnover of N15.1 million in 1979, and N7.3 million on a turnover of N19.3 million in 1980, and was ranked no. 8 and no. 6 in the two years respectively, in a survey of 14 major financial institutions in the country. Although no information on the performance of most of the manufacturing and agro-allied firms is available to us, the little there is indicates that, in their case also, losses were not as obvious or as commonplace as the advocates of privatization claim. The Nigerian Flour Mills for example earned a profit of N12.6 million before tax on a turnover of N128 million in 1979, and N13.2 million on a turnover of N147 million the next year, and was ranked for both years as no. 6 in a survey of 52 major manufacturing establishments in the country. It is slated in the decree to be fully privatized. Roads Nigeria, also slated for full privatization, earned N2.9 million and N3.6 million profits on a turnover of N37.1 million and N41.6 million in 1979 and 1980 respectively. North Breweries, also listed for full privatization, has been making fabulous profits.[13]

Among the firms to be fully commercialized is Nigerian Telecommunications Limited. In the case of this firm, although commercialization may be rational in the long run, it makes sense to subsidize it in the short run so as to enable a substantial expansion of its domestic services, particularly in the area of the provision of domestic telephones. When a mass market for telephones has developed, hopefully along with the capacity to pay, it would then make sense fully to commercialize it. Premature commercialization may just throttle the market, maintain a relatively small clientele, and inhibit the emergence of scale economies.

On the whole, it is clear from the schedule, and from the kinds of firms already privatized, that the argument on perennial losses or inefficiency was not the determining factor in the privatization of SOEs, although it was probably more relevant to the enterprises scheduled for commercialization. It is also significant that, except for a handful of the firms (no more than 10 out of 139), no thorough appraisal of the economic, social and financial performance of the enterprises was conducted before the decision to privatize them was undertaken. Rather, the most significant impetus for privatization was the pressure of international financial institutions and Nigeria's trading partners in the industrialized world on the government, following the onset of the country's economic crisis, to adopt a programme of privatization as part of a structural adjustment package. This context of internal economic crisis and external pressure has in turn reinforced the hand of domestic capitalists whose expansion has been facilitated by the oil boom of the 1970s. The oil boom expanded the scope for private accumulation in manufacturing, commerce and distribution, road haulage and transportation, real estate, construction, speculation and other spheres of business. The way in which the state handled the disbursement of the oil revenues certainly played a central role in the expansion of local capital. Furthermore, the expansion of the domestic bourgeoisie was facilitated by the activities of the state through measures such as indigenization, loans and credits etc., which enabled them gradually to expand their capital base, and diversify into medium level manufacturing production, often in partnership with foreign capital or the state, or both.[14]

V. State Investments in the Manufacturing Sector: The Kano Experience

The Historical Background

Historically, Kano occupied an important position as one of the Hausa Kingdoms which served as a central trading entrepôt linking the other Hausa Kingdoms, through the trans-Saharan trade routes, to North Africa. In the first decade of the nineteenth century, it was conquered by the jihadists and formed part of the Sokoto caliphate. The British colonialists in turn took Kano in 1903 and established a colonial administration as part of Northern Nigeria. In 1960, with the country's independence, it became one of the 13 provinces of Northern Nigeria, and evolved into a state in 1967. With an estimated population of about 10 million people, Kano State is the most populous of the 21 states in Nigeria. Its capital, Kano municipality, with a population of about 832,000, is reckoned to be the third largest city in Nigeria.

By the end of the colonial period, the pre-colonial economy based on handicraft production, extensive trade networks with North and West Africa, peasant agricultural production, an exchange system based on barter and the use of cowrie shells, and a political system based on the authority of the emirs and chiefs had been substantially transformed. A budding capitalist economy, still based on small-scale agricultural production, a rapidly developing manufacturing sector, an extensive network of roads and railways, extensive monetization, increasing importance of financial institutions, and a parliamentary system of Western democracy, complete with a house of assembly, had come into existence. The economy of Kano, along with the rest of the country, had become firmly integrated into the international capitalist system. The post-independence period saw an acceleration of this process of capitalist transformation, in which indigenous forces played an increasingly active role.[15]

The government and its agencies have been important in this transformation through their indigenization policies, provision of free industrial plots, information, physical infrastructure and direct investments. The Kano State Investment and Properties Ltd (KSIP), established in 1971, has been especially important, being responsible for all the industrial investments and shareholdings of the Kano State government. These investments and shareholdings increased dramatically between 1973 and 1978, as a result of the indigenization decrees of 1972 and 1977.

What has the performance of public sector industrial investment in Kano been like and what does this tell us about the drive towards the privatization of state-owned enterprises? In the empirical examination which follows, the analysis will focus primarily on the 15 manufacturing enterprises in which the KSIP and other government agencies (including the NIDB, NNIL, the federal government, as well as other state governments) have invested with a view to answering this question.

The Empirical Results
The enterprises analysed had varying degrees of state involvement, ranging from 9 per cent to 100 per cent. They spanned the textile, wood and metal products, food, leather products, aluminium products, cement products and vehicle assembly industries. Eleven other privately-owned enterprises, of similar sizes, producing similar products, which include aluminium products, leather goods, food, roofing sheets, ceramics and textiles, were analysed. The data is for the period between 1975 and 1986.

The variables used to measure the comparative performance of these enterprises are value-added, total and partial factor productivities, factor intensity, economic and financial profits, return on physical investment, backward and forward linkages, income distribution, net social benefits and capacity utilization. These are used to measure economic efficiency, social efficiency, as well as capacity for promoting capitalist development within the domestic economy.

The statistical analysis yielded some unexpected results. Contrary to the general view of public enterprises as financially inefficient and wasteful, no significant relationships emerged between the mode of ownership of manufacturing enterprises in the sample and financial or economic profitability. Furthermore, there was no evidence that the private or privately-controlled enterprises had achieved higher levels of factor productivity, labour productivity or capacity utilization. However, government-owned and -controlled enterprises achieved poorer returns on physical capital.

On the other hand, the government-owned and -controlled enterprises did not indicate a greater capacity to generate forward and backward linkages, or a greater emphasis on technological research, functions which have been shown to be important in the review of the theoretical justification for public enterprises. Indeed, they have used more capital-intensive methods of production, which are considered to be inappropriate to the circumstances of labour-surplus economies like Nigeria.[16] In addition, their attitudes towards the unionization of their workers is by no means superior to those of the private industrialists. However, they showed some tendency for achieving better results in terms of income distribution and net social benefits, although the evidence for this is somewhat tentative.

VI.   Implications and Conclusion

It is obvious that we cannot conclude from the above findings that public enterprises in the Nigerian manufacturing sector have comparative levels of economic and financial profitability and factor/labour productivity with private firms, and thereby claim that the argument for privatization, which has tended to be pushed in terms of the poor performance of public enterprises, is unjustified. Conversely, the results do not provide any unambiguous grounds for arguing that the enterprises have failed in their primary objective of promoting an integrated capitalist development. Quite apart from the methodological dangers of this kind of extrapolation, there has also been some clear evidence that many other public enterprises elsewhere in the country have performed abysmally on financial efficiency grounds, and many are tottering on the brink of collapse.

The main lesson to be derived is that there is no basis for concluding that public enterprises in general have been a failure. Rather, it is necessary to make a concrete analysis which recognizes that there may be substantial differences between different settings and circumstances, even between different countries and at different historical periods. Secondly, it is necessary to distinguish between different kinds of performance, or different kinds of inefficiency.

The results of the analyses in this study suggest that the correct approach is not to engage in arbitrary forms of privatization, but to recognize that certain kinds of functions can only be performed by public enterprises, and to organize towards gearing up to undertake these tasks effectively. However, for such an approach to be embarked upon and sustained within the capitalist framework in Nigeria, it requires that a bourgeoisie which has firm roots in industrial and agricultural production is able to have a dominant or at least stronger hold on the state and its apparatus. To put it in another way, a significant element of the problems of state enterprises in the Nigerian manufacturing sector concerns the fact that, in spite of the increasing importance of a domestic industrial bourgeoisie, the commercial bourgeoisie in Nigeria have been dominant, and have, along with the international bourgeoisie, mainly determined the outcome of state policy in relation to industrial development. Not surprisingly, therefore, these state policies have mainly responded to the needs of commercial interests, even if there are occasional and unavoidable concessions to the industrial bourgeoisie and the oppressed classes. The current crisis has forced a more serious attitude on the part of the state to the problems of domestic linkages and local technological research capacity. In the short term, this will trim the manufacturing sector, by forcing out some enterprises, and probably succeed in generating some linkages. The position of the domestic bourgeoisie will be strengthened, especially since the threat to commercial interests will still be minimal (they will continue to import much of the machinery, raw materials and consumer goods, and export agricultural commodities). But in the longer run, these policies will tend to be threatened unless the fraction of the bourgeoisie that has a greater stake in industrial and agricultural production is consolidated, or unless a regime that has its base in the working classes is born. Then the conditions for a more integrated development process could begin to be created or strengthened.

Notes

1. This refers to the debates that occurred in parliament, following proposals by the Action Group for the nationalization of insurance companies. In the course of the debate, it was clear that the leading members of all the political parties regarded the role of government intervention in industry as mainly one of enabling the private sector to grow and establish itself (The House of Representatives Debates,

March–April 1960, col. 1046–7). The rest of the discussion on privatization will be limited to the more recent period.

2. One member of the Committee, Mahmud Tukur, disagreed with the report on the specific issue of privatization. He emphasized the need for reforms rather than divestiture.
3. These are discussed in Blomstrom and Hettne, 1984.
4. Anne Krueger has been one of the leading critics of the negative consequences of ISI, and has also been prominent in extolling the performance of NICs. See Krueger et al., 1981–3.
5. A brief discussion of the ideas on public choice theory is contained in the *IDS Bulletin*, vol. 18, no. 3, July 1987.
6. His argument is that the big push policy of generating complementarities assumes a closed economy where exports and import-substitution do not occur, yet in advocating for a labour-intensive consumer goods industry subsequently, Rosenstein–Rodan implies the existence of an open economy where capital goods and intermediate products can be imported.
7. This argument has been imputed from Sender and Smith, 1986.
8. These kinds of arguments have been developed and discussed extensively in Xirinachs, 1985.
9. Actually, the takeover threat is minimal in most developing countries because private firms generally have a greater resort to inflated contracts, political connections, soft loans, favourable import licences, etc., which will allow them to continue operating, even flourish, despite gross operational inefficiences. G. Yarrow has also argued that market failure in corporate control, even in the industrialized countries, substantially reduces the takeover threat, and is not very effective as a deterrent against the pursuit of non-profit goals by managers of private enterprises (Yarrow, 1986).
10. Notwithstanding, the theoretical and empirical studies of the last few decades have clearly made a case for a thorough re-examination of the ISI strategies, have discredited many of the blunt administrative measures used, and have highlighted important difficulties with various forms of state intervention and public enterprises.
11. The importance of this point is not diminished by the fact that in practice, particular state-owned enterprises at particular times may be established for all kinds of objectives which may only be partially connected with this theoretical function.
12. A Review of the State of the Economy presented to Media Executives by E. 'Ukiwe, Chief of General Staff, in *Business Times*, 16.12.1985: 12–13. This came in the wake of revelations from the Study Group on Parastatals in 1984 that the Nigerian Coal Corporation had sustained losses of N5.2 million in 1978, N5.2 million in 1979, N9.6 million in 1980; the Nigerian Airways had suffered huge losses in 1977 and 1982; Nigerian Railway Corporation losses had amounted to N44 million, N56.9 million, N56.9 million, N80 million, N70.4 million and N91 million in 1978/79, 1979/80, April–Dec. 1980, 1981, 1982 and 1983 respectively. Even the Nigerian Ports Authority had negative net margins in 1979, 1980 and 1981 (The Report of the Commission, 1984).
13. The figures on the NIDB and other firms are obtained from *Daily Times of Nigeria*: 'A Survey of Fifty Business Enterprises', 1979 and 1980.
14. Undoubtedly, issues of national security (as in the case of the Security and Minting Corporation) and strategic interest of government (as in the case of some newspaper and radio stations) have played an important role in determining which enterprises are not to be privatized. But this was applicable to only a few cases.
15. For more elaborate discussions of the political economy of Kano, see, among others, Olukoshi, 1986; Bashir, 1984; Lubeck, 1983; Bello, 1982; Babura, 1987; Shenton, 1986.
16. There is considerable controversy, however, as to whether labour-intensive production techniques are necessarily more appropriate to labour-surplus and capital-poor countries. Some have argued that even in such situations, capital intensive methods may be used, if they will enable the generation of higher levels of surplus; these can then be reinvested to accelerate growth, which will expand employment opportunities in more labour-intensive sectors such as construction, services, etc. For a discussion of these issues, see Yahaya, 1983.

References

A. Abdulkadir (1987), 'Privatisation: Pros and Cons'. Paper presented at the Barewa Old Boys Association Annual General Meeting. Kaduna, 16 April.

L. Adamolekun and O.M. Laleye (1986), 'Privatisation and State Control of the Nigerian Economy', *Nigerian Journal of Policy and Strategy*, June.

M. Babura (1987), 'Primitive Accumulation and Transformation in Kano'. Ph.D. Thesis, University of East Anglia.

I.L. Bashir (1984), *Sources of Capital Accumulation among Kano Entrepreneurs*. Boston University, African Studies Center, Working Paper 117.

Y. Bangura (1987), 'IMF and World Bank Conditionality and Nigeria's Structural Adjustment Program', in H.V. Havnenik (ed.), *The IMF and the World Bank in Africa. Conditionality, Impact and Alternatives*. Uppsala: Scandinavian Institute of African Studies.

B. Beckman (1981), 'Imperialism and the National Bourgeoisie', *Review of African Political Economy*, no. 22, October–December.

—— (1982), 'Whose State: State and Capitalist Development in Nigeria', *Review of African Political Economy*, no. 23, January–April.

—— (1983), 'Public Investment and Agrarian Transformation in Northern Nigeria', CSER Reprint no. 13. Zaria.

—— (1989), 'When Does Democracy Make Sense? Political Economy and Political Rights in the Third World' (mimeo). Uppsala.

S. Bello (1982), 'State and Economy in Kano, 1894–1960: A Case Study of Colonial Domination'. Ph.D. Thesis, ABU.

M. Blomstrom and B. Hettne (1984), *Development Theory in Transition*. London: Zed.

D. Booth (1987), 'Alternatives in the Restructuring of State–Society Relations: Research Issues for Tropical Africa', *IDS/EADI Workshop on the Developmental State in Retreat*. IDS, 30 June–1 July.

CBN (1981–4), *Annual Report and Statement of Accounts*.

P. Collins (1977), 'Public Policy and the Development of Indigenous Capitalism: The Nigerian Experience', *Journal of Commonwealth and Comparative Studies*, vol. XV, no. 2, July.

A. Dahiru (1987), 'The Prospects for Transformation through SAP' (mimeo). Kano: Bayero University, September.

S.O. Falae (1988), Interview with S.O. Falae, Secretary to the Federal Military Government on NTA (Nigerian Television Authority), cited in *The Reporter*, 8 February.

T. Forrest (1982), 'Agricultural Policies in Nigeria: 1900–1978', (mimeo). Oxford.

A.H. Gantt and G. Dutto (1968), 'Financial Performance of Government-Owned Corporations in LDCs', *IMF Staff Papers*, no. 15.

A.O. Hirschman (1968), 'The Political Economy of ISI in Latin America', *The Quarterly Review of Economics*, vol. LXXXII, no. 1, February.

R. Joseph (1983), 'Class, State and Prebendal Politics in Nigeria', *The Journal of Commonwealth and Comparative Politics*, vol. XXI, 3 November.

T. Killick (1983), 'The Role of the Public Sector in the Industrialisation of African Developing Countries', *Industry and Development*, no. 7.

C. Kirkpatrick et al. (1984), *Industrial Structure and Policy in LDCs*. London: Allen & Unwin.

A.O. Krueger et al. (eds) (1981–3), *Trade and Employment in Developing Countries*, vols 1–3. Chicago: NBER.

D. Lal (1983), *The Poverty of Development Economics*. London: IEA.

I.M.D. Little (1982), *Economic Development*. New York: Basic Books.

P.M. Lubeck (1983), 'Industrial Labour in Kano: Historical Origins, Social Characteristics and Sources of Differentiation', in B.M. Barkindo (ed.), *Studies in the History of Kano*. Ibadan: Heinemann.

L. Mjoset and Jan Bohlin (1985), 'Introduksjon Til Reguleringskolen', *Aberjidspapier fra Nsu*, No. 21, Nordisk Summeruniversitety.

A.O. Olukoshi (1986), 'The Multinational Corporation and Industrialisation in Nigeria: A Case Study of Kano c.1903–1985'. Ph.D. Thesis, University of Leeds.

S. Osoba (1978), 'The Deepening Crisis of the Nigerian National Bourgeoisie', in *Review of African Political Economy*, no. 13, May–August.

A. Phillips (1987), 'A General Overview of the Structural Adjustment Programme', in A.O. Phillips and E. Ndekwu (eds), *Structural Adjustment Programme in a Developing Economy: The Case of Nigeria*. Ibadan: NISER.

The Presidential Commission on Parastatals (1981). Lagos: Federal Government Press.

The Report of the Commission on Statutory Corporations and State-owned Enterprises and Public Utilities, Lagos, 1984.

A. Saulniers (1985), 'Public Enterprises in Latin America: The New Look?', *Technical Papers Series*, no. 44. ILAS, University of Texas at Austin.

J. Sender and S. Smith (1986), *The Development of Capitalism in Africa*. London: Methuen.

R. Shenton (1986), *The Development of Capitalism in Northern Nigeria*. London: James Currey.

R. Sobhan (1979), 'Public Enterprises and the Nature of the State', *Development and Change*, vol. 10, no. 1.

E. Toyo (1984), 'The Cause of Depression in the Nigerian Economy', *Africa Development*, vol. IX, no. 3.

T.J. Trebat (1983), *Brazil's State Owned Enterprises: A Case Study of State as Entrepreneur*. Cambridge: Cambridge University Press.

T. Turner (1980), 'Nigeria: Imperialism, Oil Technology and the Camprador State', in P. Nore and T. Turner (eds), *Oil and Class Struggle*. London: Zed.

G.M. Tyler (1979), 'The Public Sector Debate and Industrial Development', (mimeo).

B. Usman (1984), 'Middlemen, Consultants, Contractors and the Solutions to the Current Economic Crisis', *Studies in Politics and Society*, no. 2.

G. Williams (ed.) (1976), *Nigeria: Economy and Society*. London: Rex Collings.

K. Wiltshire (1987), *Privatisation: The British Experience*. Melbourne: CEDA/Longman.

J. Xirinachs (1985), 'Re-asserting the Case for State Intervention: A Theoretical Critique of the Free Market Values on Economic Incentives and Development Strategy'. University of Costa Rica, February.

S. Yahaya (1983), 'The Technological Implications of the Nigerian Industrialisation Experience'. M.Sc. thesis. ABU.

G. Yarrow (1986), 'Privatisation in Theory and Policy', *Economic Policy*, 2 April.

AKIN FADAHUNSI

3

Devaluation:
Implications for Employment,
Inflation, Growth & Development

I. Introduction

The Nigerian economy, for most of the 1980s, was, like the great majority of African economies, in a state of crisis. This crisis cannot, in the tradition of neo-classical economic theory, simply be attributed to disequilibria in the demand for and supply of goods and services resulting from gaps in the available savings and investment funds and in the earnings from exports and imports. Rather, it is the outcome of a 'constellation of destabilizing forces that have operated on one another so as to keep the African economies in a state of external and internal imbalance' (Sanusi, 1986: 52).

Faced with a deepening economic crisis which was rapidly assuming social and political dimensions, most African governments have had to approach the International Monetary Fund (IMF) and the World Bank for support. Nigeria has been no exception, even though, unlike most African countries, it did not begin to experience a crisis until 1982 when, following the collapse of the world oil market, and the drastic revenue fall which it implied, the economy started to face serious problems. The collapse of the world oil market served to expose the many contradictions that had been embedded in Nigeria's post-colonial pattern of accumulation. The crisis manifested itself not just in the form of revenue falls but also in industrial decline, inflation, a payments crisis, rising unemployment and a debt service problem, among other symptoms. In spite of the enactment, by the Shagari administration (1979–83), of the Economic Stabilization (Emergency Measures) Act 1982 which, among other measures, emphasized exchange control, as opposed to the devaluation of the naira (CBN, 1982), and in spite of the far-reaching extension of the policy elements of the Act by the Buhari regime (1983–5), the country's economic crisis continued to deepen. With this situation, and in the face of growing pressure from the country's creditors, the Babangida administration (1985–) introduced a Structural Adjustment Programme (SAP) sanctioned by the IMF and the World Bank in July 1986.

By this time, the sharp decline in the country's gross domestic product (GDP), dwindling capacity utilization in industry, widespread unemployment and a sharp drop in the general standard of living made the acceptance of an IMF/World Bank-inspired programme of adjustment seem inevitable to sections of the ruling class and some state officials. The country's external debt had grown from about N2 billion in 1979 to N12.8 billion in 1981 and subsequently to N21.2 billion in 1985. Similarly, debt service payments grew as rapidly from N77.8 million in 1978 to N3.6 billion in 1985 (*Monthly Business and Economic Digest*, July 1987). In accepting the implementation of the IMF/World Bank SAP, the Babangida regime set itself the task, primarily with external support, of redressing the effects on the economy of '25 years of administrative controls, legal restrictions and bureaucratic regulations. The culture of controls is [having] in its place ... a new philosophy of economic liberalism and deregulation' (*Monthly Business and Economic Digest*, July 1987).

At the heart of the IMF/World Bank strategy of structural adjustment in every crisis-ridden developing country is currency devaluation. The Fund and the Bank, dominated as they are by the leading Western countries, accord priority to the protection of their interests, which, in contemporary times, are partly defined in terms of the maintenance of 'stability' in the international economic system. This goes some way towards explaining the almost automatic resort to devaluation in IMF/World Bank-sponsored policies, but there is always an arbitrariness to it because neither theory nor practice has been able to provide a useful guide to the amount of devaluation which will return any given economy to the path of equilibrium. Little wonder then that there is always a divergence of views between the Fund and African governments 'as to the appropriate exchange rates and levels, ... how to reach them, and their likely effects' (Nyirabu, 1986: 36).

It may, however, be pertinent at this stage to ask the question: What is the essence of structural adjustment? In normal usage in economic analysis, structural adjustment connotes quantitative and qualitative changes in the relations among the major sectors of the economy – the components of the GDP. Thus, for a developing economy like Nigeria where a majority of the population is engaged in comparatively less productive agricultural and informal sector activities, policy will be directed towards raising productivity. An industrialization strategy aimed at creating technological capacity that will facilitate efficiency in rural sector activities, social and other services would therefore be accorded a priority role. The effect will be to change the structure of the economy in terms of the labour employed and output in favour of the modernizing sectors of the economy. But this conventional usage of the notion of structural adjustment in economic analysis is not the same as the IMF/World Bank application of the notion, the thrust of which is the attainment of equilibrium in international transactions, hence the central role which they give to devaluation.

This chapter is concerned with an assessment of the impact on the Nigerian economy of devaluation. The central questions which it seeks to address are as follows: Are the monetary and fiscal policy elements associated with the orthodox IMF/World Bank package of economic reforms for Third World countries capable of solving the immediate and long-term adjustment problems of the Nigerian economy? What are the repercussions of devaluation, which is at the heart of IMF/World Bank SAP, on employment, investment and output, and hence on the long-term growth and development of the Nigerian economy? In attempting to address these questions, we shall begin by highlighting the country's experience with currency exchange movements immediately before and after the introduction of SAP. We shall then proceed to analyse the impact of devaluation on Nigeria's major development and growth variables before concluding the chapter with some policy recommendations.

If nations must devalue, then at what rate should this be? What will be the value of the correct or equilibrium exchange rate? The answers are not easy, either theoretically or empirically. Theoretically, 'these notions can only be defined for a particular set of monetary and fiscal policies; a given level of net capital inflows, a given structure of protection and given world prices of tradable goods. For practical purposes it can be supposed that an exchange rate requiring strong support by quantitative restrictions is overvalued', thereby necessitating a devaluation in real terms (Wulf, 1988: 586).

Since the determination of a correct exchange rate in the context of a dependent neo-capitalist economy will be quite illusory, what is required in coping with the crisis of the Nigerian economy, for instance, is pragmatism, a pragmatism informed not just by the intricacies of the bourgeois economic system but also by its geo-political dimensions. In the subsequent sections of this chapter I hope to be able to discuss how realistically the Nigerian state has been trying to cope with the implications of the drastic devaluation of the national currency – the naira – since 1986.

II. Devaluation: The Nigerian Experience

Because the prime objective of devaluation in an economy operating within the existing international economic order is the sustainment of the exchange rate of the local currency at a rate which keeps the balance of payments at equilibrium, policy under SAP in Nigeria has been preoccupied with finding the 'correct' exchange rate for the naira. The mechanism for the determination of such an exchange rate became a public issue only very recently when the Nigerian economic crisis worsened as a result of the glut in the world oil market which led to a fall in price from about $28 per barrel in December 1985 to an all-time low of less than $10 per barrel in July 1986. Nigeria's 1986 budget was premised on $20 per barrel. The sharp decline in the foreign exchange revenue accruing to the state was a key factor in the march by the government to SAP and the resort to a policy instrument like devaluation which is usually more suited for dealing with short-term economic objectives as against the longer-term fundamental problems of sectoral rigidities and imbalance in the economy.

The policy measures that were adopted within the framework of SAP – originally intended to last from (July) 1986 to (June) 1988 – for the management of Nigeria's foreign exchange system can, in comparison with previous practices, be described as radical and indeed revolutionary. Let us proceed to demonstrate this with a discussion of the country's foreign exchange regimes in the periods before and after the intro-duction of SAP. Our discussion of the pre-SAP period is divided into two phases – 1962–83 and 1983–6. As for exchange rate policy in the period following the adoption of SAP, our discussion covers the periods 1986–8 and after. Statistics relevant for illustrating some of the issues raised in this section are summarized in Tables 1, 2 and 3.

Foreign Exchange Management: 1962–83

Oblivious of the likely impact on the country of the monetary policies of the United Kingdom – Nigeria's major trading partner during most of this period – the Central Bank of Nigeria (CBN) sought to pursue a regime of a stable exchange rate between 1962 and 1983. This policy was maintained in spite of the major devaluation of the British pound sterling in November 1967. It was carried over into the oil boom period (1973–82) when activities outside the control of Nigeria's economic managers led to the overvaluation of the naira. If the CBN did not actively monitor the consequences for the naira exchange of the monetary policies of Nigeria's major trading partners, it was basically because it accepted the philosophy of maintaining a fixed link to an external standard. This was considered desirable for a developing economy as it provided a framework within which to organize consistent monetary, fiscal and demand management policies (Abdullahi, 1987; Wickham, 1985).

In pursuance of a policy of maintaining an external link in the determination of 'a viable exchange rate that would minimise inflation, equilibrate the balance of payments and optimise the external reserves position' (see Table 2), Nigerian monetary authorities chose to peg the naira to the US dollar in 1973 (Omoruyi, 1989). This was in response to the generalized floating of the major world currencies in 1973 following the collapse of the Bretton Woods (adjustable peg) system in 1971. Thus the fate of the naira was hitched to the fortunes of the dollar in the international money market. For instance, the naira experienced a *de facto* devaluation as a result of the devaluation of the dollar soon after the naira was pegged to it. A weak US dollar only worsened the inflationary situation in the country, especially during the first quarter of 1974 (Omoruyi, 1989).

To stem the inflationary pressure arising from the weakness of the dollar, the policy of pegging the naira solely to the dollar was abandoned and from 1974 to 1976 the naira was pegged to either the dollar or pound sterling, whichever of the two currencies was stronger in the foreign exchange market. The oil boom, and the huge external surpluses which it brought in its wake, resulted in an increasing overvaluation of the naira. Because the pegging of the naira to the two convertible currencies did not ensure its stability and viability, a policy reversal was effected in the management of the naira exchange rate. Hence, from late 1976, the naira was pegged to a basket of weighted seven currencies comprising the US dollar, the British pound sterling, the Japanese Yen, the German mark, the French Franc, the Swiss Franc and the Dutch Guilder (Abdullahi, 1987; Omoruyi, 1989). This exchange rate regime was continued until 1983.

Exchange Rate Management: 1983–6

Following the onset of a recession in the Nigerian economy from about 1982, a recession triggered by the collapse of the world oil market, the monetary authorities became increasingly aware of the consequences of the overvaluation of the naira and of the need to devalue it (see Table 1). Up to 1982, the exchange rate of the naira to the dollar was still below N0.70 for $1.00. In the mean time, the country's total outstanding debt had risen from N500 million in 1970 to about N2,331 million in 1981 and almost N10,081 million in 1983. At this stage it became clear that some drastic measures had to be taken regarding the naira exchange rate. A deliberate policy was therefore embarked upon to depreciate the naira administratively. The exchange rate management became characterized by the 'crawling-peg' approach to depreciation.

The military administration which overthrew the civilian regime at the end of 1983 inherited an economy that was in a very bad shape. Not only had the country's total external debt risen more than four-fold between 1981 and 1983, total external reserves declined at an alarming rate from about US$8.5 billion in May 1981 to about US$2.5 billion at the end of that year (*Democrat Weekly*, 14 January 1990) and US$1.53 billion or N1.03 billion at the end of 1982 (see Table 3). The balance of trade was in deficit every year from 1981 to 1983. From a favourable trade balance of over N5.1 billion in 1980, there was a deficit of over N2.0 billion during 1982. There was a balance of payments deficit of over N3.0 billion in 1981 (see Table 2). The economic balance sheet of the nation was indeed dismal. The evidence of an overvalued currency was overwhelming and the consequences frightening.

Some of the more obvious indicators of an overvalued naira during the period under review were as follows (Abdullahi, 1987):

(a) The wide divergence between the official exchange rate and the rate at the parallel market, with the latter between two and three times lower than the former before

Table 1 *Nigeria Exchange Rate and Total Outstanding External Debt, 1970–89*

Year	Average Exchange Rate (US$: N)	Total Outstanding Debt US$ Million	Total Outstanding Debt N Million	Percentage Change in Naira Debt
1970	0.71	688.5	488.8	–
1975	0.63	555.4	349.9	– 28.4
1980	0.54	3457.0	1866.8	433.5
1981	0.64	3642.5	2331.2	24.9
1982	0.67	13163.3	8819.4	278.3
1983	0.75	14103.6	10577.7	19.9
1984	0.81	17946.4	14536.6	37.4
1985	1.00	17290.6	17290.6	18.9
1986	2.22	18540.9	41160.9	138.1
1987	4.03	25009.3	100787.6	144.9
1988	4.52	29636.3	133956.3	32.9
1989	7.36	29163.5	214643.5*	60.2
1989/70	10.37	42.36	439.12	
1989/85	7.36	1.67	12.41	

* As at the end of September 1989.
Source: CBN, *Annual Report and Statement of Accounts* for several years.

Table 2 *Balance of Payment, 1979–89 (N Million)*

Year	Export	Import	Balance of Trade	Overall Balance of Payment
1979	10836.8	6169.2	+ 4667.6	+ 1868.9
1980	14186.7	9095.6	+ 5091,1	+ 2402.2
1981	10876.3	12719.8	– 1843.5	– 3020.8
1982	8722.5	10770.5	– 2048.0	– 1398.3
1983	7502.5	8903.7	– 1401.2	– 301.3
1984	9088.0	6788.2	+ 2299.8	+ 354.9
1985	11720.8	6655.7	+ 5065.1	+ 349.1
1986	8920.5	5476.6	+ 3443.9	– 784.1
1987	30360.6	16392.5	+ 13968.1	+ 159.2
1988	33138.1	22790.7	+ 10347.4	– 2294.1
1989	48747.8	–	–	+ 9803.6

Source: CBN, *Annual Report and Statement of Accounts*, 1973–88.

Table 3 *Total External Reserves, 1973–88 (Current Values)*

Year	N Million	US$ Million
1973	241.0	365.2
1974	3112.5	5020.2
1980	2424.8	3788.8
1981	–	8500.0
1982	1026.5	1532.1
1985	1591.1	1591.1
1986	3587.4	1630.6
1987	4643.3	1152.2
1988	3272.7	724.0
1989	10666.6	1399.2

Source: Various issues of CBN, *Annual Report and Statement of Accounts*, 1973–88.

the introduction of the second-tier foreign exchange market (SFEM) in September 1986.

(b) The naira equivalent of a foreign currency bought far fewer goods in the local market than it could fetch in a foreign market. This development was in line with the purchasing power parity (PPP) theory of exchange rate determination which postulates that when domestic prices are higher than the foreign prices of traded and non-traded goods, the currency should depreciate in a flexible exchange rate regime to the point where the prices are the same after adjustments in transport and custom duties differentials.

(c) Excessive demand for foreign exchange for imported goods resulting from the increase in personal incomes made possible by the oil boom in a context of an inadequate domestic supply of required goods by local producers.

The consequence for the Nigerian economy of the overvaluation of the naira was the introduction of distortions to the process of resource allocation. Dependence on imports, including food, led to the neglect of the agricultural sector both for the supply of traditional food items and for the generation of earnings from export crops. The administrative management of the exchange rate of the overvalued naira and the use of import licences to allocate the diminishing foreign exchange earnings accruing to the state from oil resulted in official abuses such as nepotism and corruption. Smuggling of cheaper foreign goods into the country became widespread while the more expensive local substitutes produced within Nigeria faced a growing problem of market realization with adverse consequences for capacity utilization in industry and employment levels. The exchange rate policy of this period also induced capital flight and discouraged foreign investment.

The continuing deterioration of the Nigerian economy as the 1980s wore on made a major change in exchange rate inevitable. That change came in July 1986 when SAP was introduced by the government of General Ibrahim Babangida. According to President Babangida, in a nation-wide address to Nigerians in June 1986, 'the SAP puts emphasis on price mechanism as a means of strengthening the existing demand management policies; it encourages . . . a more realistic exchange rate of the naira; promotes replacement of direct administrative controls with greater reliance on market forces and the rationalisation of public enterprises'. In September 1986, a two-tier foreign exchange system was introduced with the creation by the government of the first-tier and second-tier foreign exchange market, the former to be used, for an interim period of between 12 and 18 months, primarily for servicing and amortizing the country's sovereign debt, the latter for all other transactions. The naira exchange rate on the first-tier market was to be determined administratively through the crawling-peg approach while on the second-tier market it was to be determined solely by the market forces of demand and supply. The hope was that by gradually depreciating the naira on the first-tier market, a convergence would eventually be achieved with the second-tier rate to create a unified, realistic, market-determined rate within a period of 12 to 18 months from September 1986.

Exchange Rate Policy from 1986 to 1988
The introduction of SAP in 1986 signalled the effective abandonment by the Nigerian state of some 25 years of administrative controls, legal restrictions and administrative regulations in the management of the foreign exchange value of the naira. It heralded the arrival of a new era of exchange rate management informed by the philosophy of economic liberalism and deregulation. Our earlier analysis suggests quite clearly

that the naira had been overvalued for over a decade prior to the establishment of SFEM in September 1986. In the face of this, the key question which confronted policy-makers was how and when to devalue and by how much. As earlier indicated, foreign exchange management in Nigeria has been influenced more by events outside Nigeria than by the logic of internal developments and the direction of the economy. Yet, it would seem that the period when the national economy was embroiled in a deep crisis was not the most auspicious or appropriate time for a radical devaluation exercise. Little wonder then that exchange management under (S)FEM has been marked more by panicky moves than by rational and deliberate action.

A poorly designed programme of devaluation in the context of the deep economic crisis faced by Nigeria at the time (S)FEM was introduced was bound to have far-reaching adverse effects on the economy and society. What then was the government's motivation in embarking on devaluation as and when it did? It is quite significant to note that even when Nigeria had a triple-A rating among creditors, the currency was overvalued. It is therefore dishonest to suggest 'for instance that export credit agencies and overseas suppliers were refusing cover for Nigeria's imports and charging excessively before confirming letters of credit merely because the currency was overvalued' (Abdullahi, 1987). Abdullahi is broadly correct when he argues that the devaluation was substantially associated with a desire by the government to be seen to be adequately accommodating the interests of the country's creditors. According to him:

> Even though the creditor banks and multilateral financial institutions claim that a devaluation of the naira is the signal to them that the country was willing and able to carry out appropriate economic reforms at home, this is no more than a subterfuge. The true position seems to be that only a devaluation in their calculation can guarantee that balance of payments surpluses can be generated with which to service existing debts . . . though it is not officially admitted it can be said with some justification that the government has evolved the new exchange rate policy largely in order to appease its external creditors. (Abdullahi, 1987)

It is therefore not surprising that a major preoccupation of the (S)FEM-determined exchange rate of the naira is 'to eliminate the overvaluation of the naira and reduce the drain on foreign exchange reserves, thereby reducing pressure on the balance of payments which arose from unrealistic pricing of imports and exports . . . it was also expected to facilitate the elimination of further payments arrears on imports and the eventual elimination of trade and exchange restrictions' (Omoruyi, 1989).

We have already noted that for much of the period between 1986 and 1988, exchange rate policy was pursued within the framework of the first- and second-tier markets. The first-tier exchange rate, while it lasted, was used for servicing the country's external debts, subscriptions to international organizations, settlement of transitional imports for which letters of credit were opened before the commencement of SFEM, and disbursement in respect of public sector letters of credit. All other transactions imports, exports, investments – were conducted on the second-tier market. In order to ensure some appearance of fairness in the operation of SFEM, all Nigerian banks were initially classified into two groups, namely, the large and the small banks. Each large bank that made a successful bid at the foreign exchange auction was permitted to buy a maximum of 10 per cent of the total available foreign exchange while each successful small bank was allocated a maximum of 7 per cent. The bidding session was characterized by each dealer trying to outbid the other by quoting higher rates. The result was the drastic depreciation of the naira at the first and second bidding sessions.

Table 4   *Foreign Exchange Rates Movement Monthly Averages – Effective 1986 to 1989 (N/US Dollar)*

Month	1986	1987	1988	1989
January	0.9996	2.7020	4.1749	7.0389
February	0.9996	3.0788	4.2611	7.3828
March	1.0097	3.4888	4.3169	7.5871
April	1.0199	3.4734	4.2023	7.5808
May	1.7240	3.5088	4.1103	7.5051
June	1.1872	3.7257	4.1913	7.3471
July	1.3294	3.8081	4.6087	7.1600
August	1.3299	3.9982	4.5830	7.2579
September	1.6010	4.2073	4.7167	7.3433
October	2.0593	4.2761	4.7748	7.3877
November	2.4931	4.2990	5.1479	7.5050
December	2.5954	4.1665	5.3530	7.5827
Yearly (Dec.) change (%)		37.71	22.17	29.39

Source: CBN, *Annual Report and Statement of Accounts* 31 December 1987 and 1988. UBA, *Monthly Business and Economic Digest* for 1989 data.

To stem the further depreciation of the naira, the CBN decided to introduce the marginal rate system as a mechanism for setting the exchange rate. And in pursuance of fairness and viability in the market some other amendments were made to the rules. In order to increase the number of successful bids, banks were re-classified into 'large', 'medium' and 'new', with maximum allocations of 5, 2 and 1.5 per cent respectively. It is noteworthy that under the pretext of deregulation and the so-called 'under-banking' in the Nigerian monetary system, many new banks were established, and are still being established, mostly by retired military personnel and their close civilian collaborators. These new banks have been a central source of the malfunctioning and corruption in (S)FEM.

In spite of changes to the rules governing the operation of the auction system following its introduction in 1986, the naira exchange rate has continued to fluctuate widely from one bidding session to another. The CBN was in fact forced to intervene on two occasions during 1986 – the 6th and 10th bidding sessions – in order to moderate the amplitude of exchange rate fluctuation (Omoruyi, 1989). (See Table 4 for the average monthly foreign exchange rate movement.) It was also primarily because of the persistent and continued depreciation of the naira during the first quarter of 1987 that the Dutch Auction System (DAS) was introduced in April 1987. Again, the naira continued to weaken (see Table 4). Meanwhile, the autonomous inter-bank rate which was linked to the SFEM rate had assumed some importance and added another source of instability to the naira exchange rate. The link between SFEM and IFEM was later broken and the banks were only permitted to buy and sell foreign exchange at the rate determined in that market subject only to the condition of 1 per cent spread between their buying and selling rates.

The decline and fluctuations in the exchange rate continued through 1988 and 1989 (see Table 4). In spite of rules and regulations for exchange rate control at the FEM (the result of the merger between the SFEM and official naira rates), 'the multiplicity of rates under the DAS as well as the large differential between the FEM and autonomous rates exerted pressure on the exchange rate and intensified the problem of resource misallocation' (Omoruyi, 1989). It was therefore felt that a single naira exchange rate should be established. Hence, 'the autonomous market and the official foreign exchange market were merged with effect from January 1989 to form the Interbank Foreign Exchange Market (IFEM)' (Omoruyi, 1989).

During 1989, licences were issued to a number of financial companies to establish and operate bureaux de change. It marked another attempt by the government to improve the allocative efficiency of the foreign exchange market. It was also an attempt to diminish or eliminate the informal sector activities of parallel dealers in the market. Yet apart from the rather dubious occasional improvement in the balance of payments position which was achieved more through a reduction in real income and effective demand than through an expansion of exports (Abdullahi, 1987), the Nigerian devaluation experience since 1986 has been an unmitigated failure. Following the experiences of Zambia, Zaïre, Ghana, Brazil, Argentina, Bolivia, etc., the result of successive and competitive devaluations has been increasing levels of inflation, unemployment, poverty, gross income inequalities, crushing debt burden and subordination of the economies to Western capitalist interests. Let us elaborate further on this by looking more closely at the impact of devaluation on the major sectors of the Nigerian economy in the period since 1986.

III. The Impact of Devaluation on Growth and Development in Nigeria

The seven-year period from 1982 to 1989 which, according to McRaè, was one of the fastest expansionary phases in the history of the contemporary world economy was also one of the leanest for Africa, a period when the continent experienced a sharp and unprecedented fall in living standards (McRae, 1989). The overall African experience of social and economic decline was shared by Nigeria, where the optimistic sentiments expressed by government officials notwithstanding, structural adjustment had led to a steep fall in the standard of living of the majority of the people. As with much of Africa, living standards in Nigeria at the end of the 1980s had fallen below their 1974 levels. There is no doubt that the free fall of African currencies, including the Nigerian naira, in the guise of a search for 'realistic' exchange rates, has been central to this sharp deterioration in the African condition.

Before proceeding to discuss the impact of devaluation on the major sectors of the Nigerian economy, let us first of all highlight the benefits which its most ardent proponents in Nigerian government circles and within the IMF and the World Bank claim it would bring to the economy. According to Victor Odozie (1986), Deputy Governor of the Central Bank, these benefits include:

(a) the achievement of a realistic rate of exchange for the naira through the forces of supply and demand;
(b) greater utilization of industrial capacity and the expansion of domestic production, and, consequently, a reduction in the level of unemployment;
(c) an increase in non-oil exports;
(d) in-flow of capital and foreign investment;
(e) the minimization, if not total elimination, of smuggling of currency and goods; and
(f) the generation of a considerable amount of naira revenues as well as the turning of the terms of trade in favour of agriculture and exports.

But has the drastic devaluation of the naira in the period since 1986 brought about these benefits? The evidence does not seem to suggest so.

In embarking on a consideration of the effects on the Nigerian economy of devaluation, it is necessary to draw attention to the limitations of the data used in the analysis. The main limitations are in respect of the real value of the monetary figures and also in the conflicting figures from some of the data sources. For our analysis, we shall be relying mostly on the current values of the specified economic variables. It is not realistic to attempt to construct any series for deflating the current monetary value series to values at constant prices. The violent fluctuations in the values of most of the variables, especially since the inauguration of the so-called 'freemarket'- determination of the exchange rate of the naira, has made such an exercise more unrealistic. The expectation in accepting the analysis based on values at current prices is that the longer the series (Table 4, average monthly series for 1986-9), the more likely that some definite pattern will become observable. Thus, the direction of change can be captured.

With respect to the conflicts in data sources we cannot do much; it is inherent in the nature of Nigeria's statistical system. Although the Federal Office of Statistics (FOS) and other statistical offices in the States of the Federation are statutorily empowered to produce national statistics, for various reasons, some of them justifiable, other government and some private institutions and agencies try to generate their own statistics. Because no effort is made by the various institutions to establish common theoretical premises and survey procedures for the generation of the required statistics, the production of conflicting figures becomes inevitable. Again, our hope is that the reconciled figures will capture the underlying long-term trends in the movements of the major variables.

We shall now briefly discuss how far the consequences of devaluation have manifested themselves in the relevant sectors of the Nigerian economy since SAP was introduced. Since the exchange rate of the naira has been central to the adjustment policy and the economic revival policy measures, it will be pertinent to consider the changes in the exchange rate (revaluations) of the naira from 1986 to 1989.

Movements in the Naira Exchange Rate: 1986-9
During the first quarter of 1986, the exchange rate of the naira to the US dollar was almost one to one. The official administration of the crawling exchange rate policy seems to have been more active during the second quarter with the effective deprecia- tion of the naira which then exchanged in June for 1.1872 to the US dollar. The commitment of the government, expressed in its 1986 budget, to revalue the naira and the launching of the SAP policy package towards the end of June 1986 led to a greater depreciation of the naira during the third quarter. With the foreign exchange market (first and second tiers) coming into operation from the last week of September 1986, the average exchange rate of the naira to the US dollar declined during the fourth quarter to N2.3826, fluctuating from N2.0593 in October to N2.5954 in December. It is of interest to note at this point that industrial producers, organized in the Manufacturers' Association of Nigeria (MAN), and genuine traders – as against speculators – felt, and still feel, that N2.5 is about the appropriate level at which the naira should exchange to the dollar. They argued that anything more than between N2.5 and N3.0 to the dollar would be damaging to the economy (interviews in Lagos).

It is clear from Table 4 that, except on very rare occasions, the naira consistently suffered a depreciation in its value. The cumulative average annual rate of devalua- tion becomes quite substantial. By December 1987, the naira was devalued by 37.71 per cent compared with its level in December 1986. The comparative devaluation rates were 22.17 per cent and 29.39 per cent for 1988 and 1989 respectively. The devaluation of the naira since the inception of SAP towards the end of June 1986

(N1.0 = $0.8423) and December 1989 (N1.0 = $0.1319) was about 84.34 per cent, and about 86.81 per cent since January 1986 when pressure was still being exerted on the Nigerian government by the IMF for a three-stage approach to the devaluation of the naira by 60 per cent. Under the original IMF scheme, the proposal was for the naira to be devalued over a three-year period by 40 per cent in the first instance, and then by two further rounds of 10 per cent each. Assuming that this option was followed before the IMF itself abandoned it in favour of SFEM, the currency would have exchanged at N2.5 to the dollar up to the second quarter of 1987 and thereafter at between N2.5 and N3.0 to the dollar, a rate that coincides with the preferences expressed by MAN in 1986. It is clear, however, that the experience with (S)FEM and IFEM has led to a massive undervaluation of the naira and the objective of obtaining a viable and realistic exchange rate to help stabilize the monetary system as a means of economic recovery has not been attained.

Devaluation and the Gross Domestic Product
Table 5 suggests that at 1984 constant factor cost, the Nigerian economy recorded an apparent modest growth rate of about 1.8 per cent in 1987 after a full year of the operation of SAP. The improved growth rates for 1988 and 1989 were 4.16 per cent and 3.92 per cent respectively. However, when account is taken of the population growth rates averaging about 3 per cent per annum and annual inflation rates of between 40 and 50 per cent, growth rates since the introduction of SAP and the massive devaluation of the naira will be found to be actually negative in real terms. And the general decline in per capita income resulting from unemployment and low production activities is manifested by the fall in the standard of living.

The rapid fall in the standard of living as reflected in the level of per capita income was first noted in a 1987 World Bank report, in which it was revealed that the living standard of most Nigerians had fallen significantly and that per capita income had declined from 800 dollars in the early 1980s to less than 400 dollars in 1987 (see Table 6). Although some would argue that 1987, one year after SAP was introduced, was too early a period to appraise the effect of the programme on the economy, the evidence, almost five years after adjustment started, reinforces the earlier observation by the Bank of the sharp decline in living standards consequent upon the devaluation of the naira.

From Table 6 we can see that the per capita income in naira of Nigeria between 1985 and 1989 stood at between N778 to N797, a growth rate of only about 2 per cent over a four-year period. Clearly, this is a less than acceptable performance and it plainly suggests that the effect of devaluation on an economy that has remained almost stagnant cannot but lead to a drastic lowering of the standard of living of most of the population. Whatever increase in income that is recorded is likely to have accrued to a privileged property-owning minority in a context where income distribution is highly skewed.

The fall in the level of income is even more dramatic and apparent when the per capita is given in US dollars. Table 6 shows that the dollar per capita income of Nigeria which stood at $778 in 1985 dropped to $359 in 1986 and to $194 eighteen months after the implementation of SAP started and fifteen months after the commencement of the rapid devaluation of the naira through the operation of the foreign exchange market (FEM). By 1989, as a result of even more substantial devaluation of the naira, the per capita income had fallen further to $108.

The noticeable decline in the standard of living in Nigeria compares with the situation in most other African countries where incomes have, in the course of the

Table 5 *Gross Domestic Product (GDP) at 1984 Factor Cost (N Billion)*

Year	Total GDP (Naira B)	Agriculture		Crude Petroleum		Manufacturing		Utilities		Comm. Soc. & Pers. Service	
		Naira	% Share	Naira	%	Naira	%	Naira	%	Naira	%
1985	74.47	17.52	23.53	11.65	15.64	4.23	5.68	0.39	0.52	–	–
1986	77.90	23.35	29.97	11.38	14.60	7.34	9.42	0.37	0.47	0.63	0.81
1987	79.28	23.92	30.17	10.19	12.85	9.16	11.55	0.43	0.54	0.81	1.02
1988*	82.58	24.76	29.98	11.26	13.64	8.27	10.01	0.34	0.41	0.65	0.79
1989*	35.82	–		–		–		–		–	

* Estimates by the Office of Planning and Budget.
Sources: (1) CBN, *Annual Report and Statement of Accounts*, 1986–8.
          (2) 1990 Budget Speech for 1989 Figures.

Table 6 *Per Capita Income (Naira and Dollar) (at constant 1984 factor cost)*

Year	Population (Estimate) Million	Per Capita Income Naira	US Dollar
1985	95.7	778	778
1986	98.6	790	359
1987	101.5	781	194
1988	104.6	789	175
1989	107.7	797	108

Source: Estimates from the CBN (*Annual Report and Statement of Accounts*, 1985–8) and the Federal Office of Statistics (*Abstract of Statistics*, 1986).

1980s, fallen below their 1974 levels. In the case of Nigeria, whatever the weighting system that is employed to determine their naira and dollar values, income levels in 1989 cannot be more than 50 per cent of what they were in 1977. In naira terms, the GDP for Nigeria was estimated in 1986, the year that the implementation of SAP started, to be only about 80 per cent of the 1977 figures (Fadahunsi, 1988). Whatever the inadequacy of GDP as an indicator of economic development, it cannot be disputed from the preceding discussion that so far the impact of devaluation on the general well-being of Nigerians has been negative.

Devaluation and Employment
The levels of employment, unemployment and underemployment are very important macro-economic aggregates for indicating the impact of monetary and fiscal policies on development. Theoretically, devaluation is used as a policy instrument for promoting exports, replacing imports and, thereby, expanding domestic production of goods and services and consequently generating more jobs. It is of course not obvious that the implied labour-intensive development strategy of export-led industrialization and general investment activities will necessarily lead to efficient output in the domestic market that will also be competitive in the export market. The evidence so far in the implementation of SAP in Nigeria has pointed to increasing unemployment in spite of the enormous resources the government has been putting into employment-creating activities – especially through the National Directorate of Employment (NDE).

The dependent nature of the Nigerian economy is a major obstacle to the realization of the employment intention of devaluation. The approach of the United African Company (UAC), the leading multinational corporate subsidiary in Nigeria, to the problems posed for it by SAP and devaluation is particularly instructive. Describing this approach, Sam Aluko, one of Nigeria's leading economists in the Keynesian tradition, told *Business Concord* in October 1989 that it entailed shedding labour in order to cut costs. Recounting a discussion which he had in England with a top director of Unilever, the parent of UAC (Nigeria) Limited, Aluko mentioned that he was told that the main reason why the head office was pressurizing its subsidiary to reduce its work-force drastically had to do with the fact that although UAC was managing, in spite of SAP, to increase its naira earnings, the real value of the earnings was decreasing annually because of the drastic devaluation of the naira and its ever-dwindling value. 'So in terms of the pound sterling, which is what interests Unilever in England when it considers returns on its investments, Nigeria is increasingly becoming a risky investment economy' (Aluko, 1989: 8). This is why there has been profound pressure from London on the UAC to retrench staff, reduce costs and increase real returns on its investments in Nigeria. Little wonder then that:

while the UAC has been announcing increased annual naira profits since 1987, the number of its Nigerian employees has been falling. In 1980, UAC employed about 20,000 Nigerians, 22,500 in 1982, and 23,850 in 1985. But the number fell to 19,000 in 1986 shortly after the introduction of SAP. 14,000 in 1987, 9,000 in 1988 and is now about 7,500. It is planning to further reduce the number to about 6,000 employees in 1990, under pressure from its parent company, Unilever Limited of England. (Aluko, 1989: 8)

UAC's response to the effects of devaluation on its real earnings is shared by many other companies, corporate and non-corporate, Nigerian and non-Nigerian, private and state-owned. Firms in all sectors of the economy have also had to retrench staff in order to cut costs. The effects of drastic devaluation have combined with the demands of privatization and commercialization of public enterprises to exacerbate the problems of unemployment. Illustrating the way in which devaluation has affected employment in the building and construction industry, Odogwu notes that because 'the cost of building and construction materials has shot up to more than 500 per cent in the last three years, compelling the government to be concerned with mainly maintenance operations and servicing, . . . the construction industry in a bid to remain in business . . . embarked on mass retrenchment of staff' (Odogwu, 1989). Without doubt, five years of SAP has resulted in mass retrenchment, unemployment, under-employment, under-utilization of installed production capacities and has consequently led to declining output, runaway inflation and reduced income.

Devaluation, Capital Flow and Investment
One major objective of devaluation is to encourage the flow of capital into the economy given the favourable investment climate which the complete SAP package was expected to create. Contrary to the expectation of policy, devaluation has led to capital flight through speculators and in some cases through genuine business organizations which have been taking advantage of liberalization or deregulation to transfer their investment capital with ease to greener pastures like the European Economic Community (*Business Concord*, 20 January 1989).

We have already noted the acute instability that has characterized the naira exchange rate in the period since the creation of the foreign exchange auction market in September 1986. The sharp, generally downward fluctuation of the value of the naira has been blamed primarily on the activities of capital market speculators. It is clear that one result of such speculative capital movements is uncertainty in productive invest-ment (Hanson, 1974: 48–9). Prospective investors cannot be expected to engage in long-term planning, even in matters such as the acquisition of equipment and industrial raw materials, in an unstable foreign exchange environment. It is equally difficult in view of rapid changes in prices to buy spare parts and equipment to maintain or expand existing production capacity. Certainly, in the contemporary international economic environment, it will be illusory to expect any substantial inflow of foreign capital and investment in an economy without a stable and viable foreign exchange mechanism.

Devaluation and Prices
The most significant and socially relevant indicator of the impact of devaluation is the movement in the prices of goods and services; that is, the impact on the rate of inflation.

The multiple increases in the prices of goods (food, clothing, building materials), utilities (transport, post, electricity, water, telephones) and cost of services like educa-tion and health since the commencement of the devaluation of the naira from 1986 are the most telling pieces of evidence against any argument in favour of SAP as a

Table 7 *Movement of Prices of Selected Commodities: 1985-90*

Commodity	Prices (Naira) 1985	1990	Increase Per Cent
G/Nut oil (gal.)	15.0	51.0	240.0
Palm oil (gal.)	12.0	42.0	250.0
Measure of rice	1.3	9.0	592.3
Measure of beans	1.3	6.0	361.5
Bag of Semovita	13.0	45.0	246.2
Loaf of bread	0.6	6.0	900.0
Tin of milk	0.4	3.0	650.0
Pkt of sugar	0.8	3.0	275.0
Cooking stove	80.0	300.0	275.0
Bundle of roofing sheets	100.0	500.0	400.0

Source: Adapted from *The Democrat Weekly*, Kaduna, 28 January 1990.

strategy for economic recovery and development in Nigeria. Inflation, as is well known from the examples of Hitlerite Germany and some contemporary Latin American countries, is a major threat to individual freedom and liberal democracy. Hard as a benevolent dictator and latter-day apostle of 'human rights' may try, spiralling inflation and the social upheavals that it engenders can only result in political repression.

In Nigeria, over the past four years, enrolment in educational institutions has been on the decline and withdrawals have been on the increase. This is the result of parental reaction to the removal of subsidies on educational services and the imposition of levies and increases in fees. Thus, fewer and fewer Nigerians are attending primary, secondary and post-secondary institutions – universities, polytechnics and colleges of education. When it is realized that knowledge and skill are probably the most critical of the variables impinging positively on the development process, then the damage which SAP and devaluation are doing to Nigeria's development will be fully appreciated.

Similarly the increasing escalation in the cost of medical treatment has had a devastating effect on the health of the vulnerable sections of the population. More worrying is the increase in Kwashiokor, a disease caused by malnutrition in children. It was once prevalent in parts of Nigeria where the civil war was fought, and was hardly reported since the years immediately following the end of the war in 1970. The long-term consequence of malnutrition in children is said to be the impairment of the brain. Devaluation therefore has the effect of not only impairing the productivity of the present generation of Nigerian workers, who, overall, are becoming less healthy, it also poses the danger of damaging the capability of a group of potential workers from making an optimal contribution to the development of their nation in the future.

Table 7 shows the movement of prices of selected goods between 1985 and 1990 in one Nigerian urban centre. We only note from the table the rather sharp increases in the prices of banned imported food items like rice – about 600 per cent increase – and bread made from wheat – 900 per cent. The response of the government to the inflationary pressures generated by devaluation was to increase and extend the period of the annual salary increments (the so-called elongated salary structure – ESS) while keeping the starting-point of the salary grades constant. For most salary scales, the terminal increment is put at an average of about 50 per cent, while the rate of inflation since 1986 has averaged between 40 and 50 per cent annually.

The irony of the government's policy is that while prices are supposed to reflect the so-called international prices of commodities like petroleum products, for instance, a tight rein is put on the wages and salaries of labour. The removal of subsidies on essential goods and services is supposedly intended to make economic management practices in Nigeria accord with what obtains in the advanced capitalist state. It is known, however, that the institutional arrangements that have been made by the advanced capitalist states to reduce the burden of these 'free market' operations are not available to a country like Nigeria and no effort has been made since 1986 to introduce them.

In the medium term, the inflationary impact of devaluation is a major obstacle to getting the economy out of recession, and the fear is that the present intransigence of the political and monetary authorities to reconsider the present IMF/World Bank-inspired SAP policies will only spell doom for the long-term development of the country.

Devaluation and the Major Production Sectors of the Nigerian Economy
Until 1989, the proponents of SAP always pointed to the great benefits which they claimed were accruing to Nigeria's rural majority – especially the cocoa farmers – as a result of devaluation. Since the dramatic collapse in the course of 1989 of the price paid per tonne to cocoa farmers, fewer voices have been heard advocating the benefits of SAP to the peasant community. In the classical IMF package for reviving the agricultural sector of crisis-ridden Third World economies, a major plank of policy is the reduction of agricultural subsidies as a means for reducing the level of budget deficits and contributing to the restoration of sound market prices. For instance, according to the policy, 'subsidizing of fertilizer prices contributes to excessive application of fertilizers or to smuggling, while the subsidization of (staple) consumer prices fuel growing urban demand' (Sano, 1988: 565). In the Nigerian situation, the government has adopted the IMF/World Bank strategy for solving the agrarian problem which partly centres on the inadequate production of food items and export crops.

It is true that, following the introduction of SAP and the devaluation of the naira, the prices of some agricultural crops rose, as did, initially, the incomes of farmers. But once the inflationary consequences of devaluation started to catch up with the cost of farm inputs and labour in a context of subsidy withdrawal on tractor hiring, seeds and fertilizer, the farmers began to experience a diminishing income. The costs of other non-farm goods and services also turned the terms of trade against the rural producers. Another dimension to the problems faced by the farmers is the smuggling of Nigerian foodstuffs to neighbouring countries – Cameroon, Chad, Niger, Benin. The middlemen who organize the smuggling activities do so in order to be able to earn CFAs, the convertible currency of Francophone African countries which has appreciated considerably since the policy of devaluation of the naira started with SAP. Cheap Nigerian farm labour is now being employed to meet the demand of Nigeria's erstwhile relatively underdeveloped neighbours for food items.

No commodity better illustrates the consequences of devaluation for Nigeria's agricultural sector and rural community than cocoa. Between 1987 and 1989, bogus cocoa merchants invaded the cocoa trade once government yielded to IMF/World Bank pressure to disband the cocoa and other commodity marketing boards. The newbreed cocoa merchants turned out to be mostly foreigners and their Nigerian fronts who were desperately trying to repatriate some of their genuine and ill-gotten profits that had accumulated in Nigeria during the regime of controlled exchange rates. Because these foreign entrepreneurs no longer had confidence in the viability of the Nigerian monetary system and the economy, they were seeking for means to take their money out of Nigeria at any cost. The activities of these cocoa merchants contributed a great deal to the rapid devaluation of the naira which exchanged at the beginning of the cocoa season in September 1986 at about N1.6 to the dollar, at N4.3 to the dollar in September 1987, N4.8 in September 1988 and at about N7.3 at the close of the 1988/9 cocoa season in June 1989 (See Table 4).

While the Nigerian government was pushing through its policy of deregulating the country's domestic agricultural commodity trade, the international environment was becoming increasingly less favourable. This is evidenced by international cocoa price movements: in 1987 it averaged £1,500 per tonne; in October 1988, it stood at £725 per tonne and fell to £670 at a point during the 1988/9 season (Falusi, 1988). The increased domestic production of cocoa from 1987 onwards, and the increase in the amount of the commodity exported by Nigeria, while it did not lead to increased earnings by the state itself, resulted, because of the depreciation of the naira and the activities of speculators in the cocoa trade, in fabulous naira returns to the farmers. But, for reasons which we have explained earlier, the 'cocoa boom' was artificial and it was not to last. Fakorede summarizes the ramifications for the cocoa farmers as follows (Fakorede, 1990: 5):

> According to the Patron of the Farmers' congress (Ondo State), it became unthinkable that cocoa which sold at about N25,000 per tonne in March would dive so low to N3,500 by year end. At the opening of the season in September, when the price stood at N10,000, we thought it would appreciate but the opposite was the case. . . . About the end of November, 1989, Afrocontinental (the biggest buyer of the merchant firms) graded on credit at N6,000 per tonne while other merchants who could afford to pay offered between N4,000 and N5,200 oer tonne.

What makes the cocoa experience particularly unfortunate, and with it the blind ideological pursuit of the policy of deregulation by the political authorities, is the damage that has been done to the country's leading potential non-oil export and to the welfare of the cocoa farmers. There was no moment during the period when the 'newbreed' cocoa traders were offering over N20,000 per tonne to farmers that the export value of the commodity was over more than £1,000 or N15,000 FOB. A more caring government should have become suspicious of the intentions of the merchants and therefore interfered in the interest of the nation and the farmers. The hands of the Nigerian state are apparently still tied by its avowed commitment to 'deregulation' and the interplay of market forces in the commodity and foreign exchange markets. It is clear, however, from our discussion of devaluation as it affects the agricultural sector that whatever the farmers might have gained individually has been lost by them as a group and by the nation through the massive flight of capital that has been perpetrated as a result of SAP and devaluation.

The other important productive sector that has suffered tremendously from the devaluation of the naira is manufacturing. The immediate impact of the rapid depreciation of the naira against the currencies of Nigeria's major trading partners, such as the EC, USA and Japan, is the decline in the level of capacity utilization. Some of the other problems that are confronting the manufacturing sector are frequently highlighted in the reports of MAN. They include the following.

(a) Capacity Utilization: From the various reports of MAN and information available from other government documents, the level of industrial capacity utilization in Nigeria has generally hovered between 30 per cent and 40 per cent. In 1986, for example, industrial capacity utilization was put at an average of 30 per cent, in 1987, 36.7 per cent, in 1988, 40.7 per cent, and in 1989, 31.0 per cent. The figure for 1990 was 37.0 per cent. There is no doubt that the persistently low level of capacity

utilization in a modernizing industrial sector like manufacturing represents a great waste of resources and an obstacle to an early attainment of national economic recovery.

(b) Domestic Demand: The drastic devaluation of the naira resulted in a sharp increase in the cost of machinery and equipment, industrial raw materials and other inputs necessary for sustaining factory production. This in turn meant that the prices of manufactured goods rose steeply, thereby adversely affecting the domestic demand for industrial products. Many manufacturers became saddled with unsold stocks of goods and consumer purchasing power dwindled (Fadahunsi, 1989).

(c) Smuggling: According to MAN, the period since the introduction of SAP has been characterized by wide-scale smuggling, especially of wheat flour, vegetable oils and rice. In the 1988 MAN report it was stated that:

> It will be recalled that the government last year imposed a ban on the importation of wheat in order to encourage the milling and use of local cereals. Following this, the various flour mills in the country went ahead and made substantial investment to convert their plants for maize milling. The widespread smuggling of wheat and wheat flour has not only vitiated government's policy on local sourcing of raw materials, it has also put the enormous investment by flour mills in jeopardy. Furthermore, it has made investment into local wheat growing completely unattractive while at the same time resulting in the loss of about 60,000 jobs in the flour milling and bakery industry. The same situation applies to a number of other local industries which are being strangulated by rampant smuggling.

Deregulation and devaluation are not operating in favour of the manufacturing sector. The banks, speculators and traders are the main beneficiaries of SAP. The prevailing situation in the banking sector which is forcing 'cash-strapped Anambra Motor Manufacturing Company (ANAMCO) to look beyond its primary business of vehicles (Mercedes components) assembly for survival' represents the experience of most manufacturers (Fadahunsi, 1989). According to Ahlbrecht of ANAMCO:

> banks were no longer willing to sell foreign exchange to manufacturers, . . . who were mostly outbidded by traders who only buy and sell articles without much overhead commitments. . . . Moves by ANAMCO's parent company, Daimler Benz of Western Germany, since 1986 to enter into a counter trade pact with the Federal Government in which fuel would exchange to CKD [i.e. completely knocked down parts] had been blocked. (Ahlbrecht 1989)

Clearly, if the manufacturing sector has to be made to continue to operate in an environment where banking practices are hostile to genuine productive investments, then the slow pace of de-industrialization which was already noticeable in the pre-SAP period will be accelerated. A dying and unviable manufacturing sector can hardly constitute a basis for the structural adjustment of the Nigerian economy.

IV. Concluding Policy Recommendations

The prime objective of any worthwhile economic policy package is to achieve an increase in welfare through the maximization of employment possibilities and earned income. Structural adjustment in Nigeria has, however, resulted in more unemployment during the past five years. It has succeeded in increasing nominal income by the monetization of the country's petrodollar earnings through grossly undervalued naira exchange rates. Thus, it has been possible to continue to pay the wages of those workers who are lucky not to have lost their jobs during the retrenchments which began in 1984 and which are still continuing in the private and public sectors. And although some rural farmers, particularly the cocoa farmers, were beneficiaries of the 'money illusion' phenomenon that was initially created by the excessive monetization into local currency of the revenue from exports, the major point to note is that the policy measures, and especially the devaluation exercise, under SAP have led to a decline in real terms of earned income among the rural and urban population and therefore to a general fall in the standard of living of most people. The conclusion is that, so far, SAP has failed as a policy package for reviving the economy and putting it on the path of growth and development. The failure of the IMF-backed SAP in Nigeria, as in most of the developing countries, has been attributed to excessive reliance on monetary policy measures whereas what is required is an integrated stabilization and restructuring programme and 'a consistent and broad set of criteria which will . . . include monetary targets but shifts the emphasis from a purely monetary conditionality to a developmental conditionality' (Killick et al., 1984: 94; see also Wulf, 1988).

The IMF/World Bank adjustment programme, as designed, concentrates on short-term problems like the disequilibrium in the balance of payments. It is of course in the interest of Nigeria's creditors and the financial institutions under their control that deficits are eliminated from budgets, and the currency devalued so as to have a surplus in the balance of payments. While the state may feel justified to attempt to fulfil its obligations to the international economic community and financial institutions, surely this must not be at a terrible economic and social cost to the Nigerian people. The long-term goal of restructuring the economy from its primary activities base and mono-product export into a modernizing industrial and services system should never be lost sight of. The short-term adjustment measures and the more legitimate long-term requirements of the economy need to be reconciled.

The priority of policy must be a profound and fundamental restructuring of the Nigerian economy in favour of food production, industrialization and the development of a local technological capability as well as the social and physical infrastructures necessary to facilitate the attainment of the objectives of development. If devaluation is likely to frustrate these objectives, then policy ought not to resort to devaluation as an adjustment policy instrument, especially when there is no basis for determining by how much the currency should be devalued and what the economic environment that can guarantee its effectiveness should be like.

Having established the need to identify and develop some priority sectors of the Nigerian economy to meet long-term objectives, we can briefly highlight the exchange rate regime that will be required. As a basic requirement we accept the view that what is important from an investment and investor's perspective is not necessarily the level of exchange rate but its relative stability over a reasonable length of time (Kwanashie, 1984). An exchange rate stabilizing at around N2.5–3.5, calculated using PPP (purchasing power parity) and weighted in relation to the currencies of our major trading partners (Osagie and Okogu, 1988; Ogunsheye, 1990), has been recommended. The rate seems to tally with the suggestion of MAN and other corporate organizations that are genuinely engaged in productive activities within the Nigerian economy, and from an employment generation, industrial-capacity-utilization-enhancing and agricultural expansion point of view appears appropriate for us. It should by now be obvious to the political and monetary authorities in Nigeria that FEM as it is presently being managed is not serving the development objectives of the country. It is therefore necessary to make some changes. What seems to be currently a regime of 'floating exchange rate' should be replaced with a controlled flexible rate; that is, a rate which can fluctuate between a band of say 15 per cent of a given rate that will be subject to review on a quarterly basis. According to the IMF terms of agreements, a change [in the exchange rate] of up to 10 per cent could be made by any member merely by notifying the IMF of the fact. If a change in excess of 10 per cent, but not greater than 20 per cent, was desired, an application for permission had to be made to the IMF, which had to give its decision within seventy-two hours. If it was desired to change the parity of a currency by more than 20 per cent, no limit was placed on the time allowed to the IMF for the consideration of the application. (Hanson, 1974: 159)

Nigeria ought to invoke this provision of the IMF agreements in the management of its foreign exchange market. This is necessary if the developmental objectives of the country in terms of industrialization, agricultural expansion, increased employment levels, etc. are to be attained.

References

S.H. Abdullahi (1987), 'Exchange Rate Adjustment in Nigeria: The Problem, the Solution and the Cost'. Paper presented at National Conference on the Second-tier Foreign Exchange Market (SFEM) in the Context of a Developing Economy, Department of Economics, ABU, January.

M. Ahlbrecht (1989), Managing Director of Anambra Automobile Motor Company (ANAMCO) quoted in the *Guardian* (newspaper), Lagos, 9 March.

S. Aluko (1989), 'The Multinationals and SAP', *Business Concord*, Lagos, 15 December.

A. Fadahunsi (1988), 'Implication of SAP for the Planning of the Nigerian Economy'. National Workshop on the Structural Adjustment Programme, NIPSS, Kuru, April.

—— (1989), 'SAP and the Manufacturing Sector: A Review of Policy and Performance'. Paper presented at Conference on SAP and the Future of Nigeria CSER, ABU, March.

L. Fakorede (1990), 'Whither the Magic Crop?', *Business Concord*, Lagos, 6 January.

P. Falusi (1988), 'Disaster Ahead in Domestic Cocoa Market', *Business Concord*, Lagos, 11 October.

J.B. Hanson (1974), *Monetary Theory and Practice* (ELBS), London: Macdonald and Evans Ltd.

E. Hutchful, *The IMF and Ghana*, London: Zed.

T. Killick, et al. (1984), *The Quest for Economic Stabilization*, London: St Martin's Press.

M. Kwanashie (1984). Contribution to a Conference on SAP and the Financial System, Economics Department, ABU, February.

G. Lipscombe (1988), *Economics and the Banks' Role in the Economy*, London: Pitman Publishing.

J. Loxley (1986), 'Alternative Approaches'. Contribution to a Symposium on Africa and the IMF (published papers edited by G.K. Helleiner, (1986) *Africa and the IMF*, Washington, DC: International Monetary Fund.

H. McRae (1989), *Guardian Weekly*, London, 27 August.

E.J.M. Mtei (1986). Contribution to a symposium on Africa and the IMF (published papers edited by G.K. Helleiner) *op. cit.*

C.M. Nyirabu (1986). Contribution to a Symposium on Africa and the IMF (published papers edited by G.K. Helleiner), *op. cit.*

V. Odogwu (1989), 'Devaluation and Unemployment in Nigeria', (mimeo).

V. Odozie (1986), *The Standard* (daily newspaper), Jos, 13 and 14 October.

A. Ogunsheye (1990), 'Budget 90: Some Basic Issues', *Business Times*, 22 January.

S.E. Omoruyi (1989), 'Structural Adjustment and National Development: Deriving and Ensuring a Viable and Fair Exchange Rate for the Naira'. Paper presented at Seminar on Structural Transformation for Self-Reliance and Social Justice, Lagos, October.

B. Onimode (1988), *A Political Economy of the African Crisis*, London: Zed.

E. Osagie and B. Okogu (1988), 'Estimating a Realistic Exchange Rate for the Naira: Purchasing Power Parity Approach', Workshop on SAP, NIPSS, Kuru, September.

D.K. Roy (1988), 'Employment and Growth: Empirical Results from Bangladesh Industries', *The Bangladesh Development Studies*, vol. XVI, no. 1, March.

G. Saitoti (1986), 'A View from Africa'. Contribution to a Symposium on *Africa and the IMF* (published papers edited by G.K. Helleiner), June.

H.-O. Sano (1988), 'The IMF and Zambia: The Contradictions of Exchange Rate Auctioning and De-subsidization of Agriculture', *African Affairs*, vol. 87, no. 349, October.

J. Sanusi (1986), 'The Origins and Nature of the African Debt Crisis' (mimeo). Benin-city.

R. Umoren (1989), 'Sapping the Sacred Cow', *Business Concord*, 27 June.

P. Wickham (1985), 'The Choice of Exchange Rate Regime in Development Countries. A Survey of the Literature', *IMF Staff Papers*, vol. 32, no. 2, June.

J. Wulf (1988), 'Zambia under the IMF Regime', *African Affairs*, vol. 87, no. 349, October.

UBA, *Monthly Business and Economic Digest*; Lagos. June/July 1986, July 1987, November 1989 and several issues.

Business Concord, Lagos; 20 January 1989, 27 June 1989 and several issues.

National Concord, Lagos; 13 February 1990.

Business Times, Lagos, several issues.

CBN, *Annual Report and Statement of Accounts*, 1973–8.

Federal Office of Statistics, *Annual Abstract of Statistics*, 1984–1986.

ADEBAYO O. OLUKOSHI

Structural Adjustment & Nigerian Industry

I. Introduction: The Origins and Dimensions of Nigeria's Industrial Crisis

The origins of the modern industrial sector in Nigeria could be traced back to the late 1930s and early 1940s. This was the period during which the major foreign trading companies which dominated the colonial raw material economy began to modify the structure of their operations in such a way as to enable them to make a transition away from purely commercial activities into some form of import-substitution manufacturing (Olukoshi, 1986a; Kilby, 1969). By the end of the Second World War, the basic internal conditions necessary for local manufacturing to begin in Nigeria had matured sufficiently. Not only had a significant number of Nigerians been divorced from their means of production and were, therefore, available for employment as wage labourers, but a domestic market, large enough to absorb commodities manufactured locally, had also been created. Furthermore, basic infrastructural facilities such as road and rail networks as well as water and electricity necessary for supporting a process of industrialization had been put in place (Olukoshi, 1986a, especially chapter 4: 115–47). Moreover, by the 1940s, many of the colonial trading companies had accumulated sufficient capital from their years of involvement in Nigerian trade to feel confident to move into higher levels of accumulation. The transition, always in the self-interest of the companies, was made all the more urgent by their profound concern to defend their profit margins and respond to the changing context of world politics as well as the agitation by nationalist forces in Nigeria for a greater role in local business activities (Olukoshi, 1986a, especially chapter 4: 115–47).

The earliest factories that were established by the foreign trading companies, as well as a handful of other international or internationalizing firms that hitherto had no direct links with the Nigerian market but which came to establish their presence in the country during or shortly after the Second World War, were engaged in the production of light industrial commodities such as detergents, soft drinks, leather goods, textiles, confectionery and alcoholic drinks, among others. The fact that Nigeria's pioneer factories were concentrated in the light industrial sector meant that the foreign corporations did not have to engage in new research since the technology for the production of the consumer goods they were processing had already been standardized. All that the companies did was to get their parents or associates in Europe to transfer, in a package form, some of the production techniques which they needed for local manufacturing in Nigeria. This way, the companies were able to beat the tariff walls erected by the state as well as take advantage of the numerous incentives provided by the government as part of its effort to spur the import-substitution process along (Olukoshi, 1986a, especially chapter 4: 115–47; Bangura, 1987: 2–5). What is more, the fact that most of the raw materials produced locally in the country were destined for the export market meant that the majority of the early factories established in Nigeria relied on foreign sources of inputs, including raw materials, in order to produce, especially as the primary commodities that were grown or mined in the country were only those needed by the industries of Western Europe. Remarkably enough, both the concentration of industrial activities in the light manufacturing sector and the heavy reliance of the factories on foreign sources of inputs intensified in the post-colonial period, even after first the Levantines and then elements of the domestic bourgeois class joined in the establishment of local production plants (Olukoshi, 1986a, especially chapter 4: 115–47; Bangura, 1987: 2–5).

Without doubt, the seeds of the current industrial crisis in Nigeria were embedded in the early structures of manufacturing activities in the country. It would be fair to argue that the fact that trading companies pioneered the industrialization process is a major cause of at least some of the distortions that were built into the import-substitution process from the outset. For, as Geoffrey Kay convincingly argues, merchant capital imposes serious constraints on the development of a balanced and self-reliant pattern of industrialization in the epoch of advanced transnational capitalism.[1] The logic on which the foreign companies built Nigeria's import-substitution industrialization is quite simple: using foreign exchange generated by the economy, manufacturing firms would import inputs in order to produce locally consumer goods that were hitherto imported into the country. Thus, up to the early 1970s, foreign exchange earnings generated from the export of primary commodities such as cocoa, cotton, groundnuts, palm produce, tin and columbite, among others, were used to import industrial inputs such as machinery, spare parts and raw materials. There was no meaningful attempt by the manufacturing companies to source their inputs locally. What this meant was that peasant agriculture and mining activities fed the local industrialization process through the external sector, rather than directly. This way, the agricultural sector was denied the benefits of industrialization as the industrial sector itself relied on foreign sources for its raw material needs. Similarly, there was no direct organic linkage between the mining sector and local manufacturing for the same reason that industrial inputs were obtained externally to feed domestic factory production (Olukoshi, 1986a; Bangura, 1987).

There are several elements to the contradictions and distortions inherent in the pattern of Nigeria's import-substitution industrialization up to the early 1970s. First, since the essential inputs necessary for manufacturing were obtained from foreign sources, the local value-added on the commodities produced was very low. Second, the overwhelming concentration of industrial activities in light processing meant that the intermediate and capital goods sectors remained backward, thereby creating a serious problem of sectoral imbalance and lopsidedness in the industrialization process. Third, the payments position of the state was put under constant pressure by the growing import needs of the manufacturing sector and those of the rest of the economy. Fourth, the absence of direct linkages between industry and agriculture and mining underlined the fragility of the country's economic and, in particular, industrial base and reinforced the structural distortions in the entire system (Olukoshi, 1986a; Bangura, 1987;

Teriba and Kayode, 1977; Teriba et al., 1981). These distortions remained hidden for as long as the Nigerian state was able to earn sufficient foreign exchange to finance the importation of inputs necessary to keep industry going. And although attempts were made by the state from the late 1950s onwards to plan the Nigerian economy more systematically by means of periodic development plans, the crucial question of locally sourcing the raw material base of industry was not addressed as the state did not face a major shortage of foreign exchange. Even when the economy underwent a mild payments crisis in the early 1960s, the response of the Balewa administration (1960–6) was to seek foreign aid to bridge the shortfall in resources and intensify the drive, already well underway, to attract more foreign investors to the country. The internal weaknesses of the industrial sector and the structural distortions in the economy were not addressed (Olukoshi, 1986a; Bangura, 1987; Teriba and Kayode, 1977; Teriba et al., 1981).

By the second half of the 1960s, owing to the increasing tempo of manufacturing activities in the country which led to a corresponding increase in the amount of inputs imported to meet the needs of industry, and the declining fortunes of the agricultural sector which meant that foreign exchange earnings were not growing much faster than the country's import bills, a crisis of immense proportions in the Nigerian economy seemed inevitable. It seemed only a matter of time before the contradictions in the industrial sector would burst into the open. Yet, fortuitously, towards the end of the 1960s and by the beginning of the 1970s, and especially after the Organization of Petroleum Exporting Countries (OPEC) oil price increases of 1973, the revenue base of the Nigerian state underwent a major transformation as a result of the massive oil earnings accruing to it from the export of oil. From a few hundred million dollars, state revenues from oil rose to N4.733 billion in 1975, N10 billion in 1979 and N15.234 billion in 1980 (CBN, *Economic and Financial Review*, vol. 21, no. 1, March 1983). Apart from helping to stave off a potential crisis in the country's industrial sector, the exponential growth in oil revenues also served to prevent the refraction into the Nigerian economy of the generalized recession that got underway in the world capitalist system in the early 1970s. Nigerian policy planners as well as the leading industrial groups therefore did not feel any compulsion to reduce the import-dependence of the manufacturing sector. Indeed, it is a reflection of the complete neglect of the possibility of developing a local raw material base for industry that the agricultural sector of the economy whose decline was already underway in the 1960s went into further decline as the agrarian basis of accumulation collapsed and the oil economy took its place. By the second half of the 1970s, precisely at the time Nigeria's oil revenues were undergoing a massive and rapid growth, the country ceased to be a major exporter of cocoa, cotton, groundnut, palm produce, coffee and sisal. Indeed, towards the end of the 1970s, Nigeria became a net importer of cotton, groundnut oil and palm oil (Olukoshi, 1986a; Bangura, 1987).

The oil boom of the 1970s deepened the structure of Nigeria's import-dependent industrialization. Many local and foreign business interests, eager to take advantage of Nigeria's growing domestic market and partake in the disbursement of the huge amount of petrodollars accruing to the state, established many more manufacturing plants to produce light consumer goods using inputs imported from foreign sources. In the course of the 1970s, the rate of manufacturing investment in the country became so rapid that Nigeria became, after South Africa, the second most sought-after investment outlet in Africa (Olukoshi, 1986a). By 1977 and 1978, the rate of gross investments in the economy was as high as 68 per cent and 60 per cent respectively (Bangura, 1987: 4). To be sure, not all of these massive investments was attributable to the activities of private capital, whether local or foreign. In fact, with the growth of the oil economy, the Nigerian state came to assume a central role in the economy in part by using some of the petroleum revenues accruing to it to pursue rather exhorbitant capital projects, pay expensive foreign consultancy fees, support the external commercial needs of industry and the repatriation of company profits (Bangura, 1987: 4). The indigenization decrees of 1972 and 1977 further strengthened the role of the state in the economy as it had to play a central part in encouraging greater equity participation in the economy by the growing domestic bourgeoisie. Institutions such as the Nigerian Enterprises Promotion Board (NEPB), the Nigerian Industrial Development Bank (NIDB), the Nigerian Bank for Commerce and Industry (NBCI) and the Securities and Exchange Commission (SEC) were set up to facilitate this process. These institutions, and many others, formed the bedrock of Nigeria's pattern of state capitalist accumulation that was to become, in the 1980s, the focus of attack by the International Monetary Fund (IMF) and the World Bank (Bangura, 1987: 4).

For much of the 1970s, the growing import needs of industry and the rest of the economy were easily met by the huge amounts of petrodollars accruing to the state. Indeed, the country was able to build up and maintain a respectable reserve and balance of payments position. This was so in spite of the massive over-invoicing that was associated with Nigeria's international trade transactions, the unbridled inflation of contracts and the reckless misappropriation of public funds. And yet although the country's gross fixed capital formation and net fixed capital formation jumped from 22.8 per cent and 18.2 per cent respectively in 1973–4 to 40.1 per cent and 35.7 per cent in 1978–9, the contribution of the manufacturing sector to the gross domestic product was only about 6 to 8 per cent (Bangura, 1987: 4–5). What is more, the commodity composition of Nigeria's industrial output showed clearly that transport equipment, chemicals and engineering were almost non-existent in the manufacturing sector as 90 per cent of commodities produced were made up of consumer goods. It is a mark of the virtual absence of capital and intermediate goods production in Nigeria that in the course of the 1970s the country relied to the tune of 98.8 per cent and 93.9 per cent respectively on foreign sources for the supply of its industrial and agricultural machinery and equipment needs. The engineering sector of industry, despite the 16.4 per cent of value-added in manufacturing attributed to it, remained heavily dominated by metal furniture and fixtures, structural metal products and fabricated metal – all very elementary engineering activities. Primary engineering activities such as the production of agricultural and industrial machinery and equipment or even the manufacture of household electrical apparatus and transport equipment accounted for only about 2.3 per cent of value-added in manufacturing for much of the 1970s (Bangura, 1987: 4–5; Ekuerhare, 1985).

An early warning of the impending industrial crisis that was to grip the Nigerian economy from the early 1980s came by way of a relatively mild depression in 1977–8 occasioned by a 16 per cent drop in the country's oil revenues in 1977 (Olukoshi, 1984; Bangura et al., 1984). In response to a decline in Nigeria's oil exports, the government of General Olusegun Obasanjo (1976–9) effected a slight increase in the posted price of the country's high-grade, low-sulphur content oil in order to maintain the level of foreign exchange earnings accruing to the state in the face of an ever-growing import bill. This move led to a further drop in the amount of oil exported by the country as the leading oil companies opted for cheaper oil from the North Sea and on-the-spot market. As a result of the decline in the government's revenue from the overseas sale of oil, a set of mild deflationary measures was announced with the overall aim of curtailing imports and reducing the public expenditure (Olukoshi, 1984; Bangura et al., 1984). As with the Balewa administration's response to the payments crisis of the early 1960s, the regime of General Obasanjo made no effort to tackle the roots of the crisis, namely the excessive import-dependence of industry. The commodities whose importation was banned under the regime's deflationary measures were not those needed by industry but rather consisted basically of finished consumer goods and food items. The government also sought to bridge the shortfall in its revenue by raising two jumbo loans from the Euro-dollar and Euro-currency markets (Olukoshi, 1984; Bangura et al., 1984). By the time the military handed over governmental power to the civilians in 1979, Nigeria's oil exports had started to recover again, thereby postponing the possibility that the question of a local raw material base for industry would be seriously addressed by the state in the immediate future.

The advent of the civilian administration of Shehu Shagari (1979–83) coincided with a dramatic, unprecedented increase in the international price of oil, and, therefore, in the revenue accruing to the Nigerian state. From $14.9 a barrel in 1978, Nigeria's oil sold for $33 in 1979 and $44.4 in 1980. Government revenue rose from N10 billion in 1979 to some N15 billion in 1980 (Olukoshi, 1984; Bangura et al., 1984; CBN, 1983).With such massive revenue windfalls, the government of Shehu Shagari did not find it difficult at all to reverse the deflationary measures put in place by the Obasanjo regime, the more so as the ruling National Party of Nigeria (NPN) relied on an extensive patronage network to maintain its cohesiveness. Imports were liberalized, tariffs were reduced, the public expenditure was increased and various fiscal measures, such as the Approved User Scheme, which enabled manufacturers to bring in inputs at concessional rates of duty, were introduced. Increasingly, the focus of economic activity in the country shifted sharply to international trade, international and domestic finance, services, construction and real estate (Olukoshi, 1984; Bangura et al., 1984). Consumer goods imports rose from N440 million in 1974 to N2.136 billion in 1978 and N3.897 billion in 1981. Similarly, capital goods imports increased from N670 million in 1974 to N3.968 billion in 1978 and N4.667 billion in 1979. Raw material imports too grew dramatically from N519.3 million in 1974 to N1.880 billion in 1978 and N3.038 billion in 1981 (National Economic Council Expert Committee, 1983). With such a high level of import dependence, it became clear that the slightest drop in Nigeria's oil earnings would set in motion one form of crisis or another in the economy.

When, therefore, a dramatic drop occurred in the international price of oil in the early 1980s as a result of the glut in the world market, the corresponding fall in Nigeria's oil revenues triggered an unprecedented crisis of immense dimensions in the economy. From a peak of $22.4 billion in 1980, Nigeria's oil earnings fell to $16.7 billion in 1981, $12.8 billion in 1982 and $10 billion in 1983 (National Economic Council Expert Committee, 1983). Considering that imports into the country had been growing very rapidly, the level of earnings accruing to the state became unable to sustain them. The immediate consequences of this development were reflected in Nigeria's balance of payments position, which went into the red. Similarly, public finances were thrown into disarray as the country suffered a resource gap of N3 billion in 1981 compared to a surplus of N2.6 billion in 1980. As the revenue deficit of both the federal and state governments grew, the country's GDP fell by 2 per cent in 1982 and declined further by 4.4 per cent in 1983. The current account of the country recorded a shortfall of N4.9 billion in 1982 and N2.9 billion in 1983 while the budget deficit for 1983 stood at a staggering N6.231 billion more than 50 per cent of total government expenditure (Olukoshi, 1987: 7–8). The deficit was to grow even bigger in later years. Needless to mention, the collapse of Nigeria's oil revenue also had an immediate impact on industry as many factories folded up in the face of an acute shortage of inputs, particularly spare parts and raw materials. It is reckoned that in the period between 1983 and 1985, about 50 per cent of the factories operating in the country collapsed outright. As for the remaining 50 per cent that remained in business, they could only run skeletal operations and, in the majority of cases, capacity utilization dropped to about 40 per cent or less (Olukoshi, n.d.: 7–8; Bangura, 1987). Industrial turnover and value-added came under considerable strain and many tens of thousands of industrial workers were either retrenched or sent on compulsory and indefinite leave. The difficulties encountered by the manufacturing sector were not helped by the fact that the allocation of scarce foreign exchange was organized through a corrupt and highly bureaucratic system of import licensing.

As a result of the widespread collapse of factories, and also because the shortage of foreign exchange made it more difficult to import various items, an acute shortage of consumer goods developed in Nigeria between 1983 and 1985. This, in turn, fuelled the inflationary spiral in the economy, especially as traders and middlemen took to hoarding the commodities that were in greatest demand but in short supply. In addition to the decline of industry and a spiralling inflation, the agricultural sector too suffered further setbacks as poultries, piggeries, fisheries and even maize farms were forced to fold up because they were no longer able to procure inputs such as feeds and fertilizer from foreign sources (Olukoshi, n.d.: 7–8; Bangura, 1987). In addition to all this, the economy was saddled with a heavy debt burden. Internal public debts rose from N4.6 billion in 1979 to N22.2 billion in 1983. The increase in 1983 alone was N7.2 billion. At the external level, the heavy borrowing spree embarked upon by the politicians at both the federal and state levels began to take its toll from 1983 onwards when the repayment of principal and interest on the country's foreign debt rose to N1.3 billion, an increase of 72 per cent when compared with payments in 1982. Nigeria's debt service ratio jumped from 8.9 per cent in 1982 to 17.4 per cent in 1983 (Olukoshi, n.d.: 7–8; Bangura, 1987; Olukoshi, 1990a). Quite clearly, the country's economy was in serious trouble and the industrial sector in particular was faced with a major crisis which necessitated an adjustment programme. Let us now proceed to outline the aims and objectives of the Structural Adjustment Programme (SAP) of the Babangida administration as these relate to industry before examining the consequences of the programme for the performance of the manufacturing sector.

II. The Place of Industry in the Aims and Objectives of the Structural Adjustment Programme

In many respects, the Babangida administration's SAP is a logical outcome of the earlier efforts at adjustment and recovery articulated and implemented by the Shagari and Buhari (1983–5) regimes. These earlier efforts came under the rubric of austerity measures designed to curb the Nigerian appetite for imports and reduce the level of public expenditure. The Shagari administration's Economic Stabilization Act of 1982, promulgated to contain the crisis of accumulation, relied mainly on a combination of import restrictions, monetary controls and fiscal policies. All unused import licences issued by the government were recalled for review, capital projects not yet started were deferred, the public investment expenditure was reduced by 40 per cent, compulsory advanced deposits ranging from 50–250 per cent were imposed on a wide range of imports, restrictions were placed on the external transfer of capital, the price of gasoline was raised marginally and the interest rate increased by 2 per cent (Bangura et al., 1984; Olukoshi, n.d.; NIPSS, n.d). These measures were pushed forward by the Buhari administration, following the overthrow, on 31 December 1983, of the government of Shehu Shagari. The main thrust of Buhari's economic recovery pro-gramme was basically to further rationalize the domestic economic base by retrenching many allegedly superfluous public sector employees and reducing the public expen-diture. The regime sought to impose more discipline in the implementation of the Shagari administration's austerity programme, a programme whose full application had been compromised by the elaborate patronage network that characterized the politics of the Second Republic, and, particularly, of the ruling National Party of Nigeria (Olukoshi and Abdulraheem, 1985).

When General Ibrahim Babangida came to power on 27 August 1985 in a palace *coup d'état* against General Buhari, his government did not reject the harsh austerity mea-sures that had been imposed by its predecessors. Instead, General Babangida opted to carry them forward to their IMF/World Bank-inspired logical conclusion. The main difference between the adjustment programme of the Babangida administration and the various measures implemented by its predecessors centres on the role which they were prepared to assign to the so-called forces of the free market. Whereas the Shagari and Buhari administrations showed no inclination to abandon the Nigerian economy to market forces as demanded by the IMF and the World Bank, the Babangida regime had no hesitation in making the market the centre-piece of its adjustment programme. This should not be surprising as the *coup* of 27 August 1985 was the outcome of a re-alignment of forces and a shift in the power base away from the forces of state control in favour of the advocates of free market policies. In the view of the proponents of the free market in Nigeria, the roots of the Nigerian economic crisis and the increasing decline witnessed since it started were attributable to the state controls and inter-ventionism. The long-term interests of the economy and the country would be best served by the rolling back of the frontiers of the state (Olukoshi, n.d.). The clearest indication of the Babangida administration's commitment to market-oriented policies for Nigeria's economic recovery came on 27 June 1986 when a comprehensive pro-gramme of structural adjustment was spelt out, its centre-piece being the devaluation of the naira through flotation on the market. To be sure, the adoption of SAP by the Babangida administration was fraught with difficulties, not least because vested interests had developed around the allocation of import licences, the contract content of public expenditure and the regulated interest rates which, among other elements, were to form the focus of attack by the free marketeers. Much has already been written about various aspects of the politics of the adoption and implementation of SAP and so we need not detain ourselves here with this issue. Suffice it to note that domestic and external pressures from various contending class interests have continually served to shape, even distort, aspects of the programme as its implementation continues (Olukoshi, n.d.; Phillips and Ndekwu, 1987).

As officially spelt out by the government, the objectives of SAP include (Olukoshi, n.d.; Phillips and Ndekwu, 1987; Okongwu, 1987):

(a) the restructuring and diversification of the Nigerian economy in order to reduce the country's dependence on the oil sector and imports;
(b) the achievement of fiscal and balance of payment viability for the country in the short to medium term;
(c) the establishment of the basis for a sustainable non-inflationary or minimal infla-tionary growth; and
(d) the reduction of the dominance of unproductive investments in the public sector, the improvement of that sector's efficiency, as well as the enhancement of the growth potential of the private sector.

These broad objectives are to be achieved through (Olukoshi, n.d.; Phillips and Ndekwu, 1987; Okongwu, 1987):

(a) the strengthening of demand management policies;
(b) the adoption of measures to stimulate domestic production and broaden the supply base of the economy;
(c) the adoption of a realistic exchange rate policy through the establishment of a Second-tier Foreign Exchange Market (SFEM), later renamed the Foreign Exchange Market (FEM);
(d) the rationalization and restructuring of the country's tariff regime in order to aid the promotion of industrial diversification;
(e) the progressive liberalization of trade and payments;
(f) the reduction of complex administrative controls and the fostering of reliance on market forces;
(g) the adoption of appropriate pricing policies for public enterprises;
(h) the rationalization and commercialization/privatization of public sector enterprises.

As it relates specifically to the Nigerian industrial sector, SAP aims to:[2]

(a) encourage the accelerated development and use of local raw materials and inter-mediate inputs while at the same time discouraging the importation of these inputs;
(b) encourage the development and utilization of local technology;
(c) increase substantially the level of local value-added in the manufacturing sector;
(d) promote the development of export-oriented industries;
(e) generate factory employment through the encouragement of private sector small- and medium-scale manufacturing concerns;
(f) remove bottlenecks and constraints that hamper industrial development, including infrastructural and administrative deficiencies;
(g) attract foreign investment through the creation of a more liberal investment climate, the establishment of local foreign exchange domiciliary accounts and the adoption of an incomes policy favourable to international capital; and
(h) liberalize controls to facilitate greater indigenous and foreign investment.

As we pointed out earlier, the adjustment of the exchange rate of the naira is the pivot of SAP. The IMF and the World Bank had, prior to the introduction of the programme, argued that the naira was grossly over-valued. As a consequence of this over-valuation, Nigeria had an unjustifiably high import profile, the economy suffered capital flight and shifts in relative prices were unfavourable to the manufacturing sector. The Fund and the Bank further argued that since the naira was over-valued by about 60 per cent in 1983, 'there should be a 25 to 30 per cent initial devaluation, to be followed by a quarterly review until the element of over-valuation was elimi-nated'.[3] In the event, the Babangida administration's adjustment programme deviated from this gradualist approach as the government opted for the determination of the naira's value by 'market forces', first at SFEM and later FEM when the first- and second-tier markets converged in 1988. Since the introduction of SFEM on 29 September 1986, the value of the naira, which enjoyed a parity rate with the US dollar in January 1986, has dropped dramatically. For much of the last quarter of 1986, the naira fluctuated between N5.05 to the dollar on 2 October 1986 to N3.00 on 4 December 1986. This more or less continued into 1987 and 1988 with the naira officially gravitating around N4.00 to the dollar. By 31 March 1989, the value of the naira had declined much further, standing officially at N7.40 to the dollar

(Bangura, 1987: 11; *West Africa*, 10–16 April 1989: 495). By the end of December 1990, it was almost N10.00 to the dollar officially. Thus between 1986 and 1990, the naira has suffered an almost ten-fold devaluation in relation to the dollar. Beyond the official exchange rate, on the autonomous inter-bank market, the naira performed even worse with its exchange rate to the dollar rising from N5.00 in 1987 to about N10.00 towards the end of 1989 and about N11.50 throughout most of 1990. The parallel market rate was even higher, standing at N12.00 to the dollar as at 31 March 1989. The fluctuating and dwindling value of the naira forced the government to attempt to achieve a merger of the FEM and autonomous inter-bank rates of the naira through the introduction of the Inter-bank Foreign Exchange Market (IFEM) (*West Africa*, 24–30 April 1989: 565), but this has failed to have a stabilizing effect on the value of the naira as its free fall continues. As of the end of 1990, there were effectively three exchange rates in the country – the official Central Bank rate arrived at with the leading banks, the rate offered by bureaux de change and merchant banks, and the parallel market rate.

The adjustment of the naira exchange rate is closely related to the review of the tariff structure. According to World Bank sources, Nigerian tariffs were generally low between 1973 and 1980, amounting to between 5 and 10 per cent for intermediate and capital goods and 50 per cent for non-food consumer goods. In the view of the Bank, this tariff structure placed serious pressures on Nigeria's domestic production sectors and encouraged industries to look outwards for their raw materials rather than source them locally. This was exacerbated as the naira was, according to the Bank, over-valued (World Bank, 1983). Although the Shagari administration extended the tariff net to cover all imports and tightened customs procedures, the new levels of tariff were not adequate to provide incentives to the productive sectors. Furthermore, there were variations in tariffs between individual commodities, and the application of quotas and quantitative restrictions led to a distorted structure of industrial protection. According to the Bank, industrial commodities had negative protection levels for export industries and positive protection in excess of 200 per cent for assembly plants (World Bank, 1983). In order to protect local industries, discourage the importation of raw materials and unessential commodities and generate additional revenue for the government, the IMF and the Bank recommended a review of the customs tariff structure in order to rationalize and simplify it. The review had to go hand in hand with the adjustment of the exchange rate (World Bank, 1983). In September 1986, in line with IMF suggestions, the Babangida regime announced an interim tariff structure in which the duty on raw materials was put in the range of 10 to 18 per cent, intermediate inputs at 5 to 30 per cent, final capital goods at 5 to 20 per cent, final durable consumer goods at 20 to 30 per cent and final non-durable non-basic consumer goods at 100 to 120 per cent (Bangura, 1987). This was followed in January 1988 by a fully revised tariff structure which replaced the interim one and is meant, according to the government, to encourage inward-looking industrial production, a view disputed by many manufacturers for reasons which we shall see below.

One other vital component of SAP which has a direct bearing on industry is the deregulation of interest rates. In the period up to July 1987, the Babangida administration had resisted pressures from the IMF and the World Bank to allow the market to determine the rates of interest. This way, interest rates would fall in line with the floating exchange rates and the general re-alignment of prices in the domestic economy as well as mop up the excess liquidity in the system. The IMF and the Bank, supported by the leading financial houses in the country, condemned the system whereby interest rates remained fixed under the tight control of the Central Bank. The decision of the government, through the 1987 budget, to fix at 11 per cent the minimum interest rate payable on bank savings deposits and at 13–15 per cent the maximum bank lending rate also came in for harsh criticism, the chief argument being that it encouraged consumption and trading activities to the detriment of production. After a great deal of domestic and external pressure, the government finally agreed to deregulate interests. By the Central Bank of Nigeria (CBN) Circular no. 21 of 31 July 1987, all forms of control on interest rates were abolished. Henceforth, market forces were to determine the rate. The CBN raised its minimum rediscount rate from 11 per cent to 15 per cent thereby effectively preventing commercial banks from charging interest at a rate below 15 per cent if transactions were to be profitable (Bangura, 1987). As a consequence, interest rates averaged 18 per cent in 1987 and at one point, in 1988, threatened to exceed 20 per cent until pressure from the Manufacturers' Association of Nigeria (MAN) and other business groups forced the government to reduce the CBN's minimum discount rate to 12.75 per cent. But during 1990, interest rates shot up again, ranging between 28 and 30 per cent in the course of the year, much to the chagrin of MAN which once again launched a spirited campaign that compelled the government to issue guidelines in 1991 effectively reducing interests to 21 per cent.

The CBN also raised interest rates on treasury bills from 10 per cent to 14 per cent in 1987 and increased the liquidity ratio of commercial banks from 25 per cent to 30 per cent, thereby reducing their ability to lend. Furthermore, through Circular no. 21, the CBN reduced the rate of credit expansion to the private sector to 7.4 per cent from 8 per cent between 31 July 1987 and 31 December 1987. These monetary policies were meant to restrict the amount of money in circulation in the economy (Bangura, 1987). Although in 1988, as a result of popular domestic pressure, the government was forced to concede some reflationary policies, these were reversed in the 1989 budget, which sought to promote the kind of deflationary measures that were put in place in 1987. Thus, in order to check the inflationary spiral associated with the devaluation of the naira and the reflationary budget of 1988, the growth in money supply to the economy was reduced from 15 per cent in 1988 to 14.6 per cent in 1989. Similarly, the growth of credit to the private sector was reduced from 13.3 per cent in 1988 to 10.7 per cent in 1989. Merchant and commercial bank loans and advances were frozen at their 1988 levels as were the liquidity ratios of 27.5 per cent and 20 per cent for the commercial and merchant banks respectively. And shortly after the announcement in January of the 1989 budget, the CBN, exercising its preserve of fixing the rediscount rate, added a percentage point to the 1988 rediscount rate thereby raising the figure to 13.75 per cent. Also, in April 1989, through Monetary Policy Circular 23, the CBN raised the cash reserve ratio of both commercial and merchant banks by one percentage point. The liquidity ratio of commercial banks was raised from 27.5 per cent to 30 per cent while that of merchant banks was increased to 22.5 per cent from 20 per cent (*West Africa*, 24–30 April 1989: 656).

In adopting SAP and various cost rationalization measures, including the devaluation of the naira and wage rates as well as the raising of interest rates and review of the tariff structure, the Babangida administration expected that foreign capital would be attracted to the country to boost industrial production. The promulgation of a decree creating foreign exchange domiciliary accounts in the country was designed to assist in this process. A series of incentive measures was also introduced as part of SAP to encourage industrial expansion. For example, companies which have to import raw materials in order to produce for the export market are guaranteed favourable tariffs on their import needs. The compulsory import surcharge of 30 per cent imposed in 1985/6 was abolished as another step aimed at encouraging industrial investment. Excise duties paid by manufacturers of export goods would be fully refunded.

Furthermore, support services of various kinds are being made freely available to manufacturers searching for export markets. Also, exporters, originally permitted to retain up to 25 per cent of the foreign exchange earned from their overseas transactions, can now keep up to 50 per cent of their hard currency export proceeds. An export credit guarantee and insurance scheme is being set up as further evidence of the government's commitment to the promotion of industrial exports. In addition, through the 1987 budget, corporate profits tax was reduced from 45 to 40 per cent and capital allowance rates were modified in favour of corporate Research and Development expenditure. Companies can also enjoy tax-free dividends for a period of three years provided that (a) the firm paying the dividend is registered in Nigeria; (b) the equity participation is imported between 1 January 1987 and 31 December 1992; and (c) the recipient's equity constitutes at least 10 per cent of the company's share capital. If the dividend-paying company is engaged in agricultural production or processing or in petro-chemical and liquified natural gas production, then it is entitled to a tax holiday of five years. As part of the new national industrial policy, the Nigerian Enterprises Promotion Decree (NEPD) has been amended to enable foreign firms to participate in domestic agricultural production and processing and enjoy a dominant equity position. If the foreign firms so wish, they could have 100 per cent equity ownership. An attempt in 1987 to amend the 1981 Minimum Wage Act by exempting employers with less than 500 workers from paying the N125 monthly minimum wage had to be withdrawn following a spirited opposition from workers and their unions. The government had hoped through the reversed amendment further to cheapen the cost of labour for investors, regardless of the massive devaluation in real income that has been associated with the massive deprecation of the naira since September 1986 (Ohiorhenuan, 1987; Federal Ministry of Finance and Economic Development, 1988). Quite clearly, through SAP, the Babangida administration has sought to re-structure the industrial sector of the Nigerian economy. But how have industries responded to this attempt and what impact has the programme had on them? This is the question to which we now turn our attention.

III. The Impact of the Structural Adjustment Programme on Nigerian Industry

Some five years after its introduction, there is no doubt that SAP has had considerable and far-reaching consequences for Nigerian industry. As we have already pointed out, one of the main objectives of the programme is to force industries to look inwards for their raw materials and other inputs. In the face of the various measures that have been introduced by the government since the middle of 1986, the level of performance of individual firms in the manufacturing sector has been uneven. Indeed, even at a sub-sectoral level, performance has been unequal. In general, those firms that have been able easily to find local substitutes for imported raw materials have performed better under SAP than those that are heavily dependent on imported inputs for which local substitutes are either not available, or are not present in commercial quantities or would require a long time and a huge capital outlay to develop. Thus, agro-allied industries, for example, have had comparatively less problems of adjustment than firms engaged in metal processing, engineering works and automobile assembly, which are heavily dependent on imported inputs. But even those companies that have fared comparatively better than heavily import-dependent ones have had to contend with other difficulties thrown up by SAP as we shall argue below. In any case, many of these companies have had to come to terms with the problems associated with producing in an economy that is in deep crisis. Furthermore, there are the large number of firms which rely on foreign inputs to supplement local raw materials. These too have been badly hit by SAP both because of the increased cost of importing raw materials and the increased cost of locally available inputs (Bangura, 1987).

In general terms, the massive, almost ten-fold, devaluation which the naira has undergone since September 1986 has resulted in a considerable increase in the cost of production for all industrialists. As a direct consequence of devaluation, producers have found that they need many more thousands of naira to procure the same quantity of inputs and stay in business. For firms that obtain a substantial portion of their raw materials locally, the inflationary spiral associated with devaluation has led to major price increases. Matters have not been helped by the fact that increased demand for local raw materials by firms adjusting to the economic crisis and SAP has not been matched by sufficiently large increases in production. Some of these inputs such as groundnut, sorghum, maize and cassava are also important food crops consumed by many rural and urban households, a fact which adds to the demand profile for these commodities. The export promotion policy of the government, popularized by the slogan 'export all exportables', has led to a situation where local manufacturers requiring raw materials like cotton, cocoa, coffee, groundnuts and others needed by companies operating in the food and beverages, textiles and rubber footwear, tyre-retreading and foam production sub-sectors of the economy have to compete with exporters (both individuals and corporate groups) eager to earn foreign exchange from the overseas sale of these commodities or a means of exporting capital, or even quite simply for speculative purposes. Most of these exporters and speculators are often prepared to pay vast amounts of naira for the commodities and are able to outbid industrialists who obviously have to keep a tab on their costs of production. Even where some of the bigger firms like Cadbury (Nigeria) Limited, producers of food drinks among other products, have attempted to go into the production of their raw material needs by acquiring agricultural land, the generally increased costs associated with so massive a devaluation in so short a space of time has made the task ahead of them really difficult. As a result, many of these firms have had to maintain low levels of capacity utilization both as a means of reducing overall costs and in response to the increased costs associated with SAP.[4]

As for firms that for one reason or another cannot yet look inwards in any meaningful manner for their inputs, the consequences of the devaluation of the naira are more obvious and direct. These firms fall into three categories. First, there are those which need to continue to import raw materials until an adequate local raw material base is established. Some of these firms are striving to develop a raw material base for themselves while others are awaiting the completion of the federal government's steel and petrochemical projects to get a supply of inputs which they need. Companies in this category include those in metal and steel production, engineering works, plastic and battery production, among other sectors. Second, there are firms for which in the foreseeable future a local raw material base cannot be developed simply because the inputs which they need are, for now, either not available at all or are to be found in uncommercial quantities. Third, as we have noted earlier, there are many companies which, although they are able to meet some of their raw material needs locally, still have to import inputs to supplement what is available within the country. For all three categories of companies, the devaluation of the naira has meant an astronomical rise in the naira cost of their import needs and, therefore, in their cost of production. The wild, downward fluctuation which the naira exchange rate has suffered in the past years has also meant that many of the firms have had to budget ahead for possible increases in the naira amounts needed to meet their import needs. According to MAN, not surprisingly, between 1986 and the end of 1987, average unit cost of production rose by 107 per cent. The cost of imported raw materials rose by 229 per cent over the same period while that of locally sourced raw materials rose by 96 per cent (MAN, *Half-Yearly Economic Review*, July–December 1987: 3).

Ordinarily, the increased cost of industrial production arising from the devaluation of the naira should have been easily remedied by resort to bank loans by manufacturing concerns. However, this has not been an easy option for many firms precisely because, in the attempt to check the inflationary fall-outs of devaluation, the Babangida administration has imposed an almost rigid liquidity squeeze on the economy. With the decision to raise the CBN minimum rediscount rate, the government has effectively made it much more expensive for manufacturers and other business groups to borrow money. This move has been reinforced by the periodic increase in the liquidity ratio which the CBN expects banks to maintain in any given financial year. The liquidity squeeze which has been a central aspect of SAP has also been further strengthened by a deliberate policy of curtailing the rate of credit expansion to the private sector. In a climate in which borrowing has become very exorbitant, many manufacturers have found themselves unable to compete for loans needed to develop a local raw material base, or pay for the foreign exchange needed to bring in foreign inputs or even reorganize their production techniques or cover their basic overhead costs. The cash flow problems of manufacturers have been compounded by the fact that those of them that require foreign exchange must lodge the naira equivalent of the amount of hard currency they need with their bankers before submitting their application (through their bankers) to the CBN. Many producers have found that their working capital has thus been tied down in banks while they await the result of their application for foreign exchange. Quite clearly, the liquidity squeeze on the economy had made the process of adjustment by industry much more difficult and has worked with devaluation to increase, tremendously, the cost of production (MAN, *Half-Yearly Economic Review*, July–December 1987: 3; Bangura, 1987).

The increased cost of industrial production which arises from devaluation as well as the very high cost of borrowing have, as can be expected, led to exorbitantly priced goods which are beyond the real purchasing power of most Nigerians. As a result of SAP, a vicious inflationary cycle is presently at work in the Nigerian economy in which devaluation and high interest rates lead to high costs of production which, in turn, reflect themselves in highly priced commodities and an ever-growing wholesale and retail price index which, in turn, leads the government to tighten further the liquidity and credit squeeze, thereby increasing the cost of production in the context of an ever-dwindling naira, and which, in turn, means even higher costs of production and higher wholesale and retail prices. The problem which this cycle poses for manufacturers is that commodities which they produce can hardly find a sufficiently large domestic market. In other words, those producers that have managed to remain in business in spite of the very high cost of production brought about by SAP are faced with a situation in which the market for their products is diminishing by the day. This is not just a question of 'consumer resistance' to highly priced consumer goods in an inflation-torn economy; it is also a result of the devaluation of the naira which has led to a massive decline in the real income of Nigerians and, therefore, in the purchasing power of the citizenry. In the context of an almost ten-fold decline in real incomes between 1986 and 1990, many Nigerians have found that they simply cannot afford basic consumer goods and even certain categories of food items which were taken for granted by most households. Consequently, many manufacturers are saddled with a major stockpile of goods in their warehouses. The slow turnover suffered by manufacturing concerns has persisted in spite of a variety of measures introduced by managers to attract customers and, in some cases, popularize hire-purchase. Needless to say, returns on investments have, in the prevailing environment, been rather depressing for manufacturers (MAN, *Half-Yearly Economic Review*, July–December 1987: 3; Bangura, 1987).

As if the higher costs of production and the diminishing domestic market for consumer goods associated with SAP were not enough, the interim tariff system introduced by the government in September 1986 had the direct consequence of encouraging dumping on the Nigerian market by foreign-based manufacturers to the detriment of local producers. It also had the effect of exposing local manufacturers to major competition with more powerful foreign transnational corporations. This situation was not altered in any radical manner by the fully revised tariff regime introduced in 1988. Foreign-based producers, taking advantage of Nigeria's trade liberalization policy, dumped all manner of goods on the market and thus effectively under-cut Nigerian manufacturers of those commodities. Not surprisingly, therefore, local manufacturing groups across the country complained bitterly that both the interim tariff system and its fully revised version were excessively skewed in favour of liberalization, thereby penalizing local industries harshly. They cited evidence to show that from September 1986 to the end of December 1988 it had become much more profitable to import finished goods into the country rather than produce them locally. This explains why producers of automobiles, detergents and various chemicals, for example, opted for the importation of finished goods rather than produce those commodities within the country, a development which, according to MAN posed a very serious danger to the survival of those industries. Other industries that were very adversely affected by the tariff regimes in operation in the country in the period up to the end of December 1988 include those engaged in the production of batteries, enamelware and fishing nets (Bangura, 1987: 28–30).

Just how negative a consequence the interim tariff system introduced in September 1986 had on many industries can be seen from the experience of the country's automobile plants and fishing net industries. In the case of the automobile industry, Bangura, Kayode and Mogaha have shown how the tariff system failed to protect local plants by making it more profitable to import fully finished vehicles. Thus, whereas fully-built cars with an unclassified cubic capacity had their tariff reduced from 70 per cent to 30 per cent, and those with cubic capacities of between 1,600 to 1,800 and 1,801 to 2,000 had their tariffs cut from 70 per cent to 40 per cent and 200 per cent to 50 per cent respectively, tariffs for the 1,600 cubic capacity imported completely knocked down (CKD) parts needed by local automobile plants showed only a very marginal difference of 15 per cent between the old structure and the new one. Similarly, the customs duty for CKD parts between 1,801 and 2,000 cubic capacity was reduced from 40 per cent to only 33 per cent. Given the disadvantage suffered by the automobile plants under the interim tariff structure, it is not surprising that they were at the forefront of the campaign against it. They expressed similar displeasure with the 1988 fully revised tariff regime, joining other manufacturers to dub it the 'traders' tariff'. In response to the campaigns and criticisms, the government decided through its 1989 budget to reduce the import duty on parts for commercial vehicles from 25 per cent to 5 per cent (Bangura, 1987: 28–30; Kayode, 1987; Mogaha, 1988).

As to the fishing net industries, the interim tariff structure had the consequence of robbing them of about 30 per cent of their domestic market as importers of finished nets took advantage of the trade liberalization policy of the government to bring in the commodity at a rate of duty that was favourable. The four fishing net companies in the country claimed that, with an installed capacity of over 200 machines, they were capable of producing over 1.2 million fishing nets annually, a level of production that is sufficient to satisfy the national demand. Yet, as a result of the decision to impose a 20 per cent duty on the raw material needed by the industries, the cost per kilogram of fishing nets produced locally was slightly over N33,000, whereas, at a duty of only 5 per cent, the total landed cost per kilogram of complete fishing net imported from foreign sources stood at N28,730. Quite clearly, local manufacturers of fishing nets were placed at a serious disadvantage by the interim tariff structure (Bangura, 1987).

Side by side with the general liberalization of trade, the de-control of the foreign exchange market has encouraged the importation of finished goods into the country. Ohiorhenuan has pointed to the fact that in the first five months of the operation of the SFEM about 25 per cent of the total amount of foreign exchange sold on the market was used to finance the importation of finished, mostly consumer, goods. This trend has generally continued although since 1988 the government has gradually increased the number of items whose importation into the country is absolutely prohibited. For many local producers of consumer goods the liberalization of exchange rules has mainy exacerbated the problem of market realization created by the diminishing purchasing power of Nigerians and reinforced by dumping activities encouraged by the liberalized tariff structure of the country (Ohiorhenuan, 1987).

Given the increased cost of production and diminishing domestic market suffered by most manufacturing firms under SAP, it is not surprising that since July 1986 the industrial sector has, at best, been more or less stagnant in its overall performance. This fact is amply demonstrated by the level of capacity utilization in industry, which has not undergone any appreciable increase. Average capacity utilization between 1986 and 1990 generally remained in the 30–40 per cent range for the industrial sector as a whole, a performance which does not represent any serious improvement on the pre-1986 levels. Indeed, for some manufacturing sub-sectors capacity utilization fell, in many cases substantially, below the pre-1986 levels. Such sub-sectors include heavily import-dependent ones like producers of electrical and electronic goods, metal, iron and steel and fabricated metal products, plastic and rubber goods, motor vehicles and trucks, and chemicals and pharmaceutical products whose level of capacity utilization stood on average at between 3 per cent and 25 per cent. However, for firms whose raw material needs were being met by local suppliers capacity utilization underwent some growth. For the textile mills, for example, average capacity utilization stood at well over 50 per cent in 1987. Similarly, producers of glass and glass products, tyre and tubes, and footwear and beverages recorded increases in their capacity utilization, with some of them attaining 90 per cent of their installed capacity. Yet, firms using local raw materials are few, and local inputs constituted only about 49 per cent of total raw materials used by industry in 1988, a marginal increase on the 40 per cent figure recorded in the pre-SAP years (Bangura, 1987; MAN, *Half-Yearly Economic Review*, 1986–9; *West Africa*, 16–22 January 1989: 50–1). In 1989 and 1990, MAN reported that average overall capacity utilization in industry stood at 31 per cent and 37 per cent respectively.

A stagnant average capacity utilization level went hand in hand with abjectly low sales turnover for many companies. Although, as with capacity utilization, some firms have recorded increases in sales since the introduction of SAP, for the majority of industrial producers turnover has either remained static or even undergone declines. MAN, in a report on a survey it carried out, noted that the 31 companies which it covered had a huge stock of finished goods valued at over N70 million, representing about 15 per cent of their total production (MAN, *Half-Yearly Economic Review*, January–June 1987). It is needless to point out that, faced with this situation, the profit margin of many manufacturers has fallen drastically. Even manufacturers, like those engaged in beer brewing, whose absolute profit margins grew in spite of SAP recorded lower returns per share. Production levels which in 1988 declined by 3.4 per cent either remained stagnant or fell for most firms in 1987, 1988 and 1989, with the plastic and rubber industry and motor vehicle and assembly plants recording declines of 6 per cent and 48 per cent respectively between the first and second halves of 1987 (MAN, *Half-Yearly Economic Review*, July–December 1987: 3). High operational costs, low sales and declining profitability also meant that manufacturers had further to rationalize their operations in order to save costs, with the consequence that employment in the industrial sector fell by 6 per cent in 1987 compared to the corresponding figure in 1986. Many firms, faced with low sales and cash flow problems, took to the retrenchment of workers in order to reduce their production costs (MAN, *Half-Yearly Economic Review*, July–December 1987: 3).

The broad climate of industrial stagnation and decline engendered by SAP has not lifted as the massive inflow of foreign investment that was expected to follow the introduction of the programme has not materialized. The foreign exchange domiciliary accounts have not sufficiently won the confidence of investors and Nigerian holders of foreign exchange. Consequently, the accounts remain very small, standing at a mere $68 million at the end of June 1987 (Bangura, 1987). Fresh capital inflows from foreign sources have remained very negligible. In fact if Nigeria's debt service obligations are taken together with other transfers of capital from the economy, it would be seen that for much of the period since 1986 the country has been a net exporter of capital. The economy has suffered a high level of capital flight through non-oil exports in particular as various groups engaged in the export of primary commodities have generally externalized their foreign exchange earnings rather than lodge these in local domiciliary accounts. In 1987, some 215 companies which, through their export activities, encouraged or exacerbated the flight of capital were barred from further participation in the domestic foreign exchange market, a move which has not done much to discourage the flight (MAN, *Half-Yearly Economic Review*, July–December 1987: 5). Not surprisingly, the country's balance of payments and foreign reserves continued, as in the immediate pre-SAP period, to be under considerable strain up to the end of 1990. It is, in part, because it is keen to mitigate the consequences of the absence of major fresh foreign investments in the economy and the flight of capital that the Babangida administration took to the policy of debt-equity conversion towards the end of 1988 (Olukoshi, 1990b).

If fresh foreign investment flows into the economy did not, as the government anticipated, accompany the introduction of SAP, investment expenditure by the various concerns already established in local manufacturing was also very minimal. Most new investment proposals by local businesses were negated by the combined effects of an unfavourable tariff structure, low sales arising from depressed domestic demand and the deregulation of interest rates. According to MAN, many manufacturing firms had to suspend on-going projects in the face of unclear market prospects and the high cost of capital (MAN, *Half-Yearly Economic Review*, July–December 1989: 6). Matters were not helped by the stalemate which developed over the settlement rates for all pre-SFEM transactions. The manufacturers and the bankers were unable to agree on how to share the burden of the consequences of the devaluation of the naira on uncompleted transactions conducted prior to the introduction of SFEM and for which naira lodgements had already been made by the manufacturers. Particularly hard hit by the stalemate were manufacturing capital projects initiated under deferred payments (i.e. external loans) arrangements. The only investment projects not abandoned by manufacturers were those that entailed equipment replacement or the adaptation of machinery to use local raw materials. The decision by the CBN in December 1987 to attempt to resolve the controversy on the settlement rate for pre-SFEM transactions did not significantly affect the low rate of investment by local manufacturers. In its Circular no. TED/AD/280/87 of 11 December 1987, the CBN ruled that the various pre-SFEM transactions covered by the SFEM transitional arrangements should be settled at the official exchange rate prevailing as at 26 September 1986. According to the CBN, 'where an importer paid the local currency equivalent in respect of the transaction before 26/9/86, he shall be responsible for the exchange loss arising up to that date while the government will be responsible for the exchange loss thereafter. The importer shall also be liable for the off-shore interest charges payable up to the date of lodgement of the naira equivalent of the transaction with his bank.' But 'where an importer paid the local currency equivalent to his bank in respect of the transaction after 26/9/86, he shall be responsible for the burden of exchange rate depreciation up to 26/9/86 as well as the naira equivalent of off-shore interest charges to the date of payment of local currency to his bank'. As can be imagined, the manufacturers affected by the CBN's ruling were not pleased with the settlement rate and they argued forcefully that it would further adversely affect industry (MAN, *Half-Yearly Economic Review*, July–December 1987: 6–7).

Despite the vast array of incentive measures that have been introduced since 1986, the production of manufactured commodities for export which the Babangida administration hoped would boost industrial activities in the country has not really taken off. The absence of any noticeable development in the export of manufactured goods can be attributed to several factors, all associated with the internal contradictions of SAP. First, the massive devaluation of the naira and its widely fluctuating value at the weekly, later fortnightly, and then daily foreign exchange bidding sessions were important disincentives for would-be investors in export production. Second, for reasons which we have already discussed, various aspects of SAP actually discouraged investment expenditure in the country by manufacturers. Third, the expectation of the government to attract foreign investors into the area of export production has also not materialized as foreign investment capital has not responded to the incentive measures put in place under SAP (Bangura, 1987).

The stagnation and general decline of industrial production in Nigeria was reinforced by the overall negative impact of SAP on small-scale industries. Proponents of SAP had argued that small-scale industries would benefit from the adjustment programme because of their reliance on domestic sources of raw materials. This optimism rested on the false assumption that all small-scale industries in Nigeria source their raw materials locally. The reality is, in fact, much more complex. As Bangura has pointed out, capitalism in Nigeria has generated different levels and degrees of development among small-scale industries. First there are those, mostly of the traditional type, which depend on local raw materials and whose operations have not been too adversely affected by SAP except for the higher cost of production which they are faced with and the fact that the liquidity squeeze may restrict their expansion. Examples of small-scale industries in this category include firms engaged in the production of local garments, basket weaving, leather works, rice husking, wood work, local farming, traditional soap and cosmetics production and the fabrication of traditional construction implements. This group of firms has benefited immensely from the shift, necessitated by SAP, by the urban poor and some members of the middle class towards the use of its products, which used to be the preserve of rural and semi-urban communities. The case of soap, to cite an example, is quite revealing. In the wake of SAP, various types of unrefined soaps have penetrated the urban market to fill the vacuum created by the massive increase in the price of 'modern' soaps and detergents manufactured by transnational companies (Bangura, 1987: 30–1).

Then there are the small-scale industries that use local inputs to engage in the production of commodities that are a direct outcome of the dynamics of modern capitalism in Nigeria. Many of the firms in this category are producers of snacks (like packaged cocoa-nut cakes, *chin chin*, plantain and popcorn), petroleum vaseline, sand paper, starch, modern shoes, handkerchiefs and polythene bags. Like the traditional small-scale industries, the only problems which they face under SAP centre around increased production costs and the effects of the liquidity squeeze. They enjoy a respectable domestic market for their products, however, and have made giant strides in creating new markets in urban centres throughout the country. Ever since the introduction of SAP in the middle of 1986, there has been a veritable explosion in the fast-food business as many small-scale firms have been set up to take advantage of a new and rapidly expanding market in the urban centres (Bangura, 1987: 30–1).

Finally, there are thousands of small-scale industries that have been integrated into the system of import dependence either because they act as suppliers of raw materials and spare parts to bigger companies or because they are engaged in the manufacture of finished goods whose production depends upon a steady supply of foreign exchange needed for acquiring necessary inputs from foreign markets. Examples of small-scale industries in this category include those that produce battery acid, glue, modern cosmetics, baby oil, pencils and crayons, socks, ink, exercise books, crown corks, candles, shoe polish, nails, wires, screws, aluminium utensils, PVC pipes, bolts and nuts, among other products. Because of their low capital base, they have been unable to compete effectively with the bigger companies in the acquisition of foreign exchange on the foreign exchange market. Their problem has been compounded by the fact that many cannot afford to raise loans at the high rates of interest that have prevailed in the Nigerian economy since 1987. The serious cash flow problem which many of these companies have faced has meant, among other things, that they have not been able to procure the raw materials and other inputs which they need to remain in production. Not surprisingly, many of these small-scale industries have had to fold up, especially as even those that managed to import inputs at very high naira costs have suffered a dwindling market as a result of the very high price tags carried by their products (Bangura, 1987: 30–1). According to MAN, many of the companies 'are faced with the grim reality of permanent closure with threats of receivership hanging over their neck' (MAN, *Half-Yearly Economic Review*, July–December 1987: 4).

The picture which we have painted so far is one in which the adjustment process in Nigeria's industries has had dramatic and, largely, negative consequences for manufacturing concerns in the country. To be sure, the restructuring and reorganization of the basis of industrial accumulation in the country, while adversely affecting the majority of manufacturers in Nigeria, has, at the same time, compelled an increasing number of firms to seek survival by exploring local sources of raw materials and investing in them in order to reduce their import dependence and integrate more directly with the agricultural sector of the economy. Among the manufacturing groups that have invested in and, in some cases, are already using local raw materials are those engaged in the production of beer, beverages, flour and flour products such as bread, as well as leather products, textile goods, and so on. Some of the firms engaged in the production of these commodities have, as part of their adjustment strategy, acquired and put under cultivation vast tracts of land for the production of cotton, sorghum and even wheat. Others have established direct contact with farmers who cultivate primary commodities such as cocoa, coffee and cotton to ensure regular supply of these inputs to their factories. And as for firms engaged in the production of chemical products, the commissioning in 1988 of a government-owned petrochemical plant producing linear akyl benzene, among other substances, has helped to meet some of their local raw material needs. Several firms have also invested in the modification of their existing plants in order to facilitate their switch to local raw materials. Notable among these firms are those engaged in beer brewing. A number of breweries have modified their equipment to enable them to switch from the use of imported barley to locally-produced malted sorghum.

However, both because the process of local sourcing of raw materials has been painfully slow and the level of fresh investment in industrial activities for which local raw materials are available in abundance has been virtually non-existent, the Nigerian industrial sector has, at best, been basically stagnant in its overall performance since the introduction of SAP. The rate of closure of firms has not been matched by the rate of formation of new ones. The loss of capacity arising from raw materials shortage has not been matched by significant expansion of production by firms for which inputs are available locally. The retrenchment of workers on a large scale has not been matched by significant fresh recruitments in new 'sunshine' industries which the advocates of SAP had hoped would spring up in the wake of the introduction of the programme. In other words, since 1986 when it was introduced, SAP has severely undermined the old structure of manufacturing in the country without appearing capable of replacing it with new, inward-looking production firms on a scale that will enable the manufacturing sector to retain its share of the Nigerian gross domestic product (GDP). It is in the light of this fact that scholars like Bangura have spoken of a process of de-industrialization in Nigeria under SAP (Bangura, 1987).

IV. Concluding Remarks

There is no doubt that SAP is the most far-reaching economic programme to be implemented in Nigeria in the post-colonial period. As we have argued, the response of industry to the programme has been very uneven. Whereas some firms, still a minority, have taken steps to adjust their production structure in line with the dictates of SAP, others, the majority, have either collapsed outright under the weight of the programme or have retained their old production structures but on a reduced level of capacity utilization. In the face of this reality, MAN has been campaigning for the adoption of policies that will enable the majority of industrial producers to enjoy a greater chance of survival. The government, in response, has generally taken the attitude that those firms that cannot break even under the new economic climate should be allowed to die. There is optimism in official circles that manufacturers that make adequate arrangements for self-reliance will survive and serve as the bedrock for a new, long-overdue, inward-looking industrial system in Nigeria. Quite often, government officials point to the resilience of the small number of agro-allied industries in the country which have displayed a greater ability to absorb the shocks of drastic adjustment as examples of firms that have a bright future under the Babangida administration's new industrialization policy. The crucial problem though is that there is no guarantee that a sufficient number of new industries will spring up to take the place of the old ones which the government is willing to allow to die. And this lack of guarantee lies at the heart of the contradictions of the industrial policy induced by the adjustment programme. On present evidence, it is clear that economic recovery in general, and industrial recovery in particular, if and when they come under the current SAP climate, will be very long-term indeed and are bound to be riddled with contradictions which defy the textbookishness of Nigeria's latter-day monetarists and their political and intellectual supporters in the counsels of the IMF, the World Bank and the donor/private credit agencies.

Notes

1. See Kay, 1975. For an attempt to apply Kay to the study of Nigerian capitalism, see Shenton, 1986. For a critical review of Shenton's book, see Olukoshi, 1986b: 116–18.
2. Olukoshi, 1987, Okongwu, 1987. Also Ohiorhenuan, 1987, and Kayode, 1987. The proceedings of the Nigerian Economic Society's 1988 Annual Conference put together under the title *Structural Adjustment and the Nigerian Economy* also contain useful analyses of the aims, objectives and instruments of SAP. As they relate to industry, see the papers presented in the Fourth Group Session.
3. Statement issued by the Presidential Committee set up to co-ordinate the 1985 national debate on the IMF loan as cited in Bangura, 1987: 11.
4. Bangura, 1987. Also see the various issues of the Manufacturers' Association of Nigeria (MAN) *Half-Yearly Economic Review* between 1986 and 1989.

References

Y. Bangura (1987), 'Structural Adjustment and De-industrialization in Nigeria' (mimeo).
—— et al. (1984), 'The Deepening Economic Crisis and its Political Implications', *Africa Development*, vol. IX, no. 3.
CBN (1983), *Annual Report and Statement of Accounts*. Lagos: CBN.
B. Ekuerhare (1985), 'Recent Pattern of Accumulation in the Nigerian Economy', *Nigerian Journal of Political Science*, vol. 4, nos 1 and 2.
Federal Ministry of Finance and Economic Development (1988), 'Assessment and Evaluation of the Structural Adjustment Programme'.
G. Kay (1975), *Development and Underdevelopment: A Marxist Critique*. London: New Left Books.
M.O. Kayode (1987), 'The Structural Adjustment Programme and the Industrial Sector', in Phillips and Ndekwu (1987).
P. Kilby (1969), *Industrialisation in an Open Economy: Nigeria 1945–1966*. Cambridge: Cambridge University Press.
P. Mogaha (1988), quoted in news report, *Business Times*, 15 December.
National Economic Council Expert Committee (1983), *Report on the State of the Economy*. Lagos: Government Printer.
National Institute for Policy and Strategic Studies (NIPSS) (n.d.), *Proceedings of the Workshop on the Economic Stabilisation Act of 1982*. Kuru, Nigeria.
J. Ohiorhenuan (1987), 'Recolonising Nigerian Industry: The First Year of the Structural Adjustment Programme', in Phillips and Ndekwu (1987).
C.S.P. Okongwu (1987), 'Review and Appraisal of the Structural Adjustment Programme', September.
A. Olukoshi (1987), 'The Politics of Structural Adjustment in Nigeria, 1982–1988' (research proposal).
—— (1984), 'The Origins, Dimensions and Consequences of the Nigerian Economic Crisis' (mimeo).
—— (1986a), 'The Multinational Corporation and Industrialisation in Northern Nigeria: A Case-Study of Kano c.1903–1985'. PhD thesis, University of Leeds, September.
—— (1986b), Review of Shenton (1986) in *Review of African Political Economy*, no. 37, December.
—— (ed.) (1990a), *The Nigerian External Debt Crisis: Its Management*. Lagos: Malthouse.
—— (1990b), 'Debt-Equity Conversion as an Instrument of Structural Adjustment in Nigeria: A Critique', in Olukoshi (1990a).
—— (n.d.). 'The Crisis in the Nigerian Economy', (mimeo).
—— and T. Abdulraheem (1985), 'Nigeria: Crisis Management Under the Buhari Administration', *Review of African Political Economy*, no. 34, December.

A. Phillips and E. Ndekwu (eds) (1987), *Structural Adjustment Programme in a Developing Economy: The Case of Nigeria*. Ibadan: NISER.

R. Shenton (1986), *The Development of Capitalism in Northern Nigeria*. London: James Currey.

O. Teriba and M.O. Kayode (eds) (1987), *Industrial Development in Nigeria*. Ibadan: Ibadan University Press.

O. Teriba et al. (1981), *The Structure of Manufacturing in Nigeria*. Ibadan: Ibadan University Press.

World Bank (1983), *Nigeria: Macro-Economic Policies for Structural Change*, Report no. 4506 – UNI, 15 August.

YUSUF BANGURA
& BJORN BECKMAN

5

African Workers
& Structural Adjustment:
A Nigerian Case-Study

I. The Case against the African Workers

Workers as an Obstacle to Structural Adjustment

In their attempts to pursue policies of 'structural adjustment', African governments meet resistance from African workers. The workers oppose wage freezes, privatization, public sector cuts and increases in the prices of essential commodities and services. The opposition is seen by governments as obstructionist and irresponsible. Workers are accused of failing to make their due share of the sacrifices necessary for national economic recovery. Their demands are seen as unreasonable and unrealistic.

Workers' opposition is treated as particularly illegitimate as it is viewed as coming from a small, privileged minority, pursuing narrow self-interests at the expense of the mass of the people, the poor and underprivileged peasants. Workers are accused of taking undue advantage of being better placed, more organized, more articulate. What right do they have to speak for the common people, the silent majority? African governments therefore feel justified in applying repressive policies against workers and their organizations. They draw support not only from neo-liberal theories but also from populist positions, including those concerned with 'labour aristocracy' and 'urban bias'. The limited rights of unionization and bargaining, where these obtain at all, are often suppressed to facilitate the passage of IMF- and World Bank-sponsored adjustment programmes.

The transnational institutions and the foreign aid agencies with which the African governments closely work show little concern for such anti-working-class repression. On the contrary, there seem to be more worries that African governments are not firm enough with such irresponsible opposition. By making unwarranted concessions to workers' agitation, weak governments jeopardize the reform programme. The state is too 'soft'. It is held to ransom by an articulate and well-organized minority.

How justified is this view of workers as irresponsible and obstructionist? This chapter draws primarily on the Nigerian experience of the 1980s but it seeks to broaden the argument. We begin by sketching a Nigerian scenario as a backdrop to a presentation of the case against the workers. We distinguish an 'economic' and a 'political' case, the latter with a focus on the role of trade unions. We highlight and discuss some of the theoretical perspectives by which such a case is informed. In the second part, we look more closely at the Nigerian experience. In the third and final part we ask whether

75

the case against the workers holds. Is there an alternative way of relating to workers' opposition? We conclude by arguing the need to address the political context of structural adjustment.

The Battle of the 'Oil Subsidy': A Nigerian Scenario

In Nigeria, in April 1988, an increase in the price of petrol precipitated a month of protest. What began as a peaceful students' demonstration in the city of Jos escalated into riots and a nation-wide strike by workers (*Analyst*, 3: 1, 1988; *Newswatch*, 2 May 1988; *West Africa*, 25 April and 2 May 1988). Why did a minor price increase cause such uproar and conflagration?

Central to the structural adjustment policies sponsored by the IMF and the World Bank, in Africa as elsewhere, is the demand that governments should remove 'subsidies' of prices of consumer goods. In most cases conflicts have concerned the prices of basic food items, as in the case of wheat in Egypt, maize in Zambia and rice in Sierra Leone. When such goods are imported the subsidy is most apparent. But domestically produced items are also said to be subsidized when they sell locally at prices fixed by the state below the world market price, if calculated on the basis of current exchange rates.

This has been the case with petrol in Nigeria. In the early 1980s, at a time when the naira was kept at par with the US dollar, a litre of petrol would sell at 20 kobo (= 20 cents). In 1986, as the economic crisis deepened, the government decided to almost double the price, removing what government then claimed to be 80 per cent of the 'subsidy'. In the context of a government proclaimed wage freeze and fast declining real incomes, the price increase hit people hard. But this was only the beginning. As the naira was allowed to drop drastically to a six-to-one relation with the dollar, the 'subsidy' 'grew' correspondingly. The government came under pressure from the IMF and the World Bank to 'adjust' the price upwards in tune with the declining value of the naira.

Workers objected. In November 1987, government-sponsored advertisements sought to prepare the way for a 'removal of the oil subsidy'. The Nigeria Labour Congress (NLC), the central trade union body, responded with a counter-campaign. It published hard-hitting anti-removal posters and organized protest rallies (*West Africa*, 28 December 1987). The state responded with repression. Leading union officials were detained and threatened with sedition charges. The Director of Public Prosecution declared that the position of the NLC was 'unreasonable in the extreme', designed to meet the 'selfish interests of a few leaders' and to cause general dissatisfaction with the government (*West Africa*, 28 December 1987).

The state backed down. The unionists were released and workers were jubilant when the January 1988 Budget did not include the expected increase in petrol prices (*West Africa*, 11 January 1988). But the truce was temporary. The standby agreement with the IMF expired at the end of 1987 and the Fund refused to endorse the performance of SAP. The World Bank withheld a US$500 million structural adjustment loan. Debt rescheduling and commercial credits were also held up (*West Africa*, 7 March and 25 April 1988). In February 1988, the government hit out again, taking advantage of the division between 'moderates' and 'radicals' within the unions. The NLC leaders were suspended and a Sole Administrator was appointed to 'bring about unity'. The suppression of the union leadership came in the wake of a national conference where the government was condemned for trying to cripple the organization so as to prepare the way for an increase in the petroleum price (*West Africa*, 7 March 1988; *Newswatch*, 14 March 1988; NLC, 1988).

While the government succeeded, for the time being, in silencing the union leaders, it failed to contain workers' opposition. Although the April 1988 price increase was marginal, it was believed to be the first step in a gradual removal of the 'oil subsidy'. In the absence of the official leadership, unionists formed local 'Action Committees' to sustain the strikes. Local leaders were arrested and workers threatened with summary dismissals and long prison sentences as 'saboteurs' under government emergency laws. According to a spokesman for the President the disturbances were caused by the 'urban élites', not the peaceful rural majority (*West Africa*, 2 May 1988).

Again, the government was obliged to back down, confronted with this unprecedented spate of popular unrest and strikes. It was forced to the negotiation table. Union leaders, worried about their capacity to sustain action and feeling that their point had been made, agreed to call off the strikes. Their opposition to the fuel price increase, however, was reiterated. Also the 'moderates' who had co-operated with the state in engineering the breakup of the NLC were obliged to join a unity platform rejecting the price increase (Ejiofoh, 1988). The stalemate persisted.

The 'Economic' Case: There are too many Workers and They are too Costly
How 'legitimate' is the opposition of African workers to structural adjustment? How 'irresponsible' and 'selfish' is it? Is it true that it primarily reflects the politicking of a disgruntled urban-based labour élite, representing neither the interests of rank and file workers, nor the silent majority of the rural areas? How far does such workers' opposition offer an alternative road out of the crisis? Or does it merely obstruct the efforts of the government?

Let us look closer at the case against the workers, beginning with the 'economic' side of the argument. It is an old debate but one greatly boosted by the economic crisis. The basic contention of the structural adjusters is that there are too many workers and they are too costly.[1] This is due to misconceived policies, including the development of an overprotected and therefore oversized industrial sector. Another problem is the growth of overstaffed state enterprises and public services with wage bills out of proportion to their carrying capacity and with deficits paid for by state subsidies. There is a combination of budgetary laxity and the influence of corrupt, nepotistic and/or clientelist modes of labour recruitment.

The inflation of overpaid wage employment is reinforced by the policy bias against the private sector. The public sector is more insulated from market pressures and can therefore resort to administrative and monopolistic methods to prop up employment and high wages. The result has been to inflate the demand for public sector employment. Overprotection, subsidies and monopolistic practices have led to wage levels which do not reflect the productivity of labour. African workers, it is argued, have been overpaid when compared with workers in 'comparable' Asian countries (World Bank, 1986: 21). Uneconomic public sector wages have been imposed on the private sector directly or indirectly by means of minimum wage legislation and the generalization of public wage awards. An excessive (artificial) demand for wage jobs has been further encouraged by policies that discriminate against non-wage employment. This takes two basic forms: one is the suppression of non-wage income, especially farmers' income, through taxation and price controls (marketing boards etc.); the other is the allocation of public resources in favour of the urban areas. The struggle for wage employment is therefore also a struggle to secure access to better education, health care, water supply, electricity, etc.

The 'Political' Case: Workers are Powerful and Selfish

The 'political' case focuses on the place of the workers in the structure of power relations in African society.[2] The policy bias in favour of excessive wage employment, inflated wages and a pro-urban, pro-worker allocation of public services and economic opportunities is, from this point of view, a result of the political entrenchment of an urban-based coalition in which workers play an important role. Despite their small numbers, they are seen as wielding excessive power in giving direction to government policies. In part, this is supposed to be due to their physical closeness to power, including an ability to destabilize and undo governments by taking to the streets. The senior partners of such political coalitions and their primary beneficiaries are politicians, senior bureaucrats, military officers and other members of the élite proper. But the workers also benefit and provide support for pro-élitist and pro-urban policies.

It is in the context of such economic distortions and urban policy bias that workers' opposition to structural adjustment is seen as illegitimate, selfish and unrepresentative of wider popular interests. Workers take undue advantage of their closeness to political power. They fail to take their due share of the sacrifices necessitated by the economic crisis. They look neither to the national interest, nor to the interests of the vast, mainly rural, mainly silent population whose mouthpiece they mistakenly claim to be. The interests of the workers, it is argued, are opposed to those of other popular classes, the peasants in particular. The workers participate in the exploitation of the latter, sharing responsibility for the neglect of agriculture, premature or stunted industrialization and a swollen, inefficient and predatory public sector. Workers use their strategic location to extort preferential treatment, subsidies, high wages and special access to commodities and services that are denied the rest of the (rural) population. They use their power to distort and obstruct national development.

African governments are either too weak to impose the programmes against the opposition of the workers or too permeated by élitist self-interests to be prepared to act resolutely in the interest of the nation and the suffering rural majority.

Problems with the Economic Case against the Workers

On the economic side, much of the case against the workers may seem to be validated by the sheer inability of employers, whether state or private, to pay wages and engage workers in productive activity. Factories close down or operate at a fraction of their installed capacity because of lack of foreign exchange to pay for basic inputs. School teachers and railway workers absent themselves *en masse* in search of alternative means of survival after months of non-payment of wages. Public institutions including hospitals are turned into empty shells without necessary equipment. Wages collapse, not just as a result of a conscious policy but because of the shortage of basic wage goods in the markets.

In much of Africa, strong forces are thus at work causing contraction in employment and a reduction in wages. Cutting costs, reducing budgetary deficits, withdrawing subsidies, shedding 'unviable' activities, trimming wage bills, laying off workers, are the imperatives everywhere. The case for cuts is often overwhelming, as in Nigeria, where, within the span of a few years, export earnings were reduced to one-quarter by the combined fall in the price and volume of petroleum sales.

Much of the public case against the workers is argued on such 'prima facie' grounds. How can workers and their friends fail to recognize the imperatives of the situation? The perceived strength of the economic case makes opposition to structural adjustment appear not just unrealistic but irresponsible, selfish and unpatriotic.

On closer inspection, however, the validity of the case against the workers is less than self-evident. It dissolves into a range of controversies. At one level it is a problem of facts and evidence, at another of policy and options. At a third level, the controversies concern the theoretical premises that underlie the selection and evaluation of both evidence and options.[3] What, for instance, are acceptable levels of protection for infant industries? How sensitive are particular industries to variations in production costs? What price 'distortions' are acceptable in the interest of the national economy? What 'subsidies' are 'distortions' and what is an acceptable way of financing public services? What is a 'correct' exchange rate?

Problems of theory and policy are compounded by difficulties at the level of methodology when constructing the data base for any such argument. How, for instance, can wage levels be compared? How relevant are conversions on the basis of official exchange rates? What do relative wages mean in terms of actual consumption baskets? How should such baskets be constructed in societies where both the structure of market-derived consumption and household organization differ so much? The problem is further exacerbated when turning to comparisons between urban and rural income, between wages and household production for own consumption. What is a meaningful comparison between the provision of public services in fragmented, only partially commercialized rural economies, on the one hand, and in cities, on the other?

Crucial to the case against the African worker are notions of low productivity, giving the impression that workers do not work hard enough and that wage demands therefore are unreasonable. How much of this must be attributed to organizational problems, for instance, in the access to inputs and maintenance that have little to do with labour performance? The policy implications differ. Is it a question of shedding labour or using it more efficiently? Moreover, the impact of high wage bills on the economy is also contested. To some, high wages lead to a contraction of overall employment either because labour saving methods are introduced or because entrepreneurs abstain from investing. To others, high wages fuel demand and contribute to the expansion of employment and income in other sectors, including the peasant food production.

The controversies are further complicated by the specific dislocations caused by crises and crises policies. What is the balance to be struck between abandoning and protecting existing assets? What are the relevant 'economic' criteria for assessing 'viability' in the volatile context of collapsing money markets? Pointing to the resource constraints and the need for drastic adjustment is merely stating the obvious. There is very little that is obvious, however, when it comes to the content of the adjustment programmes. The controversy over the allocation of the scarce resources is intense. It is not just a question of policy preferences but rather of deep divisions over facts and theory. Moreover, the issues must be addressed in the context of specific social formations and historical conjunctures.

Theoretical Aspects of the Political Case

At the core of the political case against the workers is the notion of irresponsible and unrepresentative trade unions. It draws on different political and theoretical perspectives. For some neo-liberals, trade unions are cases of entrenched 'special-interests' and 'social rigidities' that stand in the way of market forces and economic growth. Unions, according to Mancur Olson (1982), use their power to obtain wages for their members above competitive levels. In doing so, they cause economic stagnation, inflation and unemployment. Neo-liberals seek to use the economic crisis to roll back union power. Other liberal positions are less extreme. Unions may serve useful purposes, but they should not be too strong, otherwise they pose a threat to national economic policies and economic growth (Ubeku, 1983: 192–3).

In the African context, liberal objections to strong unions are reinforced by statist and developmentalist positions. While acknowledging the distinct contributions of radical unionism during the independence struggle, the imperative of national development in the post-independence period was that unions should be firmly subordinated to the state (Hashim, 1987; Damachi et al., 1979). The statist view covers a wide range of positions, including those of 'radicals' such as Nkrumah and Nyerere and 'conservatives' such as Senghor and Houphouet Boigny. Unions that refuse to toe the line have been repressed, whether in Sankara's Burkina Faso, Rawlings's Ghana or Babangida's Nigeria. There is a confluence of liberal, managerial and statist/developmentalist positions of both left and right coloration in opposition to strong and autonomous unions. Both liberals and statists draw additional support from populist and 'peasantist' positions that pit selfish, privileged and vociferous workers against silent, suffering peasants.

The radical, populist position has borrowed arguments from a Marxist tradition concerned with the problem of 'labour aristocracy' (Waterman, 1975, 1983). A section of the working class is seen as having been bought off and co-opted and thereby turned into an ally of the bourgeoisie. The transfer of surplus from the oppressed nations made this policy of co-optation possible in the advanced capitalist countries. On similar lines, it has been suggested that a section of the African working class has been co-opted as a labour aristocracy and that it is bought off with surpluses extracted from the peasants.

African trade unions, from this point of view, represent a small and relatively privileged section of the working people. They often draw their membership from a small number of establishments, mostly in the state and transnational sectors. The bulk of the workers in transport, construction, trade and commercial agriculture, for instance, are non-unionized. Moreover, the assumed lack of democracy within the unions has resulted in the entrenchment of labour élites, whose interests are similar to the parasitic, exploitative state bureaucracies into which they have been co-opted. The aristocracy argument is therefore applied either to the unionized working class as a whole or more specifically to the 'labour leaders'.

In the Marxist tradition, the working class and its organizations are credited with a leading political role in social transformation. The labour aristocracy argument aims at explaining why it does not always turn out that way. Another Marxist-type argument has similarly been used to reinforce the anti-unionist case. It focuses on the question of class formation and class consciousness. Working-class political leadership is expected to emerge out of a process of class consolidation, including an awareness of a common identity and common interests.

In the populist anti-union argument, such class cohesion and consciousness are assumed to be absent among African workers. From this perspective, the African working class is not 'real', either because so much of it is clerical (non-productive, non-industrial) and/or because it is structurally unsettled, migrant, with one foot in petty commodity production, and with a consciousness that is dominated by non-class identities of community, ethnicity and religion (cf. Lloyd, 1982).

The class argument has been incorporated in the populist, anti-union argument. It can be used in rejecting claims by the labour leaders to speak on behalf of a 'working class' when opposing the state and structural adjustment. It is also helpful in denouncing working-class claims to offer leadership to wider popular forces.

The political case against the workers, as the economic one, needs to be evaluated in the context of concrete historical experiences. Let us look closer at one such context. We shall begin by outlining the Nigerian crisis and how it has affected workers. We then look at the development of the working class and its organizations. We shall discuss worker strategies of fighting the crisis at the workplace and at the level of national policies. Finally, we shall conclude the empirical case by looking at the role of workers in wider alliances for surviving economic crisis and state repression.

II. Nigerian Workers and Structural Adjustment

Crisis and Adjustment Hit the Workers

Oil replaced agriculture as the backbone of the Nigerian economy in the 1970s. It accounted for more than 90 per cent of export earnings and 95 per cent of public expenditure by 1974. The large oil revenue of N65 billion that was received between 1973 and 1981 shielded the economy from the early phase of the world recession (World Bank, 1983a). State expenditure rose sharply from N8.3 billion in 1975 to N23.7 billion in 1980. Investment expenditure, estimated at about N70 billion in current prices over the period between 1973 and 1981, exceeded the value of oil revenues received. Import-substitution industries expanded and foreign exchange-based agricultural projects proliferated. The naira was allowed to appreciate in value.

The failure of industrial accumulation to generate its own autonomous sources of foreign exchange strained the external account. The importation of consumer goods rose from N440 million in 1974 to N3.9 billion in 1981; that of capital goods increased from N760 million in 1974 to N4.7 billion in 1979; and raw material imports jumped from N519.3 million in 1974 to N3 billion in 1981 (National Economic Council Export Committee, 1983). The dramatic increase in revenue which followed the oil price hikes of 1979 and 1980 facilitated the relaxation of import controls. Federal and state governments resorted to heavy borrowing from the international capital market as a result of improved creditworthiness and the availability of cheap credits from suppliers and bankers anxious to overcome the glut in demand for new investments in Western countries. Short-term trade credits accumulated rapidly. The cumulative external loans commitment, estimated at N18.5 billion at the end of 1983, was in sharp contrast to the total outstanding debt of US$2.35 billion in 1978. The public debt service ratio jumped from 8.9 per cent in 1982 to 17.4 per cent in 1983 (CBN, 1983).

The sudden drop in oil revenues from US$22.4 billion in 1980 to US$16.7 billion in 1981 and US$12.8 billion in 1982, following the decline in world oil prices, accentuated the structural problems of the economy. There was a serious fiscal crisis affecting both the federal and the state governments. The economy experienced a resource gap of about N3 billion in 1981 (6 per cent of GDP) compared to a resource surplus of N2.6 billion in 1980 (World Bank, 1983a: 4); the balance of payments was in persistent deficit; capacity utilization in industry dropped to below 40 per cent in 1983, leading to massive retrenchment; and the prices of basic commodities escalated.

The imbalances in the domestic and external accounts called for major structural reforms. The stabilization programmes of the Shagari (1979–83) and Buhari (1984–5) administrations emphasized state controls, even though both regimes agreed with the IMF and the World Bank on the need to eliminate distortions, prune the public sector and introduce 'realistic' domestic price systems. Buhari's regime encountered problems with the IMF over devaluation, the withdrawal of the subsidy on petroleum products and trade liberalization. Alternative strategies of counter-trade, raising debt servicing to 44 per cent and cultivating new sources of foreign finance proved unsuccessful. Foreign credit lines were blocked and external debt rescheduling stalled. This affected the supply of essential commodities and industrial inputs. Massive cuts in public expenditure led to retrenchment and cuts in social benefits in the public sector.

Difficulties in the negotiations with the IMF were accompanied by repressive policies at home. Several decrees were introduced curtailing civil liberties and workers' rights. Decrees 17 and 19, for instance, prevented workers from appealing against retrenchment and the automatic receipt of retrenchment benefits. Babangida's administration (1985–) re-opened the negotiations with the IMF. The regime substituted the World Bank for the IMF when the public rejected the IMF loan, but continued to work with the IMF to get its necessary support for the debt talks with the creditors. Most of the IMF's demands on structural reforms were accepted without the standard accompanying IMF loan. Currency overvaluations were to be removed through a second-tier foreign exchange market (SFEM); price distortions were to be eliminated through privatization, the rationalization of tariffs and the removal of subsidies; and general imbalances were to be corrected through a policy of tight money supply and the regulation of public expenditure.

Workers have been hit by the shift in policy. Further cuts in public expenditure have led to new rounds of retrenchment. Rates of retrenchment have tended to correspond with the declines in turnover. Several industries have slashed their work-force by more than 60 per cent between 1982 and 1988. The worst hit have been the construction, automobile, pharmaceutical and electrical equipment industries. Capacity utilization in the automobile firms, for instance, was only about 10 per cent in 1988. Most of the companies maintain a skeletal work-force.

Many social benefits have either been cut or suspended. Workers have had to pay high prices for drugs and declining health services; school fees have been reintroduced in most parts of the country; and levies of various kinds have been imposed by state governments to make up for the fiscal crisis. In Niger State, for instance, a compulsory levy of 5 per cent of gross monthly salary and wages was introduced for public sector workers in 1984. This was buttressed by a purchase tax of 5 per cent and an education levy of N20. Repressive methods have been used to enforce compliance. Wages and salaries were cut at the federal level in 1985 as part of contributions to an economic emergency fund; new employment and wage increases have been tightly controlled. The rate of inflation has increased sharply. Prices of food items such as gari, yams, beans, maize, plantains and rice rose from an average of about 150 per cent to 330 per cent between 1981 and 1987; those of sugar, milk and fish rose by more than 350 per cent. Real wages have indeed fallen sharply. Estimates by the Nigeria Labour Congress show that the minimum wage of N125 was worth only about 25 per cent of its value in 1987 (NLC, 1987).

The naira has deteriorated sharply from N1:US$1.83 in 1980 to N1:US$1 in January 1986, N3.3:US$1 in January 1987, to about N7.3:US$1 in February 1989. Many companies cannot cope with the current rate of exchange (MAN, 1987). Some industries, like the breweries and textiles, that can find local substitutes, are doing slightly better. Most industries have, however, experienced reduced turnovers and low capacity utilization. The Manufacturers' Association of Nigeria's half-yearly report puts the capacity utilization at 25 per cent in 1987, compared with 30 per cent in 1986. The rationalization of costs in industry have led to generalized retrenchment, more compulsory leaves and an increase in the work-load. Workers' living standards have fallen sharply. The withdrawal of petroleum subsidies has further worsened the situation. Workers are bound to react.

The Nigerian Working Class and its Organizations
The development of the Nigerian working class dates back to the colonial period when labour was required to establish and run the colonial infrastructure and to extract mineral resources for export. From just a few thousand in the colonial period, the

working class has grown in strength to several millions, covering a wide range of industrial activities and located in all the major towns of the federation. Industrialization has attracted a substantial number of workers into the manufacturing and service sectors. The commercialization of agriculture has also seen the rise of a small, but growing, working class in the rural areas. Small-scale industrial activities have flourished. The boom of the 1970s was significant in creating a large force of construction workers.

Workers have formed their own organizations to defend specific interests at the workplace and in the wider society. Apart from the early civil service union of 1912, trade union organization started in earnest in the 1930s, with the formation of the National Union of Teachers and the National Union of Railwaymen. The issues of material living conditions, the right of unions to participate in politics and to be independent, and the establishment of a central organization have dominated the history of the trade union movement since colonial times. The trade unions provided a platform for nationalists to challenge colonial rule. But labour unity has been affected by state interference and ideological differences that partly mirror the divisions among the international trade union organizations (Otobo, 1986). The state has consistently sided with the moderate factions to blunt the militant interventions of the unions in national affairs. No government has succeeded in either co-opting or completely subordinating the general movement, but trade unions have also not been able to float their own political parties. Attempts to do this in 1964, following the successful national strikes, ended in failure (Cohen, 1974).

The trade unions came to play a prominent role in national affairs in the 1970s, articulating a broad range of demands which affected several other social groups. Workers' protests were instrumental in bringing about the package of wage/salary increases and social benefits announced in the Adebo report of 1971. The shortcomings of the awards led to new rounds of agitations and culminated in the more comprehensive Udoji awards of 1974. Workers led the way in forcing the policy-makers to channel some of the new oil revenues to the lower sections of the society. They also supported the business groups and the professionals in agitating for the indigenization of the economy; and were among the social forces that protested Gowon's decision in 1974 to postpone, indefinitely, the return to civilian rule.

The limitations of workers' struggles in the early 1970s, in the face of intensified state repression, led to renewed attempts by leading labour activists to reconcile the differences among the four competing labour centres. This culminated in the formation of a central labour organization in 1975, with the radical Nigerian Trade Union Congress, dominating the leadership. But the state was anxious to impose its own version of labour unity on the workers. The petition of a faction, the United Labour Congress, against the new executive offered the new military government an excuse to intervene. The government dissolved the newly-formed Nigeria Labour Congress, arrested several unionists and appointed an administrator to look after the affairs of the unions, pending the outcome of a probe into union activities. The unions were later restructured from over a thousand bodies to forty-two, and given a new central labour organization, the Nigeria Labour Congress. A ban was placed on affiliations with foreign trade union organizations; a system for deducting worker's contributions from their wages to support the new trade unions was introduced; and a labour bureaucracy with remunerations similar to those of the civil service was created. The victory of the radical unionists in the elections of 1978, however, underscored the concern of the majority of workers to keep the trade union movement independent of state interference.

The new labour constitution, though state-imposed, gave the NLC considerable national significance. The trade unions now had a strong financial basis to employ the services of trained union officials to monitor industrial and national developments and improve upon their techniques of collective bargaining. Branches of the NLC were established in every state of the federation. Federal spread meant federal power and influence. It allowed for co-ordination of union affairs, linking up with non-workers' organizations and having access to a variety of data on a national scale. No other organization could rival the labour movement in this regard.

Workers' Strategies at the Workplace

Workers confront the effects of adjustment at the workplace. Their responses have been varied and complex, ranging from those that are planned, militant, collectivist and political to those that are spontaneous, conciliatory, individualistic and economistic. Variations reflect differences in levels of organization and consciousness, and the differential effects of adjustment on the public sector and on industry. We make a distinction between individual workers' strategies and union strategies. Non-unionized workers, especially those in the construction industry, have had a particularly raw deal. Options have been very limited; those who are lucky tend to fall back on the informal sector.

Some unionized workers have pressed for the payment of their gratuity to enable them to go into petty trading, farming or small-scale transport services. Such entrepreneurial responses have been prominent among workers in the older industries such as textiles and the railways. Those with technical skills either establish repair shops or join already existing ones. Some of the workers dismissed in the aftermath of the demonstration in the automobile industry, Steyr-Nigeria, in 1985, for instance, were able to set up a small-scale enterprise to service the vehicles of the company in downtown Bauchi. It is not uncommon to find workers combining farming with full-time waged employment. In places where salaries have not been paid, especially in the public sector, workers pay less attention to their jobs, report for work late or attend to private matters during office hours. Authorities find it difficult to enforce the rules.

Unions are concerned about minimizing the impact of rationalization on the workers, defending activists and the union against harassment and repression, and reconciling conflicting workers' interests in the various departments of the workplace. Individual workers' initiatives strengthen as well as weaken unionist strategies. In Kaduna Textiles Limited, workers opted for resignation in 1983 and 1984 in order to collect their gratuity and look for alternative means of livelihood. Such a strategy was prompted by the company's deep financial problems and the fears expressed that workers' benefits might be frozen in the event of its collapse. Several anti-workers' strategies had been pursued by the management to keep the company afloat. These varied from the frequent resort to compulsory leaves, to pay-cuts, the suspension of a wide range of social benefits, and periodic retrenchment. The national union of textile workers leaned on the option of the workers to quit the company and collect their gratuity as a strategy to force the employers to halt retrenchment and accommodate some of the demands of the workers. The company's inability to pay off the workers in one fell swoop led to a stalemate (Andrae and Beckman, 1989; Bangura, 1987c).

But individualist responses also undermine collective union initiatives and militancy. Public sector workers in Ondo State were unable to take firm decisions on whether to embark on an industrial strike to protest the non-payment of salaries for more than four months during the early stages of the crisis in 1984 and 1985. Large sections of the work-force had looked for alternative ways of survival, mainly farming, and paid less attention to their formal jobs. Unionists in the state believed that it would have been difficult to mobilize workers for a strike at that stage (Bangura, 1987a).

Unions have relied on three broad strategies to influence the adjustment programme at the workplace. The first is to operate within the logic of the programme, and to accuse the employers of being responsible for the problem. Managers and top bureaucrats are exposed as corrupt, inefficient and undisciplined. When such arguments are made workers see themselves as the embodiment of the national interest and the custodians of the factory systems on which their livelihood depends. The objective is to undermine the legitimacy of the employers and to win broad popular support for their more specific fights. Such a strategy also allows the unions to argue for the sharing of the burdens of adjustment. Even when employers do not moderate or reverse the contentious policies, the exposure of top officials as financially wasteful strengthens the morale of the rank and file workers and helps to prepare them for militant action.

The union at the Glaxo pharmaceutical company in Lagos relied on the strategy of discrediting the management credentials of the official in charge of the raw material sector of the company to mobilize the workers against the industrial rationalization programme in 1986/7. The company had resorted to large-scale retrenchment, the withholding of end of year bonuses and delays in the payment of salaries to contain the crisis. Workers contested these measures and called for prudent ways of handling the resources of the company. They demanded the resignation of the farm manager whose alleged mismanagement of the farm's resources exacerbated the raw material crisis. A bitter struggle ensued. Workers were locked out of the factory for a few weeks and stringent conditions were laid down for re-engagement. But the union remained adamant and continued to insist on the farm manager's resignation. Large numbers of workers were subsequently laid off. Industrial relations have remained tense and workers have little confidence in the crisis management policies of the company (Aremu, 1987).

A second strategy of the unions is to fight for the institutionalization of collective bargaining. This is intended to hold employers accountable for their policies, open up channels of communications and advance alternative policies. The contract of employment, often exploited by the employers to lay off workers and curtail other benefits, usually comes up for attack. The union in Steyr-Nigeria used the disadvantages in the 'Workers' Handbook', on issues pertaining to termination, as the basis for challenging the rationalization programme in 1985.

Collective bargaining allows unions to wrest concessions from the employers. Workers struggle over the yearly bonus; some compensation for the time spent on compulsory leave; the sharing of the burdens of rationalization; spacing out retrenchment if it is inevitable; ensuring that non-discriminatory procedures are followed when staff are being laid off; and insisting on retrenchment benefits to be paid on time. Despite the wage freeze and the suspension of collective bargaining between 1982 and 1987, several unions succeeded in getting employers to pay end of year bonuses, to offset some of the losses generated by the wage freeze (Andrae and Beckman, 1989). Manufacturers were worried about the effect of the liquidity squeeze on sales.

A third strategy of the unions is to use strikes and demonstrations to obstruct production. Such actions are embarked upon when management refuses to negotiate with the unions; or when employers insist in forging ahead with the contentious policies, following a breakdown in negotiations; or when management refuses to honour its own part of agreements that have already been reached by both sides. Workers react militantly when they are side-tracked or ignored. Unionists come under considerable pressures from the work-force to engage in militant actions.

In Steyr-Nigeria, it was the arrogance of the managing director (MD) and his refusal to discuss the plight of the company with union officials that provoked the workers to a militant demonstration in 1985. Apart from the problems of contending with the periodic closures of the company following the drop in the supply of completely knocked down (CKD) parts, workers were enraged to find out in one of the regional newspapers that the managing director had given an interview to the press hinting on a possible closure of the company. Attempts by the unionists to book an appointment with the MD to discuss the issue were rebuffed. A work-to-rule was declared by the union while further attempts were made to see the managers. But no one was ready to talk to them. The workers lost their patience and decided to force-march the managing director from his office to the factory gates. A crisis ensued as management dismissed the entire work-force and laid fresh requirements for re-engagement. The workers successfully resisted the conditions even though they failed to get their union leaders reinstated (Bangura, 1987b). Struggles continued to be waged in the courts and in the community to reverse the policy and compensate the sacked unionists.

The unions in Niger State were faced with a similar problem in 1984/5. They declared an industrial strike following the breakdown of negotiations with the state government and the latter's decision to press ahead with the contentious public sector cuts and levies. The military government had retrenched more than 5,000 workers in the public sector, imposed a variety of levies and suspended several allowances. Previous negotiations between the government and the unions had ended in deadlock. But in January 1985 the unions succeeded in getting the government to agree to restore the allowances after six months. The governor, however, announced in June 1985 that the allowances would not be restored. Workers, he said, would spend the money to 'drink and marry more wives'. The unionists felt insulted and aggrieved. Fresh rounds of negotiations produced no results. Workers were mobilized for an industrial strike. But the government used a section of the unions to break the strike and threatened to terminate the services of workers that refused to report for work on the day of the strike. Although the strike collapsed, it dented the image of the government and strained industrial relations in the state (Bangura, 1987a).

The experience of workers in Niger State contrasted sharply with those of workers in Ondo, Benue and Cross River states where workers were able to wage successful strikes against their respective state governments. Negotiations between management and the unions in Ondo State, for instance, were protracted. The state government was owing the workers about four months of salaries and reneged on every timetable set for their payment. Workers were much easier to mobilize and the government was on weak moral and political grounds if it intended to wield the big stick (Bangura, 1989a). The government had to raise money from federal sources and the banks to pay the salary arrears.

The Nigeria Labour Congress and the Reform Programme
Workers' strategies at the workplace are reinforced by those of the NLC at the national level. The NLC monitors the industrial relations scene, identifies with the strategies of the industrial unions and defends aggrieved unionists and workers. The Bauchi State NLC was instrumental in sustaining the opposition of the work-force to the harsh conditions laid down by the management of Steyr for readmitting the workers into the factory. The NLC acted on behalf of the national industrial union and collaborated with the in-plant union executive to negotiate the terms of re-entry (Bangura, 1987b).

The co-ordinating roles of the NLC have been more seriously felt at the state levels where public sector unions need the support of the private sector workers to strengthen their strategies. The fact that all unions in a state are represented in the state council executive of the NLC facilitates the harmonization of policies. In Niger State, for instance, private sector unions contributed to the discussions leading to the industrial relations crisis of 1985 (Bangura, 1987a). The platform of the NLC was also used by the public sector workers in Ondo State to get the support of the private sector workers in the successful strike of August 1986.

But it is at the wider national level that the impact of the NLC has been decisive. The Congress has intervened in the debate on the IMF loan, the question of oil subsidy and other vital aspects of the reform programme. It is not surprising that Nigerian governments have used different methods in trying to neutralize the power of the NLC to obstruct the stabilization programme. Shagari's government, acting through the moderate unionists, attempted to amend the trade union act of 1978 to allow for the establishment of more than one central labour organization. Buhari's approach was to keep the NLC at arm's length and rely on the repressive instrument of the state to quell any protests. Babangida initially attempted to co-opt the leadership of the unions into a tripartite committee, but finally suspended the NLC when co-optation failed to tone down the militancy of the leadership.

Retrenchment, the defence of incomes and struggles against certain aspects of price adjustments have generally occupied the attention of the NLC. The capacity of the NLC to redress these basic issues is constrained by the objective decline of the national resource base and the inability to check the downward adjustment of the exchange rate. This general weakness is more telling in the area of retrenchment. But the NLC is not completely powerless. Several aspects of the reform programme are still contestable and are being contested. The strategy of the NLC is to defend nominal gains in incomes and prices within a framework of mobilizing workers and other groups to discredit the general direction of the reforms. The strategy is premised on the fact that the government relies on a combination of market and administrative instruments to depress workers' living standards. Even though workers' incomes have already been eroded by the devaluation of the naira and inflation, the government attempted to repeal the minimum wage, imposed cuts on wages and salaries and outlawed collective bargaining in the early phase of the crisis. By waging militant struggles on these issues, the NLC seeks to expose the insensitivity of the adjustment programme to the basic survival needs of workers.

Central to the logic of the programme is the depression of wages to control inflation, attract foreign capital and facilitate the competitiveness of local industries in the export market. The government introduced wage/salary cuts in October 1985, at the peak of the debate to decide Nigeria's relations with the IMF, and announced a state of economic emergency which was to last for fifteen months. A general pay-cut for both the military and civilian employees was introduced, ranging from 2 per cent to 20 per cent. The NLC opposed the cuts. Its leaders contended that the government was implementing the contentious IMF conditions before the conclusion of the debate; that workers were not consulted before the cuts were announced; and that, unlike the business groups which appropriate profit and rent, workers have no alternative sources of income. The NLC gave an ultimatum to embark on a strike if the government pressed ahead with the deductions.

With barely two months in office, many groups were still prepared to give the government the benefit of the doubt. Journalists were still grateful to the regime for abrogating 'Decree Four' which had limited press freedom under Buhari. There was a virulent press campaign against the NLC's position. A compromise solution had to be worked out which would allow the NLC to call off the ultimatum and enter into negotiations with the government. Negotiations led to the formation of a tripartite committee, comprising of representatives of the state, labour and the business sector. The NLC later put forward a plan which recommended additional taxes on dividends, profit and rents, and it demanded that the pay-cuts should be converted into savings. Government's representatives on the committee were concerned about how to extend the cuts to other sectors. They held on to the terms of reference which stated that there would be no trade-offs and that the pay-cuts would not be rescinded (interview with A. Oshiomhole, 7 February 1986).

The failure of the NLC representatives to wrest concessions from the committee led to renewed calls among sections of the unions for an industrial action. A massive campaign to convert the pay-cuts into savings was mounted by the NLC. The announcement of the Structural Adjustment Programme (SAP) in 1986, which drastically devalued the naira and withdrew 80 per cent of subsidies from petroleum products, strengthened the NLC's case. The government announced in the 1987 budget the refund of the salary/wage cuts to lower categories of employees.

But the government was determined to keep wages down. The national minimum wage act was amended in December 1986. The amendment exempted persons or companies employing less than 500 workers and companies in agriculture from paying the minimum wage. The NLC launched a mobilization campaign against the amendment and declared a state of emergency within the labour movement. Rallies were held in several major cities denouncing the amendment and preparing the workers to resist the policy. The government was worried about the depth of the mobilization and the enthusiasm with which the rank and file workers responded to the campaign. The amendment order was revoked in April 1987 (Bangura, 1989a).

As the liberalization measures further eroded workers' incomes, the NLC intensified its struggle for the lifting of the ban on collective bargaining. A wage freeze had been imposed since 1982. The NLC called on the government to allow wages to find their 'market' value. They argued that a policy of wage freeze was inconsistent with liberalization (NLC, 1987). Manufacturers were also dissatisfied with the government's deflationary policies. A poll conducted by the Manufacturers' Association of Nigeria revealed that 31 companies alone had about N70 million of unsold stocks in their warehouses in the first half of 1987 (MAN, 1987). Manufacturers were, therefore, not opposed to an upward review of wages and a relaxation of the liquidity squeeze. But new conditions were imposed on collective bargaining. By insisting, for instance, that unions should not resort to the threat or use of strikes and other forms of pressures the government attempted to blunt the effectiveness of collective bargaining and limit the upward adjustment of wages. How would recalcitrant employers be called to order? Negotiations turned out to be messy. The unrealistic conditions were ignored. Many unions had to embark on strike before some agreements could be reached.

The Politics of Alliances

The reform measures have challenged some of the vested interests associated with the expansion of the post-colonial state and eroded general living standards. Those that stand to benefit from the reforms, such as the transnationals, exporters and sections of the agriculture lobby, have tried to build the necessary political alliances to defend the programme. Ruling class groups that thrive on profits derived from bureaucratic influence and state protection are also organizing to moderate the full impact of the reforms. Subordinate groups are demanding alternative solutions, building popular fronts and contesting some aspects of the programme. The state is constructing its own political and social base to push through the hard-hitting economic measures.

The working-class movement has unavoidably been drawn into the dynamics of alliance politics. Workers provide leadership for a broad range of social groups that have been hit by the reforms. Workers are drawn into these alliances because of the experiences they share with other groups on general questions of falling living standards, the assault on the existence and autonomy of unions, the harassment of activists and the need to relate union alternatives to the specific demands of groups in other sectors of the economy. The struggles of academics and students for a just and democratic educational system, those of doctors for an improved health care system and of journalists and lawyers for a free press and civil liberties have implications for workers' ability to challenge the reforms at the workplace and at the level of the state. Workers play leading roles in the popular struggles because of their centrality in the production process; their long history of democratic struggles; and the national networks that unions have established since 1978.

Current attempts at constructing alliances have focused primarily on urban employees of workers, journalists, academics, doctors, lawyers, traders and students, but the package of demands accommodate some of the interests of peasants and artisans. The urban popular opposition to the withdrawal of petroleum subsidy drew attention to the problems farmers would face in transporting their wares to the market. Concern was also expressed during the debate on the IMF loan about the effects of devaluation on farm inputs.

The formation of alliances has been mainly an informal process. The only exception has been the alliance between academics and workers, resulting in the affiliation of the Academic Staff Union of Universities (ASUU) to the NLC in 1984. Groups are pulled together through solidarity rather than on the basis of common structures. The strongest alliance to date is that between the NLC, ASUU and NANS, the students' body. The NANS received the support of the ASUU and the NLC in 1986 during the general students' uprising that followed the police brutalization of students in one of the universities. The three organizations boycotted the panel established by the government to investigate the crisis on the grounds that the principal characters, the police chief who ordered the use of fire-arms and the vice-chancellor who precipitated the crisis, had not been suspended from office. The groups insisted that this was a minimum requirement for the panel to function without key witnesses being compromised and crucial evidence suppressed. The composition of the panel was also challenged on democratic grounds. The NLC even planned a nation-wide demonstration to underline its concern for civil liberties and democratic rights. But the state descended heavily on the leadership, took over the secretariat of the NLC, disaffiliated the ASUU from the NLC and suspended students' unionism on the campuses. Joint struggles continue to be waged to redress the abridged rights and protect the existence and autonomy of the unions.

The workers provide the backbone to popular struggles. Even when they had not initiated popular protests, workers' interventions had often changed their character. Students and the urban unemployed, for instance, acted as a catalyst to the nation-wide protests that greeted the withdrawal of oil subsidies in April 1988. But it was the workers' intervention that forced the government to enter into negotiations with the protesters. Workers' representatives negotiated on behalf of the groups that participated in the demonstrations. The April protests underscored the power of the workers to mobilize large sections of the population against the reform programme.

III. The Case against the Workers Reconsidered

The Legitimacy of Workers' Opposition

The crisis hits the workers hard. Unlike independent producers and traders, who constitute the bulk of Africa's population, workers have little direct access to commodities with which to bargain for survival. The anti-worker logic of structural adjustment is formidable. African economies are reconstructed on the ruins of the wage sector. Whatever 'privileges' workers may have had have been swept away. How legitimate is their self-defence? How futile? Must structural adjustment mean the destruction of the African working class?

In conclusion we outline elements of an alternative case that takes its point of departure from the aspirations of the workers and the leadership they may offer for more broadly based strategies of national reconstruction. It is a critique of the repressive political programme that informs the crisis policies of most African governments. The capacity of the state to undertake social and economic reforms, we argue, depends on its ability to come to terms with the forces in the field. Attempts by governments to override, side-track or ignore workers' opposition, as illustrated in the Nigerian case, are therefore self-defeating. The stalemate is merely cemented. Moreover, governments and their backers underestimate the capacity of workers' organizations to offer both leadership and backbone to wider alliances of popular social forces. It is because of their ability in this respect, not because they defend the interests of an entrenched and privileged minority, that workers are in a position to 'obstruct' structural adjustment.

Workers are no doubt 'self-seeking', but in defending their interests as wage-earners they are obliged, as demonstrated by the Nigerian experience, to enter into wider alliances in order to fend off attempts by the state to isolate, control and repress them. It is true that the African working class is small and that its numbers have further dwindled as a result of the crisis. Politically, however, the workers are important as the popular stratum with the most advanced organizational experience. While the Nigerian working class for obvious reasons is bigger than others, experiences elsewhere, for instance in Burkina Faso, suggest that working-class political capacity is not just a matter of the size of the wage economy.

While in pursuit of their own interests, working-class organizations articulate wider popular grievances, urban and rural. This was clearly demonstrated by the popular support that rallied behind the Nigerian workers in their fight against the removal of the oil subsidy. Their defence of wage income forms part of complex household strategies, reaching deep into the peasant economy. Similarly, efforts to protect basic unionist rights brings workers, as we have seen, into wider coalitions of social forces, including the organizations of students, teachers, lawyers, journalists and other professionals with a common interest in organizational survival and autonomy in the face of state impositions. It is as part of such broader alliances that workers offer an alternative to the politically repressive, transnational restructuring project that currently dominates the African scene.

Governments apply different tactics; outright repression is only one example. The Nigerian experience also points to efforts to co-opt and to marginalize. In many cases workers take 'unreasonable' positions simply because the state refuses to reason with them. 'Obstruction' is also a strategy of forcing governments and employers to the negotiating table. But the conflict of interest is profound and finding 'solutions' is therefore not just a question of reasoning but also of recognizing the strength of the opposite side and the constraints set by the balance of forces.

The failure of the state to recognize the limits of its own power is a major reason for the stalemate that characterizes so much 'crisis management' in Africa (and elsewhere!). Foreign intervention tends to reinforce this stalemate, by propping up and shielding regimes from popular political pressures. While succeeding temporarily in shifting the balance of forces in favour of ruling coalitions, such interventions simultaneously undermine the process of accommodation that is necessary to break the stalemate.

Is There a Working-Class Alternative?
Workers are under no obligation to offer an 'alternative' structural adjustment programme. They are within their rights in defending what they see as their interests, until they are convinced that what.they are offered is the best they can get under difficult circumstances. They have as much interest as any other class in the speedy recovery and rapid development of the economy. But they are as concerned as all others that the road to such recovery should not be through the destruction of their own means of existence. It is the obligation of the state and its transnational partners to convince workers that their interests have been fully considered, otherwise the state, not the workers, stands to blame for any stalemate arising from the workers wielding whatever powers they can muster in self-defence. The state, not the workers, has the resources to explore the alternatives. It has the ministries, the central banks, the statistics, the professionals, the foreign advisers, the money, the arms. For workers to dig their heels in is neither selfish nor irresponsible. They are asserting their bargaining power, in the face of the overwhelming intellectual and repressive resources of the state. 'Obstruction' signals two things: 'We are not convinced' and 'We are not defeated'.

Attempts to challenge the legitimacy of popular resistance to structural adjustment, with reference to the 'failure to offer an alternative' must be exposed for what it is: an attempt to enforce submission by way of psychological warfare. This goes also for the accusation of selfishness and irresponsibility. This being said, however, the Nigerian experience suggests that workers have not been insensitive to the need to offer alternatives to government crisis policies, not least as part of an attempt to create alliances.

An alternative crisis programme, 'Towards National Recovery', was prepared by the NLC in 1985. It is an expansionist programme. Employment should be protected and expanded in order to avoid wasting human resources and to stimulate demand and overall growth. Finance should come from cutting costs of inflated contracts, reducing defence spending and corruption, taxing the rich and preventing tax evasion. Industrial investment should be accelerated, especially in the capital goods sector. Foreign exchange resources should be allocated in such a way as to make sure that existing industrial capacity is efficiently utilized. Raw materials and other industrial inputs should be given priority over luxury consumption. Foreign investors should have to wait to remit profits until the industrial recovery is well underway. Retrenched workers should be reabsorbed and the wage freeze lifted. A ceiling of 20 per cent of export earnings should be placed on foreign debt payments. The state, rather than privatizing, should take a lead in the expansion of productive activity. In agriculture, major state development schemes should be abandoned in favour of a focus on small peasant farmers and co-operatives.

Was this a realistic alternative to official structural adjustment? Realism in this context is of course as much a question of politics as of economics. We may argue that the NLC at this point was in no position to challenge politically the alliance of class forces, local and transnational, that saw it as its primary task to 're-establish the international credit worthiness of Nigeria' (Buhari, 1984), and to whom most of the NLC positions were objectionable. One may also question the economic realism of some of the pro-posals. In terms of its long-term strategic orientation, however, the NLC programme could not be dismissed lightly, either on political or economic grounds, representing views with strong support not only from labour leaders, but also from a wide range of intellectuals, professionals and technocrats, while simultaneously expressing the aspirations of wage-earners, unemployed, school-leavers and, very likely, a good number of their peasant parents and relatives as well.

We are not at this point entering into any substantive discussion of such alternative, working-class-based crisis programmes in Africa. We are merely stressing the fact that they exist, that they represent significant social forces and that they therefore need to be taken seriously.

Who Speaks for Whom?

But what about labour leaders exploiting, deceiving and misrepresenting workers? What about workers exploiting peasants? What about 'labour aristocracies' and 'urban bias'? Has not a case been made for rejecting such alternatives as selfish and irresponsi-ble? Are not the allies of the workers mentioned above the very urbanites and élites that benefit from the continued distortions of African economies, at the expense of the poor peasants?

Let us first affirm that such distortions and contradictions exist. Many labour leaders are privileged and élitist and hold offices with a dubious democratic mandate. There are also real conflicts of interest between peasants and workers over prices and over the allocation of public resources. Workers cannot in this respect be expected to speak for peasants and vice versa.

Peasants in Africa have suffered a raw deal. They are oppressed and their interests are neglected. But the same applies to the workers. The overwhelming numbers of Africa's workers eke out a miserable existence in unhealthy and impoverished urban environments. Most are unable to survive on the basis of their wages, many are unemployed and insecure. Only a few have been able to enjoy a sustained increase in real earnings. Only a few succeed in climbing into the middle classes or into business, as do some peasants.

Notions of workers exploiting peasants and towns exploiting rural areas funda-mentally obscure the differences in social existence within the two poles. They mis-represent the modes of exploitation and accumulation that have characterized the post-colonial economies. Workers and peasants are no fools. They can easily identify the beneficiaries of post-colonial development. The monuments of wealth and property belonging to the rich and their foreign friends are there for everybody to see.

Some labour leaders may have profited excessively from their union jobs. But little can be gauged from their personal affluence when seeking to assess their ability to voice the case of the workers. As workers' leaders they are subject to contradictory forces, including co-optation by state and management. But the pressures also come from below, and in contemporary Africa they are stronger than ever. In Nigeria, labour leaders operate in a competitive context that widens the scope for such popular pressures.

The African working class may not conform to ideal-type notions of a 'proper', indus-trial working class. Its mode of integration into a wider petty commodity economy, however, rather than detracting from, may actually enhance its ability to voice wider popular grievances and interests. A long history of trade union struggles have simul-taneously generated collective experience and identity at the level of class organization.

Nigerian labour leaders have offered a working-class programme for national recovery. Have they a right to speak for the nation? Who has? The politicians who ruined it? The generals who usurped power? When the Generals-Presidents of today reject the rights of labour leaders to speak for the 'peaceful rural majority' we are reminded of the pronouncements of the colonial Governor-Generals of yesterday. In the 1920s, Governor Clifford ridiculed the educated nationalist 'gentlemen' who claimed to represent Nigerian interests: who were they, he said, to dare to speak on behalf of the mass of the Nigerian peasant farmers? – Who was he?! Who did he represent?

As we think is evidenced in the Nigerian case, African workers may well have a stronger case than most other actors on the political scene to claim to represent broad popular interests.

Workers, State and Democracy
Global and local ruling classes have plunged post-colonial Africa into a national crisis on an unprecedented scale. Embryonic transnational state institutions dabble in experiments of 'crisis management' and 'liberalization' with little knowledge of how they will work out in poorly understood economic, social and political environments. Some interventions may be economically sound and reasonable. Others play havoc with meagre resources and cause further destabilization, as in the case of the current disastrous auctioning of foreign exchange in Nigeria. It should come as no surprise that African people have little confidence in such crisis management or in the class agents that promote it.

Workers' opposition to structural adjustment deserves to be taken seriously. To the extent that African states do so, they choose to respond with repression. This has become the political programme of 'liberal' structural adjustment (Ibrahim, 1986; Mustapha, 1988). We have argued that this is counterproductive even within the narrow parameters of the economic programme as it stands. The forces in the field have to be recognized. Even if they are too weak to enforce their own programme, they may be strong enough to obstruct that of the state.

We conclude by arguing an alternative political programme that rejects state repression and manipulation. The case may first be argued in terms of the process of state formation. It is often suggested that the state in Africa is repressive because it is too 'weak' to handle opposition more gently. Peter Lloyd (1982: 22) warns that governments are fragile and 'strikes and mob violence may well lead directly to their collapse – a consequence perhaps unintended by the poor'. The implied warning is: do not rock the boat or you are yourselves to blame. The repression or co-optation of trade unions has been explained with reference to the fragility of the state. The state can hardly afford opposition from such a quarter, especially as the unions have proven themselves to be powerful political vehicles in the past (Hashim, 1987: 2).

Let us invert this argument. Precisely because of its weakness the state should develop more advanced forms for relating to alternative sources of power in society. In our own understanding of historical experiences elsewhere, the pressures on the state from below by popular forces is critical to the process of state formation, including the development of the capacity to manage social contradictions. The state is formed and disciplined from below (Beckman, 1988a, 1988b). The challenge of structural adjustment at present is not just to try out more new, bright formulae for foreign exchange allocation, once the first set of experiments have failed; there is the need to address, politically, the social contradictions that have been aggravated by the economic crisis and exacerbated by politically repressive crisis management. Simply promoting one policy or the other will not take anybody anywhere if the political context is not simultaneously addressed. State crisis management confronts a formidable credibility gap. If that gap is to be bridged at all, governments must learn to listen and argue more and to repress less.

What about co-optation? Is it not an 'alternative' to repression as a strategy for political crisis management? It is. African governments have tried it. The Nigerian government, as we have shown, has turned from one to the other, trying out various blends. On the whole, it seems, at least for the time being, that co-optation has failed. But contradictions have not been resolved. The stalemate is as precarious and potentially explosive as ever.

The state has not succeeded in effectively co-opting Nigerian labour leaders. But even if it had, it is likely to have been counterproductive. Co-optation weakens the capacity of the labour leaders to offer leadership. It drains it of whatever popular credibility it can claim and renders it useless for the purpose of any genuine political crisis management. From this perspective, it could be argued that the preservation of union autonomy may even be in the interest of the state. There are signs that at least some members of the Nigerian ruling class have come to appreciate this, even if the repressive reflexes still dominate.

Is there a democratic option to the prevailing repressive political programme of structural adjustment? In Nigeria, the present military rulers claim that they are busy steering the ship of state towards civilian rule and democracy in 1992. They claim that structural adjustment and the return to civilian rule are two faces of the same transition programme. Both faces have ugly repressive and manipulative traits. Nigerian workers have unsuccessfully sought to impress themselves on that process of political transition by, for instance, defending their right to form a workers' party, in the face of the state's commitment to impose a two-party system of its own liking.

Whatever hopes and doubts that may be pinned on 1992, the democratic challenge does not lie in the future. It is here and now. As long as labour leaders are whisked off into detention, unions proscribed and demonstrating workers brutalized, in the name of structural adjustment and with the backing of a formidable array of repressive labour laws, the democratic agenda of the workers is clear (Bangura, 1989b). Workers are fighting for the right to have their own organizations, to express their views and to be protected against state brutalization. Workers' opposition to the crisis policies of the African states and their foreign backers is part of the struggle for such democratic rights.

It is important that we see this direct link between workers' economic and political demands. We began by asking why a minor increase in the price of petrol in Nigeria in April 1988 resulted in popular riots and a nation-wide strike movement. Was it not sufficient proof of irresponsible workers' opposition? We have explained why the petrol price issue had become a symbol of resistance, going beyond the few kobo that were added to the price at that particular time. The immediate issue at stake was the petrol price, but to understand the full meaning of the protest we need to recall the proscription of the NLC leadership that preceded it. Workers were asserting the democratic aspirations of the people.

Notes

1. The 'economic' case against the African workers is here primarily constructed from World Bank documents and reports, including the 'Berg Report' (World Bank, 1981) and World Bank, 1983b, 1984 and 1986. Many (but not all) of the points can be deduced from the section on 'Adjustment programs' in the 1986 report.
2. The political dimensions of the 'urban bias' case are forcefully argued in Bates, 1981. The World Bank documents are less explicit in this respect, although Bates's work is seen as providing support for the World Bank position (cf. Bienefeld, 1986). The political case against the workers as outlined here, however, draws primarily on the responses of Nigerian governments to workers' demands.
3. For references on the controversies over Structural Adjustment policies and their theoretical and factual basis, see Cornia, Jolly and Stewart, 1988; Havnevik, 1987; Lawrence, 1986; *IDS Bulletin*, 1983. Mkandawire, 1989, and Godfrey, 1986, address specifically the labour and employment issues.

References

G. Andrae and B. Beckman (1989), 'Workers, Unions, and the Crisis of the Nigerian Textile Industry', in I. Brandell (ed.), *Practice and Strategy: Workers in Contemporary Third World Industrialisation.* (Forthcoming.)

I. Aremu (1987), 'Glaxo Workers: A Report'. Lagos: NLC.

Y. Bangura (1987a), 'Crisis Management and Union Struggles in Niger State' (mimeo). Zaria: Department of Political Science.

—— (1987b), 'The Recession and Workers' Struggles in the Vehicle Assembly Plants: Steyr-Nigeria', *Review of African Political Economy*, no. 39, September.

—— (1987c), 'Industrial Crisis and the Struggle for National Democracy: Lessons from Kaduna Textile Ltd. and the Workers' Demonstration of January 1984' (mimeo). Zaria.

—— (1989a), 'Crisis and Adjustment: The Experience of Nigerian Workers', in B. Onimode (ed.), *The IMF, the World Bank and the African Debt*. London: Zed.

—— (1989b), 'Authoritarianism and Democracy in Africa: A Theoretical Discourse' (seminar paper). Uppsala: AKUT.

R. Bates (1981), *Markets and States in Tropical Africa. The Political Basis of Agricultural Policies*. Berkeley: University of California Press.

B. Beckman (1988a), 'The Post-Colonial State: Crisis and Reconstruction', *IDS Bulletin*, vol. 19, no. 4.

—— (1988b), 'When Does Democracy Make Sense?' (seminar paper). Uppsala: AKUT.

M. Bienefeld (1986), 'Analysing the Politics of African State Policy. Some Thoughts on Robert Bates' Work', *IDS Bulletin*, vol. 17, no. 1.

M. Buhari (1984), Statement on the Assumption of Power by the Military Government of General M. Buhari. Lagos, January.

CBN (1983), *Annual Report and Statement of Account*. Lagos: Central Bank of Nigeria.

R. Cohen (1974), *Labour and Politics in Nigeria, 1945-1974*. London: Heinemann.

G.A. Cornia, R. Jolly and F. Stewart (1988), *Adjustment with a Human Face*. Oxford: UNICEF.

U. Damachi, H.D. Seibel and L. Trachtman (eds) (1979), *Industrial Relations in Africa*. London: Macmillan.

S.O.Z. Ejiofoh (1988), 'Communiqué Issued on behalf of 42 Industrial Unions by 14-Man Negotiating Team on the Impending Negotiations with the Government on the Issue of Increases in the Prices of Petroleum and Petroleum Products and General High Cost of Living etc., etc.' Signed by S.O.Z. Ejiofoh, G.O. Ulucha, E.D. Fidelis, M.A. Kazeem, F.E. Nwachukwu and A. Ogbonna, 10 June.

M. Godfrey (1986), *Global Unemployment: The New Challenge to Economic Theory*. Brighton: Wheatsheaf.

Y. Hashim (1987), 'State Intervention in Trade Unions. A Nigerian Case Study'. MA diss. The Hague: Institute of Social Studies.

K.J. Havnevik (ed.) (1987), *The IMF and the World Bank in Africa. Conditionality, Impact and Alternatives.* Uppsala: Scandinavian Institute of African Studies.

J. Ibrahim (1986), 'The Political Debate and the Struggle for Democracy in Nigeria', *Review of African Political Economy*, no. 37, December.

IDS Bulletin (1983), 'Accelerated Development in Sub-Saharan Africa', vol. 14, no. 1.

P. Lawrence, (ed.) (1986), *World Recession and the Food Crisis in Africa*. London: James Currey/ROAPE.

P. Lloyd (1982), *A Third World Proletariat?* London: Allen & Unwin.

MAN (1987), *Half-Yearly Economic Review*. January-June. Lagos: Manufacturers' Association of Nigeria.

Mkandawire, T. (1989), 'Labour and Policy-Making in Africa' (draft). Dakar: CODESRIA.

A.R. Mustapha (1988), 'Ever-decreasing Circles: Democratic Rights in Nigeria 1978-1988'. Oxford: St Peter's College.

National Economic Council Expert Committee (1983), *Report on the State of the Economy*. Lagos: Government Printer.

NLC (1985), 'Towards National Recovery: Nigeria Labour Congress' Alternatives'. Lagos.

—— (1987), 'A Case for Wage Adjustment for Workers: A Memo Presented to the Federal Military Government'. 29 July. Lagos.

—— (1988), 'Resolutions of 3rd Congress of the Nigerian Labour Congress Holding at Saidi Centre in Benin, 24th–26th February, 1988'.

M. Olson (1982), *The Rise and Decline of Nations: Economic Growth, Stagflation, and Social Rigidities*. New Haven: Yale University Press.

D. Otobo (1986), *Foreign Interests and Nigerian Trade Unions*. Oxford: Malthouse.

R. Sandbrook and R. Cohen (eds) (1975), *The Development of An African Working Class*. London: Longman.

A.K. Ubeku (1983), *Industrial Relations in Developing Countries: The Case of Nigeria*. London: Macmillan.

P. Waterman (1975), 'The Labour Aristocracy in Africa. Introduction to a debate', *Development and Change*, vol. 6, no. 3.

—— (1983), *Aristocrats and Plebeians in African Trade Unions? Lagos Port and Dock Worker Organization and Struggle*. The Hague: Self-publication.

World Bank (1981), *Accelerated Development in Sub-Saharan Africa: An Agenda for Action*. Washington.

—— (1983a), *Nigeria: Macro-Economic Policies for Structural Change*. Report no. 4506 – UNI, 15 August.

—— (1983b), *Sub-Saharan Africa: Progress Report on Development Prospects and Programs*. Washington.

—— (1984), *Towards Sustained Development in Sub-Saharan Africa. A Joint Program of Action*. Washington.

—— (1986), *Financing Adjustment with Growth in Sub-Saharan Africa, 1986–90*. Washington.

Newspapers and Journals
Analyst. Monthly news magazine, Jos.
Newswatch. Weekly news magazine, Lagos.
West Africa. Weekly news magazine, London.

ATTAHIRU JEGA

Professional Associations & Structural Adjustment

I. Introduction

In this chapter, an attempt is made to describe and analyse the implications for Nigerian professionals and their associations of the Structural Adjustment Programme (SAP). The aim is to establish the basis for a comprehensive understanding of the way in which the dynamics of crisis and adjustment have shaped their involvement in the unfolding democratic struggle in contemporary Nigeria. It is our contention here that the introduction, by the military regime of General Ibrahim Babangida, of an International Monetary Fund (IMF)/World Bank-sponsored adjustment programme and the efforts that have been made to push it through have posed a profound problem of relevance and irrelevance for Nigerian professionals and their associations.

The degree of relevance or irrelevance of any organized professional association is seen to be related to the extent to which it struggles to advance the fundamental aspirations both of its members and of the majority of the nation. It is also related to the extent to which the association refuses to condone the erosion of the nation's democratic values and processes. In other words, the relevance of a professional association is seen in terms of its ability or willingness to make significant contributions in: (a) securing improved socio-economic conditions for its members as well as for the majority of the nation's populace; (b) enhancing the citizens' civil and democratic rights; and (c) creating a stable foundation for the nation's democratic processes. For any professional association to contribute to the erosion or negation of these conditions, rights and processes, or for it to be a passive onlooker while these are being destroyed, is to render itself virtually irrelevant.

Furthermore, it is argued that, while the general effects of SAP on the majority of the Nigerian people have resulted in a considerable deterioration of their socio-economic conditions and of civil and democratic rights, a situation which any relevant professional association cannot afford to ignore, the progressive agitations and struggles of these associations occasioned by this situation are, at the same time, increasingly being checked by the harsh and repressive political methods which the regime employs to prop up SAP. These methods are characterized by the widespread use of divide-and-rule tactics backed by an array of decrees; and they seem to have, even if only temporarily, a subduing or, at least, a constraining effect on the struggles of professional associations against SAP.

II. Professions, Professionals and the Professional Association

A fairly acceptable, conventional starting-point in defining a profession is to note that it has well-defined methods of entry and a required set of qualifications (IESS, 1969). To learn or to enter into a profession, a person generally undergoes training which 'aims at the achievement of qualification through the demonstrated mastery of a body of materials and repertory of skills' (Wolf, 1969: 19–20). Thus, a period of training and acquisition of skills through experience or by academic lessons is very essential for anybody who aspires to join a profession.

Professionals are people who, in most cases, 'profess to know better than others the nature of certain matters and to know better than their clients what ails them or their affairs' (Lynn et al., 1965: 2) because they are perceived as possessors of an 'elaborate stock of rigorously founded knowledge' (Shils, 1984: 7). They also dispense, for a fee, of course, 'certain specialized services to their fellow citizens and to the state' (Holmes, 1979: 323).

A professional association is, thus, an organization or union that brings, or seeks to bring, together members of the same profession primarily so as to advance commonly defined and agreed upon collective interests and aspirations. Generally, professional associations are democratically-run organizations – unless they are military or para-military in nature – in the sense that they are 'a self-elected, self-disciplined group of individuals' (Norman and Chadwick, 1976: xi) who have freely chosen to associate as professional colleagues. They usually have legal instruments (e.g. constitutions, programme, etc.) defining their aims and objectives, specifying their organizational structure and functional roles and subjecting their leadership positions to periodic elections guided by principles of popular representation and free and fair elections.

By virtue of their origins, professional associations are not always 'actuated by the common good', contrary to Parsonian assumptions (Johnson, 1972: 12). They mostly have selfish or very parochial objectives and inclinations. None the less, the liberal-democratic foundations of such associations can, depending on the balance of forces in their ranks and the historical conjuncture, tilt them towards objectives of broad social reforms and to the recognition, even if only tacitly, of the need for an entrenched national democratic process in which the professions they represent could grow and prosper.

III. Evolution of the Democratic Process in Nigeria

It is important to stress from the outset that the introduction, protection and guarantee of fundamental rights and civil liberties, the facilitation of peoples' involvement in managing their own affairs through popular representation and elections, in short the embrace and promotion of democratic practices, come about only through political struggles (Jega, 1988b).

Thus, the democratic process in Nigeria did not just unfold naturally, of its own account. On the contrary, it emerged as a by-product of colonialism as the forces of British imperialism started to be confronted by the peoples' determined struggles and aspirations for self-assertion and independence. Although this struggle resulted in the defeat of the forces of colonialism, the struggle for democratization was by no means over. At independence in 1960, Nigeria, governed on the basis of a Westminster-style parliamentary system, had a democratic system which was weakly founded and which, therefore, was very shaky. After Nigerian patriots and nationalists waged the political struggles that ultimately forced the British out, the colonizer was replaced by a band of political and economic wrecking crews who cared little about democracy and democratic values. Motivated solely by their selfish interests, they were wedded to their newly acquired political power which they saw as an avenue for acquiring wealth. Hence they payed little attention to the creation of a solid foundation for the emergence and sustenance of popular democracy in the country. They even threatened the survival of the nation as one sovereign entity in their determined struggles to acquire more power and wealth, or to protect what they had already acquired.

The turbulence of the First Republic (1960–6) was, therefore, characterized by only feeble, inconsequential attempts and pretensions at building democracy by those around whom the political and economic power of the state revolved. There were obviously some struggles waged by concerned Nigerians, especially through working-class unions and professional associations, which forced the ruling classes to concede some democratic reforms. But by and large, state power was crudely utilized to advance selfish ends, execute unpopular and undemocratic decisions, and generally suppress the democratic aspirations of the majority of the people.

The persistent political upheavals of the First Republic culminated in the incursion of the military into Nigerian politics. The 15 January 1966 *coup d'état* represents the first and perhaps the greatest assault on the processes of building a sound democratic tradition in Nigeria. Dudley (1982: 85) noted that 'the not uncommon practice is for the military to "abolish" all political parties and para-political organizations' as soon as they take over power. But most significantly, the first thing they actually do, which Dudley missed, is to suspend the constitution, the instrument that at least symbolizes the quest for democracy by specifying the mechanics of democratic processes of governance. With this singular act, the stage is set for the junta to do as it pleases through periodic issuance of all sorts of decrees which are imposed as substitutes for the legislative functions of a representative assembly of the people. Almost invariably these decrees curtail the fundamental rights and civil liberties of the people. The opportunities for participation, or of at least having a say, in the running of public affairs are withdrawn from all but a chosen few who are connected to, and selected by, the military rulers and given functional or advisory roles. The combined effect of the military's incursion into politics on the building of the democratic process in Nigeria is, in short, very profound. It is far greater than S.G. Ikoku's observation that the era of 'military rule had almost atrophied the art of governance' (1985: 94).

IV. Professional Associations in Nigeria before SAP

In order to set a proper context for assessing the role which Nigeria's professional associations have played in the post-SAP period, it is necessary, even if only briefly, to summarize the roles they played during the First Republic, in the post-civil war, oil-boom era and in the early 1980s prior to the introduction of SAP.

With a few exceptions (such as the Association of Nigerian Native Doctors and Herbalists formed fairly recently), most professional associations in Nigeria have a colonial origin and are patterned after similar European groups. The formation of many of them, especially the big three representing medicine, law and engineering, predated Nigerian independence in 1960. The Nigerian Bar Association (NBA) was formed in 1950; the Nigerian Society of Engineers (NSE) was founded in 1959; the Pharmaceutical Society of Nigeria (PSN) was founded in 1927, although it was only incorporated by statute in 1956; while the Nigerian Medical Association (NMA) started as a branch of the British Medical Association before it was indigenized (Norman and Chadwick, 1976).

During the First Republic, with the emergence of new associations, and the accelerated growth of others such as the Nigerian Union of Teachers (NUT) which from the outset had a large membership base, professional associations became firmly rooted in the country. But for most of this period, these associations seem to have been preoccupied solely with advancing and defending the particularistic interests of their members, especially in the area of private practice. They generally assumed a marked degree of indifference to national politics in the tradition of the aloofness and detached 'professionalism' of their British counterparts. Being few in number and treated as privileged and esteemed citizens in the early post-colonial years, Nigerian professionals, many of whom were engaged in lucrative private practices or had choice government jobs, seemed to have no cause to engage in preoccupations other than their parochial interests. Membership in a professional association was largely a status symbol, an admission into a class-oriented fraternity. It was useful in opening up new business contacts and opportunities to members, especially in those associations which were still dominated by foreigners (e.g. law, medicine). Nationalist or radical sentiments, when they were invoked, were usually intended to advance particularistic interests. As individuals, many of the professionals were probably concerned about and sympathetic to the plight of the under-privileged, as a doctor would feel professionally concerned with malnutrition and preventable diseases in the rural areas, or as a lawyer might worry about the rule of law or the crime-wave. But professional associations in the early post-colonial period hardly ever confronted the government on broad issues relating to civil and political rights, or deteriorating socio-economic conditions.

By the 1970s, many post-colonial professional associations had emerged in Nigeria. At the same time, as Western education expanded in the country, the membership of the older associations also experienced a significant increase. Associations such as the Nigerian Union of Journalists (NUJ) and the Association of University Teachers (AUT), which later became the Academic Staff Union of Universities (ASUU), attained national recognition during this period primarily on account of their periodical intervention in important national issues. In general, however, the political apathy of professional associations that characterized the First Republic persisted. This is primarily because most of the key members of and leading figures in these associations utilized the expanded opportunities of the 1970s for amassing wealth either as government advisers, consultants and contractors, or as commission agents of the multinational corporations. Not surprisingly, therefore, many of these professional associations remained virtually irrelevant in the sense of condoning and being generally indifferent to the erosion of the socio-economic well-being and democratic rights of the majority of the Nigerian people. There are hardly any concrete examples of these associations taking principled positions on the democratic future of the country, on civil rights, or even on the plight of the down-trodden during this period. Only sporadic and feeble protests were made, such as when the members of the AUT agitated against the bad deal they got from the Udoji salary review exercise of 1973/4, or when one of the then military governors ordered the shaving of a journalist's head with a broken bottle because of a news report he published, which was deemed unfavourable by the governor. But for most of the oil-boom era of the 1970s, professional associations clearly served merely and primarily as reservoirs of skilled manpower into which the military regimes constantly dipped their hands for the design, implementation and management of their 'development' programmes, or for membership of the several commissions of inquiry which they set up. The more favoured members received key positions, ministerial or extra-ministerial.

The 1980s, however, were remarkable in the sense that they were characterized by the growing concern of professional bodies with the erosion of the country's democratic values and process, their increasing demands for broad socio-economic reforms, as well as heightened agitations on their part for the restoration of denied basic democratic and human rights. This is largely because the general crisis which hit Nigeria's dependent, capitalist-oriented economy in the first half of the 1980s and which has escalated since then immediately engendered unprecedented suffering and deprivation for the majority of Nigerians, affecting even many of the members of the previously secure professions to the extent that their professional associations could no longer afford to ignore national socio-economic and political issues.

By 1985, for example, the professional associations of medicine and law, the majority of whose members in the 1960s and 1970s were either independently employed or generally well off (or both), became infested with increasing numbers of newly qualified, poverty-stricken, under-employed or unemployed members. This situation has inevitably forced some sort of radicalization within these associations, often resulting in the displacement of conservative-oriented leaderships or the compulsion of these leaderships to put the struggle against the socio-economic malaise of the times on their agenda. Increasingly, professional associations began taking hitherto inconceivable tough stands against the government and on issues of national concern.

For example, the Academic Staff Union of Universities (ASUU) suddenly shook itself out of the slumber and timidity which had engulfed it since the harshly aborted strike of its predecessor in 1973, and embarked on successful strikes in 1981 and 1982 which forced the Shagari regime to address the issue of improved conditions in the educational sector. From then on, it generally agitated against the recklessness of government functionaries (ASUU, 1984a), the deteriorating living and working conditions of the majority of Nigerians, the siege on the fundamental rights of Nigerians imposed by the Buhari and Babangida regimes, and especially the deterioration of the educational system occasioned by the economic crisis the country had been plunged into (ASUU, 1984a, 1987b). In 1984, ASUU hosted a national conference on 'The State of the Nigerian Economy', from which it derived a wide range of short- and long-term solutions to the country's economic predicament. These were published under the title *How to Save Nigeria* (1984). In 1985, it organized another national seminar on the 'Political Debate' initiated by the Babangida regime on the political future of the country. The resolutions passed at the seminar were also published and widely circulated (ASUU, 1987a).

Similarly, the Nigerian Medical Association (NMA), formerly a branch of the British Medical Association, together with the National Association of Resident Doctors (NARD), which were hardly known outside the medical profession in the 1960s and 1970s, suddenly became household names as they began to challenge the government's healthcare policies, and as they articulated demands for the improvement of healthcare services in the country and the conditions of work and service in the teaching hospitals. These culminated in the massive strike by doctors in February 1985. The strike was so successful and effective that the Buhari regime proscribed the two associations, arrested (or drove underground) their leaders, sacked 64 doctors and penalized more than 2,000 others.

One important development in the 1980s helped to reinforce the increasingly significant role that professional associations came to assume in national affairs in the period prior to the introduction of SAP. As the national economic crisis began to deepen, the Nigeria Labour Congress (NLC) appeared increasingly incapable of standing up to the assaults on the interests of Nigerian workers unleashed by successive regimes. It particularly shied away from contesting the Buhari regime's (1984–5) tough stand against labour struggles. That regime had declared strikes as 'unpatriotic' and 'undisciplined'. Hence, as the regime imposed its austerity programme, declared a general wage freeze, retrenched about 30 per cent of the workers in the civil service and proceeded to 'reduce or eliminate altogether' many hard-earned workers' benefits, the NLC looked helplessly on (Agan, 1986b). In the circumstances, even the job security and other petty-bourgeois aspirations of many professionals became threatened or fell directly on the line of assault. Professional associations had to join the fight first and foremost to protect and defend the interests and aspirations of their members, and then generally to speak up against the deterioration of the socio-economic conditions of the masses.

V. The Nigerian Professional Associations under SAP

The introduction of structural adjustment in 1986 was not solely responsible for the radicalization or militancy of professional associations in Nigeria as several of them had for many years before SAP assumed or portrayed a radical or militant posture on national issues, as we have shown in the preceding section. However, SAP has certainly hastened, reinforced and intensified that process, especially after its full effects began to be felt by the majority of the people.

When the Babangida regime came to power in August 1985 it introduced several packages of inducements and enticements which initially softened up some members of the vocal middle class and their professional associations. These associations and their members had been thoroughly intimidated, antagonized and alienated by the Buhari regime. For example, Babangida repealed Decree no. 4, which had been used by his predecessor to gag the press. He promised to respect the human rights of Nigerians and the rule of law and co-opted the President of the Nigerian Bar Association into his cabinet as Attorney-General and Minister of Justice. The NBA had been in the frontline of the campaign, during the role of General Buhari, for the respect of human rights and the rule of law. General Babangida also appointed a respected professor of medicine from one of the country's teaching hospitals as his Health Minister. Two other professors were given the Education and Science and Technology portfolios. From among the journalists and media practitioners, professionals whose members bore the wrath of Decree no. 4 under Buhari, Babangida appointed his Press Secretary and his Information Minister. Several other professionals were co-opted into the Presidential Advisory Commission (PAC) or specially created directorates. For the intellectuals in the universities, national economic and political debates were initiated (on the IMF loan and the country's political future), which created convenient intellectual diversions.

Following the IMF debate, in which the Nigerian people overwhelmingly rejected the taking of an IMF loan with its attendant conditionalities, the Babangida regime's first move was to announce, on 12 December 1985, that negotiations with the IMF would be terminated and the loan rejected in accordance with popular demand. However, Babandiga announced his intention to commence a process of restructuring the economy which would require 'belt tightening' and sacrifices by all Nigerians. Through the 1986 federal budget, the government introduced a host of measures which signalled the commencement in earnest of the restructuring process. For example, 80 per cent of the 'subsidy' on petroleum products was removed, subventions to parastatals were cut, public expenditure was further reduced, measures to reduce the import profile of the economy and boost government revenues were introduced and an intention to privatize/commercialize public enterprises and parastatals was announced.

Then, in June 1986, the regime unfolded the Structural Adjustment Programme (SAP), which specified the framework within which economic recovery was to be sought. As officially spelt out by the government, the programme aimed to:

(a) devalue the naira in order to stimulate exports and discourage imports of non-essentials;
(b) combat inflation through a generalized liquidity and credit squeeze, including the minimization of deficit budgeting and the reduction of public expenditure;
(c) liberalize the economy by removing exchange and trade restrictions and deregulating prices and interest rates; and
(d) repay the huge foreign debt of the country.

In a national broadcast to the people, Babangida sought to convince Nigerians that SAP was the only viable option available for curing the economic ailments of the nation and that, unlike the policy responses of the previous regimes, it would assure a speedy economic recovery.

Within a very short period after its introduction, SAP unleashed an unprecedented inflationary pressure in the economy. Since the devaluation of the naira entailed a reduction of real wages by at least 50 per cent in a context of a generalized wage freeze imposed on workers, SAP came to have a negative effect on Nigerians and their general socio-economic well-being. Food prices sky-rocketed, the costs of essential drugs, school uniforms, etc. became unbearable, school and hospital fees were increased and all sorts of 'development' levies were imposed on the people.

As SAP took effect, the Nigerian middle classes, already badly hit by the economic crisis, suffered more setbacks to their interests. These professionals, who are generally petty-bourgeois with fantastic aspirations and inclinations, found that the introduction of market reforms, far from restoring their economic and social fortunes, actually diminished them further. Consequently, the initial pronouncements which had endeared the Babangida regime to the professionals, relative to the Buhari regime, began to lose their appeal. As the economic hardship faced by many professionals increased, so the initial romance which they had with the regime gradually ebbed and professional associations became increasingly restive. SAP came under attack from all angles with unions and associations leading the agitations for the lifting of the wage freeze, a review of conditions of service and the scrapping of adjustment.

On its part, the government grew weary of these agitations. It became increasingly intolerant of opposition, suspected sabotage in every voice of dissent or criticism and branded every critic an 'extremist'. Above all, the regime made a sudden about-turn on its human rights posture and started employing authoritarian tactics to subdue and suppress the increasing anti-SAP sentiment gaining ground among the Nigerian people. These tactics ranged from intimidation and harassment to proscription of associations and detention of union leaders. Subtler methods of containing opposition to adjustment, such as divide-and-rule and co-optation, were also employed by the regime. The ways in which these tactics have been used to prop up SAP, and how they presently affect the struggles of professional associations in Nigeria, can be illustrated with the experience of the ASUU and the NBA.

The Academic Staff Union of Universities (ASUU)

Following the announcement of the *coup* of 27 August 1985, ASUU was sceptical about the birth of another military government, although like all the other antagonized and intimidated unions and professional associations in the country, it was much relieved to see the end of the dictatorial regime of Generals Buhari and Idiagbon. Nigeria has experienced so many *coups* and counter *coups*, all of which have contributed immensely to the prevailing crisis in the country, that many Nigerians have come to be sceptical about the value of any military government. None the less, the ASUU welcomed the Babangida regime's promise to respect human rights and seek the views of Nigerians on how to solve the country's economic and political problems. Thus it actively participated in the IMF and political debates initiated by the regime (ASUU, 1987a).

When the 1986 budget was announced, there was a considerable increase in the capital grant to the universities for uncompleted buildings and equipment acquisition. However, the actual recurrent grant came down to N395 million from N429 million in 1985. This decreased further to N316 million in 1987, a 26 per cent reduction on the 1985 figure (NUC, 1987; 1988).

By May 1986, when ASUU held its National Delegates Conference, it had enough reasons to pass resolutions condemning the recovery measures the regime had incorporated into the 1986 budget, such as the withdrawal of government subsidies on social services, underfunding of education and the proposed privatization and commercialization of public enterprises (ASUU, 1986a). Other resolutions called for granting increased autonomy to universities, as well as a demand for the removal of Jubril Aminu, the professor appointed by the regime as Minister of Education, because he was seen to be contributing to, rather than solving, the crisis affecting the Nigerian educational system (ASUU, 1986b).

Soon after the ASUU Delegates Conference in May, the government announced its SAP package in June 1986. The adverse effects of SAP, as it began to be consolidated, on the educational sector in particular, and on the socio-economic conditions of Nigerians in general, led ASUU increasingly to articulate critical views on the regime's handling of national affairs. Because of SAP, the pre-existing crisis in the Nigerian educational sector intensified, as evidenced by:

(a) chronic underfunding, relative to other sectors such as defence;
(b) increasing inadequacy as well as physical disrepair of existing infrastructure and educational facilities;
(c) insufficiency of trained staff and basic teaching aids and equipment (e.g. university teacher–student ratio of over 1:20, far in excess of UNESCO's recommended 1:10, and NUC's target of 1:12);
(d) deteriorating conditions of service of teachers relative to supporting staff; and
(e) demoralization of staff, students and even parents, due to the intolerable and oppressive conditions in the educational institutions, etc.

Although in 1988 (and 1989) government somewhat raised the absolute level of funding of education, the hike was inconsequential because of the inflationary trend unleashed by SAP. Liad Tella (*National Concord*, 5 September 1989: 7) sought to demonstrate this fact in his assessment of the amount allocated to education in the 1989 budget. N800 million was allocated to primary education with an additional grant of N40 million for the purchase of books. As Tella demonstrated, assuming that it was all disbursed, each state could expect to get N39 million out of the N800 million. In five states of the federation, this was barely sufficient to meet the salaries of teachers over a four-month period. Similarly, each state could expect to get N2 million out of the special book grant which worked out at N500 per school in each state. But N500 in 1989 could only buy a few books since SAP has ensured that the price of books has risen by almost 600 per cent relative to their pre-SAP costs.

According to UNESCO figures, even at its peak, educational expenditure per pupil, the major 'indicator of the educational priorities of eash state', has never exceeded US$24.10 in Nigeria. This placed Nigeria ahead of only 20 countries in the world (Kurain, 1979). The devaluation of the naira under SAP has obviously further reduced this rating.

The attempt by the Nigerian state under SAP to disengage from several of its responsibilities in education under the pretext that it has been spending too much has further intensified the educational crisis. This policy is pursued in spite of the fact that Nigeria's total expenditure on education as a percentage of its GNP is below 4.9 per cent (UNESCO, 1984). Today, education is fast becoming a huge private enterprise with even the World Bank coming up with loan packages (and conditionalities) for Nigerian Universities (Jega, 1988a).

Given the gross underfunding of the university sector occasioned by SAP; the deterioration of conditions of service of staff; the attack on university autonomy; the threat of retrenchment of staff and increasing arbitrariness of university authorities in violation of statutes, ASUU declared an industrial dispute with the government in 1987 and, failing to reach an amicable settlement, called out its members on a general strike on 1 July 1988 (see ASUU and SSAUTHRIAI, 1988). The strike was total and effective, halting work in virtually all the 28 universities in the country for seven days. On the eighth day of the strike, government announced a decree proscribing ASUU.

Between 1986 and 1988, the government responded to ASUU's anti-SAP comments, criticisms and demands in several ways. It would seem that these responses were informed by a preconceived notion that ASUU is an association of trouble-makers infested with 'extremists'.

For example, when, following the police massacre of Ahmadu Bello University (ABU) students in May 1986, the NLC declared 4 June a day of national mourning, the government suspected that ASUU was responsible for the decision and brutally suppressed the attempt to organize a march by students, workers and lecturers. Hence, when the Abisoye panel was set up to investigate the killings, ASUU foresaw the possibility of it being an inquisition, so it boycotted the proceedings, although some members of the ABU (Main Campus) branch defied the organization and went ahead to appear before the panel. In its report to government, the Abisoye panel absolved the police and the university authorities of all responsibility for the crisis. Instead, it claimed that 'some teachers who are members of ASUU in Ahmadu Bello University are not teaching what they are paid to teach' and recommended that 'these teachers should be flushed out of the universities'. The government accepted the recommendation and directed 'the Federal Ministry of Education to take appropriate action' (FMG, 1986: 14). About 20 lecturers would have summarily lost their jobs had ASUU not been able to secure a court injunction restraining the Minister of Education from taking any such 'flushing out' action (ASUU, 1986c).

Secondly, in July 1986, the government issued the Trade Unions (Miscellaneous Provisions) Decree 1986 which disaffiliated ASUU from the NLC and removed the mandatory check-off system whereby employers automatically deducted union dues from workers' wages and salaries and credited the union. ASUU officials believe that the decree was meant to prevent further co-operation between the central labour body and the academics as well as to cripple ASUU financially, because the government suspected academics to be responsible for the NLC's militant response to the ABU massacre of students in MAY 1986.

Thirdly, when the Abisoye panel failed conclusively to shift the blame on to ASUU for the May 1986 crisis at ABU, the government set up the Justice Akanbi Panel of Inquiry, to investigate the 'May 1986 crisis in Nigeria'. While ASUU stayed away from what it saw as the Abisoye 'kangaroo' panel, it decided to appear before an open judicial panel of inquiry in the conviction that it offered a good opportunity to protect and defend its integrity in the full view of the Nigerian people. Although state security agents testified, in camera, to the effect that ASUU wanted to overthrow the government in May 1986 with the NLC as the political party, NANS the youth wing and ASUU the intellectual vanguard, they failed to prove their outrageous claims before Justice Akanbi. Consequently, the panel exonerated ASUU and even praised it for promoting peace on many campuses. The government is yet to release the full report of the Akanbi Panel.

Subsequently, the government attempted in various ways to flush out those it considered to be the 'extremists' in ASUU. Dr Festus Iyayi, then ASUU President, was the first to fall victim to this witch-hunt when he was served with a letter summarily terminating his appointment with the University of Benin in May 1987, on the allegation that he had engaged in activities which violated university laws governing his employment. ASUU saw this onslaught as aimed at tarnishing its integrity in the eyes of the Nigerian public as well as causing confusion and disarray amongst its members. And it almost succeeded as some branch officials (notably at ABU, UI, UNIBEN and UNILAG) passed moral judgement on Dr Iyayi when both the allegations against him and the illegalities committed in terminating his appointment were before the courts. The ASUU national leadership, however, considered this as only a temporary setback as the 1988 National Delegates Conference passed a vote of confidence on Iyayi and unanimously elected a new leadership which was mandated to be as committed as the previous one in pursuing ASUU's aims and objectives.

The year 1988 proved to be eventful in ASUU–government relations. The elongated salary structure (ESS) that the government introduced under the 1988 budget raised more problems for the conditions of service of university staff than it solved. In spite of ASUU's persistent demands for negotiations and dialogue with the National Universities Commission (NUC) over the modalities for the implementation of the ESS, as well as the outstanding issues in the trade dispute declared by ASUU in 1987, the government refused to react or take appropriate remedial action. At the same time, the government illegally deported two expatriate ASUU members very crudely and on unsubstantiated charges. By June 1988, the ESS had not been implemented in the universities, six months after it had been implemented in other public sector institutions; the NUC continued to refuse to negotiate with university unions; and none of the outstanding issues in the trade dispute had been addressed. ASUU's representations and letters to top government functionaries fell on deaf ears. Consequently, ASUU and the Senior Staff Association of Universities, Teaching Hospitals, Research Institutes and Associated Institutions (SSAUTHRIAI) gave the government deadline of one month, at the expiration of which they went out on strike on 1 July 1988 (*National Concord*, 25 April 1988).

The government's reaction was swift. Suddenly the unions were ordered to appear before the Industrial Arbitration Panel (IAP), which ordered them to call off the strike pending the determination of the case. On the same day as the court order, the Minister of Education addressed a press conference at which he gave the unions 48 hours to call off the strike or face the consequences. ASUU was projected by the government as unreasonable and irresponsible and spirited efforts were made to sever the solidarity between SSAUTHRIAI and ASUU. Efforts were also made to weaken the resolve of ASUU members in several branches with dubious promises of swift payments of ESS *if* they called off the strike, or by intimidating branch officials.

ASUU's position in the circumstances was that the IAP was acting under government pressure. It had taken more than one year since ASUU declared a trade dispute, and over one month since ASUU and SSAUTHRIAI declared their intention to go on strike, before the IAP decided to arbitrate. ASUU also felt that the Minister had acted in contempt of the IAP by giving the unions a 48-hour ultimatum, several hours after the IAP had urged the unions to go back to work. In any case, ASUU immediately scheduled an emergency Tactical Committee meeting, and issued a statement to the effect that the meeting was to consider the latest developments regarding the strike. As it turned out, SSAUTHRIAI decided not to participate in the joint meeting. And while the meeting was in progress on the evening of Friday 7th, ASUU received the news of its proscription. The same news item carried the announcement of SSAUTHRIAI's decision to call off the strike (NTA, *Network News*, 7 July 1988).

Subsequently many ASUU branch officials nation-wide were ordered to surrender their passports and report daily to the State Security Services (SSS). Others were intimidated, while four officials, including the immediate past President and the incumbent President, were arrested and detained.

Two factors are central to any attempt to explain the growing relevance of ASUU as a professional association, especially in the 1980s. These are related to the rapid expansion of the Nigerian educational sector, and the crises which began to engulf it in the late 1970s and early 1980s. First, as a consequence of the expansion and the subsequent crisis of the educational sector, university students became increasingly radicalized due largely to growing dissatisfaction with the callousness and insensitivity of university administrators and the government in addressing their needs and demands (e.g. withdrawal of subsidies on meals, and the shooting dead of some of the students who demonstrated against the measure at ABU in 1978, etc.). The increasing radicalization of the student body seemed to have a spin-off effect on the university lecturers as they came under increasing pressure, dictated by the circumstances, to take sides with students, because they could no longer totally ignore the symptoms of the general crisis of the Nigerian economy as manifested in the university sector (e.g. ASUU, 1987b: 35–40).

Secondly, the balance of forces within ASUU itself altered significantly with the emergence of a leadership with a progressive and radical disposition from about 1979 onwards. This situation resulted in the placement of broader mass-oriented national issues on the agenda of ASUU struggles, side by side with, in fact sometimes ahead of, particularistic 'professional' demands of the members. While the balance of forces continued to be in favour of the progressives until ASUU's proscription by the government in July 1988, the politics of the association became increasingly characterized by intra-union factional struggles between those who thought that the association was devoting too much of its energy and resources to national politics rather than the specific interests of the members, and those who believed that the relevance of the association was only to the extent that it perceived and strived to solve the problem of its members in the context of the broader struggles for the resolution of other crucial national problems.

It is conceivable that in its determination to check the growing relevance of ASUU as a nationally recognized association agitating and struggling for progressive changes in the educational sector as well as on such national issues as SAP and the Transition

Programme, the state exploited the intra-union squabbles to its advantage. The extent to which the state succeeded in this might be even more significant than the use of coercion and intimidation in plunging ASUU into what now seems to be a profound dilemma of relevance and irrelevance even as the attempt to consolidate SAP continues. The decision, announced in August 1990, to lift the ban on ASUU has not resolved this dilemma, although it now means that ASUU can once more organize openly.

The Nigerian Bar Association (NBA)

The NBA, as noted earlier, started taking principled positions which brought it into confrontation with the government in the growing crisis period of the 1980s, especially during the Buhari regime (1984/5). The regime's use of obnoxious decrees such as Decree no. 2, permitting preventive detention for up to three months without trial, and Decree no. 4, which sought to curtail severely the freedom of the press, created unease and dissatisfaction in the NBA. The use of military tribunals to try politicians accused of various offences and the confinement of many of them to long periods of detention without trial were particularly challenged by the NBA as contrary to the rule of law and natural justice. As the regime became indifferent to the Bar's protests and increased its repression, the NBA, under the presidency of Bual Ajibola, continued doggedly and undaunted with its fight. It even took a decision to boycott the proceedings of all the military tribunals because they could not guarantee impartial dispensation of justice. Mr Ajibola became so popular as a champion of human rights and justice that as soon as Babangida came to power he appointed him as his Minister of Justice, to preside over the regime's new human rights policy. However, while the Babangida regime repealed Decree no. 4 upon assuming office, and released most detained politicians, Decree no. 2 was retained, revised and strengthened, such that not only the Chief of General Staff but also the Inspector-General of Police had powers to detain people under the decree. Also, the period over which people could be detained was increased from three to six months and renewable indefinitely.

As SAP began to bite and many groups started to protest against the government's economic policy, the Babangida regime shed all pretensions to a human rights policy. Decree no. 2 came increasingly to be used to clamp down on the opposition. New repressive decrees were promulgated and sometimes backdated to legalize certain arbitrariness. Expatriate lecturers were arbitrarily deported on trumped-up charges, and there was increasing interference in the functions of the judiciary. Abuses of the rule of law also became commonplace. Against this background, many members of the Bar became disappointed with the Babangida regime and Ajibola. The leadership of the NBA which took over from Ajibola felt unable to have meaningful dialogue with him, accusing him of having abandoned the principles which the NBA had sought to defend under his leadership.

In addition, SAP began to take its toll on the younger members of the Bar, who increasingly became restive and were frustrated by the wheeling and dealing of their senior colleagues and the commercialization of justice. The law seemed to be no longer on the side of the innocent in many respects: it went to the highest bidder. Every year, thousands of lawyers are called to the Bar, but SAP came increasingly to block their aspirations to a lucrative practice. Instead, only a few became employed in the chambers of the Senior Advocates and were compelled to do donkey work on meagre wages. Many ended up being underemployed, hovering around police stations looking for 'charge-and-bail' briefs. The most unlucky ones were completely unemployed and poverty-stricken. By early 1987, therefore, many lawyers were looking for a credible alternative to the NBA. Some, while retaining their membership of the Bar, formed a new association called the National Association of Democratic Lawyers (NADL) to try to champion the cause that the NBA seemed to have abdicated.

As the 1980s wore on, the effects of SAP bit harder and the Babangida regime abandoned its increasingly ill-fitting human rights cloak, a movement began to gather within the NBA for the election of a dynamic and principled leadership capable of standing the test of time. This movement emerged in the hope of promoting the election of a progressive, 'a peoples' lawyer', to the leadership of the NBA come the 1987 annual elections; a person who could protect and defend the interests of the younger members of the Bar in the association, and who could generally campaign for human rights, the rule of law, social justice and social reform. In August 1987, at the Ibadan Delegates Conference of the NBA, Alao Aka-Bashorun was elected as the President of the NBA on a 'progressive ticket', and with an overwhelming majority over his key opponent, Mr Ladapo Ladasu, who was alleged to be the government's favoured candidate. Mr Aka-Bashorun was also re-elected unanimously in August 1988 at the Kaduna Delegates Conference to serve his second and last term. Under his leadership, the NBA waged a running campaign against Decree no. 2; against governmental arbitrariness and interference in the dispensation of justice in the country; on issues of human rights; and against the Structural Adjustment Programme. The NBA even went on strike over interference with a court decision by the Gongola State Governor in May 1989. This was unprecedented and the government was incensed.

Clearly, Aka-Bashorun's leadership of the NBA incurred the displeasure of the Babangida regime. The Justice Ministry never had it so bad from the Association of the learned men. The NBA constantly demanded for the repeal of 'obnoxious' decrees, and for the independence of the judiciary in upholding the rule of law.

The government became determined not to allow 'radicals' and 'extremists' to take over the leadership of the NBA as it believed they had done in the case of ASUU. A tactic which failed in 1987 was repeated on a grand scale in 1989. In 1987 government sponsored lawyers from the various states' Attorney-Generals' chambers to the conference and election, all expenses paid, in the hope that they would vote for its favoured candidate. But that failed to stop the election of Aka-Bashorun. In 1989, Aka-Bashorun had finished his term and could not, therefore, run again. But the government was not taking any chances. So, government papers ran news items insinuating financial improprieties against his leadership (e.g. *New Nigeria*, August 1989). The government also once again sponsored any lawyer from the states' Ministries of Justice who wished to attend the annual conferences with clear suggestions as to who to vote for (interviews in Kano, Sokoto and Lagos, August 1989). At the opening ceremony of the conference held in Lagos, both the Attorney-General and the Chief Justice of the Federation delivered speeches against what they termed the 'irresponsibility' of Aka-Bashorun's leadership in deceiving the NBA and leading it into an unprecedented strike. They also stressed the need to discontinue his style of leadership. Aka-Bashorun was reported to have responded credibly to the allegations and charges made against him. The outcome of the elections, however, seemed generally to favour the government. Whether the man who was elected President of the NBA, Charles Idehen, was actually a government-sponsored candidate, as some members of the Bar now allege, is difficult to say, but he has been reported as making clear his determination to pursue dialogue with the government during his tenure (*Daily Times*, 1989). Moreover, as soon as he assumed office, he led courtesy calls to top government functionaries re-stating his belief in dialogue rather than 'confrontation' with the government (Fatunde, 1989: 7).

VI. Conclusion

The two case-studies presented above illustrate the attitude of the state in terms of its responses aimed at checking the growing relevance and involvement of professional associations in the politics of SAP in Nigeria. The effects of SAP make it impossible for many of the professional associations to ignore, or remain aloof from, the politics of the adjustment process. But as they become more militant in their involvement, the state uses its might to cajole, intimidate, divide and even ban the trade unions and professional associations in order to contain their opposition. In the case of ASUU, the ban imposed on it was facilitated by the activities of a minority group of reactionary elements who sought to dampen the increasingly radical tone of the union and narrow its platform. During the period when ASUU was banned, conditions in the universities deteriorated even further while negotiations were opened with the World Bank for a loan of $120 million to help restore facilities and acquire equipment, among other uses. Although ASUU was still banned when the loan negotiations opened, many lecturers, and students, did not hide their displeasure at the government's willingness to accept the conditionality of rationalizing courses, increasing fees, retrenching staff, reducing student intake and closing some departments in order to obtain the loan. The unbanning of ASUU in August 1990 was announced against the background of continuing discussions between the government, NUC and the World Bank over the loan. It is the primary challenge which ASUU has to tackle now that it can once more organize openly. The loan raises questions at the heart of structural adjustment, university autonomy and campus democracy over which ASUU fought relentlessly before it was banned.

As to the NBA, it became so relevant and credible during the period 1987–9, taking up issues on the rule of law and civil rights with the government in a manner which endeared it to Nigerians, that the government seemed to have resolved to act decisively to tame it by apparently facilitating the election of an 'acceptable' leadership for the Association. Paradoxically, the popular movement within the NBA which had installed and supported the militant Aka-Bashorun's Presidency had to settle for a thoroughbred liberal whose expressed preoccupation in office would be consultations and dialogue with the government, although it is the same government which refused to consult and dialogue with the NBA in the past on the Bar's demands for the repeal of obnoxious decrees, and an end to the violation of the rule of law.

In conclusion, it can be suggested that to the extent that the struggles of professional associations under SAP, in general, are marked by 'two steps forward and one step backward', it is indicative of progress and not of a hopeless situation. In any case, the popular resentment against SAP generates its own spontaneous dynamics independent of professional associations and trade unions, as demonstrated by the uprisings in May 1989 in Benin-City and Lagos.

References

I. Agan (1986a), 'Nigeria: Free Speech, Rising Prices', *Africasia*, nos 44 and 45, February.
—— (1986b), 'Nigeria: Troubled Trade Unions', *Africasia*, no. 52, September.
ASUU (1984a), *How to Save Nigeria*. National Secretariat.
—— (1984b), 'The Immediate Future of Higher Education in Nigeria', *Newsletter*. National Secretariat, Ibadan. 27 September.

—— (1984c), 'The New Military Administration and its Tasks', *Bulletin*. National Secretariat, Ibadan. 5 January.

—— (1986a), 'Communiqué and Resolutions of the National Delegates Conference'. Ife. 19 May.

—— (1986b), 'Professor Jibril Aminu and the Crisis in Nigerian Universities', *Press Bulletin*. National Secretariat, Ibadan. 19 August.

—— (1986c), 'We Will be Vindicated'. Memorandum to Justice Akanbi Judicial Commission of Inquiry into the Crisis in Nigerian Universities in (May) 1986. National Secretariat, Ibadan. 25 September.

—— (1987a), 'The Views of ASUU on the Government's Transition Programme'. National Secretariat, Ibadan. October.

—— (1987b), *ASUU and the 1986 Education Crisis in Nigeria*, National Secretariat, Ibadan.

—— and SSAUTHRIAI (1988), 'Why We Are on Strike'. Joint Statement published in *HOTLINE* Magazine and some selected dailies. July.

Daily Times (1989), 'NBA: The Change of Baton' (editorial). 15 September.

B. Dudley (1982), *An Introduction to Nigerian Government and Politics*. London: Macmillan.

T. Fatunde (1989), 'Letter to the New NBA President', *Vanguard*, 18 September.

FMG (1986), *White Paper on the Abisoye Panel of Inquiry into the Killing of ABU Students in May 1986*. Lagos.

G. Holmes (1979), *The Professions and Social Change in England*. Oxford: Oxford University Press.

S.G. Ikoku (1985), *Nigeria's Fourth Coup d'état*. Enugu: Fourth Dimension Publishers.

International Encyclopaedia of the Social Sciences (IESS) (1969), vol. 12. London: Macmillan.

A. Jega (1988a), 'The State of Education in Nigeria Today'. Paper delivered as a Graduation Lecture, College of Education, Sokoto. 5 February.

—— (1988b), 'The Relevance of Organized Professional Bodies under a Military Regime – The Nigerian Experience'. Paper delivered at the Annual NBA Conference, Kaduna. 28 August–2 September.

T.J. Johnson (1972), *Professions and Power*. London: Macmillan.

G.T. Kurain (1979), *Encyclopaedia of the Third World*. London: Mansell. Vol. 2.

K.S. Lynn, et al. (1965), *Professions in America*. Boston: MIT.

NBA (1988), Communiqué and Resolutions of the Annual Delegates Conference, Kaduna. 28 August–2 September.

National Universities Commission (NUC) (1987), *Annual Report*. Lagos. January to December.

—— (1988), *Annual Report*. Lagos. January to December.

T. Norman and J. Chadwick (eds) (1976), *Professional Organisations in the Commonwealth*. London: Hutchinson. 2nd Revised Edition.

E. Shils (1984), *The Academic Ethic*. Chicago: University of Chicago Press.

UNESCO (1984), *Statistical Yearbook*. Paris: UNESCO.

G. Wolf (1969), *Professions and Professionals*, New York: Indigo.

ABDUL RAUFU MUSTAPHA

Structural Adjustment & Agrarian Change in Nigeria

I. The Problematic of Nigerian Agrarian Development

Agriculture in colonial Nigeria was dominated by smallholder peasant cultivation. Although this sector was the motor for the economy, very little was done to improve peasant productivity (Shenton, 1987). By the 1960s, it became apparent that the agricultural sector could not continue to be the milk cow of the economy.[1] The mid-1970s saw concerted efforts by Nigerian governments to invest in improved agricultural productivity. A central argument of this chapter is that the efforts largely succeeded in compounding the problems.

Some have argued that despite increased commitment to agriculture in the 1970s, the sector still suffered from neglect. Others argue that the theme of agricultural neglect is a myth; the reality of the malaise lay in the misdirection of the resources committed. The argument advanced here is that the problem of Nigerian agricultural investment from the 1870s was *both* relative neglect *and* wasteful expenditure.

Refuting the theme of agricultural neglect, Toyo argues that between 1962 and 1980 agriculture's share of total public sector *capital* expenditure *allocations* ranged between 13.5 and 18.5 per cent (Toyo, 1986: 236). This is, however, a misleading picture. As Bienen points out, the share of agriculture in the *total* resources committed towards the Second Development Plan, 1970–4, was 6 per cent, of which only 5.2 per cent of Plan expenditure was actually invested. The same figures for the Third Plan period, 1975–8, were 6.5 per cent and 2.5 per cent respectively (Bienen, 1985). Relative to other sectors of the economy, agricultural investment was neglected in the 1970s.

But even the little that was invested was directed at schemes of dubious value. There was the 'mass exhortation' programme, the Operation Feed the Nation (OFN), which expended much money and effort in getting ill-prepared university undergraduates to go to the rural areas to 'teach' the peasant farmers how to farm. Secondly, there was direct government involvement in production through programmes like the National Accelerated Food Production Programme, the National Livestock Production Company and the National Grains Production Company. Thirdly, massive irrigation schemes were constructed under the River Basin Development Authorities (RBDAs). Fourthly, World Bank-sponsored Integrated Rural Development Projects (IRDPs) were initiated in many parts of the country. Finally, there was the encouragement of private large-scale capitalist farming through the Agricultural Credit Guarantee

112

Scheme Fund, specialized agricultural banks to provide cheap loans to 'newbreed' farmers, generous tax regimes, the use of government bodies like the Grains Marketing Board to guarantee the profits of 'newbreed' farmers without providing any incentives for peasant farmers, and the Land Use Decree which established the legal framework for the appropriation of peasant lands.

All these schemes were united by two factors. Firstly, there was the implicit belief that the peasantry could no longer be relied upon for increased agricultural productivity. Secondly, all the schemes were underpinned by a naïve belief that the answers to the problems of the agrarian sector lay in the acquisition of large-scale and sophisticated modern technology. The human and societal dimensions of agrarian development, especially where these concerned the peasantry, were given inadequate consideration. Despite persistent proclamations of the state's commitment to smallholder agriculture, the reality implicit in numerous state policies was that the peasantry was no longer seen as a central agrarian force. The relative importance of the various sub-sectors of agriculture for much of the 1970s and the early 1980s is reflected in the distribution of the 1982 Federal government budget for agriculture: nearly 50 per cent went to irrigation, 16 per cent went to large farms and large-farm services, and only 17 per cent went to small-farm activities, including the IRDPs (Scherr, 1989: 557).

While the potential modernization of smallholder peasant agriculture has been stymied by state non-investment, and even over-taxation in the case of some crops, the large-scale state and private capitalist production which has absorbed the bulk of public sector resources did not show any signs of producing the desired results. The dismal results of the state's efforts at intervention in direct production are obvious. All the food 'production' companies survived on massive subsidies; none has ever produced anything of noteworthy quantity.

The situation with the RBDAs is similar. For example, the Peremabiri Rice Project of the Niger Delta RBDA produced rice nearly ten years after it was established, but at a cost of between N1,400 and N2,500 per bag of 70 kilograms, while selling the rice for around N50 per bag of 50 kilograms (Toyo, 1986: 246–7), possibly because, at around the same time, a 50 kilogram bag of rice could be obtained on the international market, at the official exchange rate, for about N30. Similarly, wheat produced by the RBDAs was six to eight times the cost of imported wheat (Andrae and Beckman, 1985: 126), and government subsidy per ton of wheat grown on many projects ranged from N57 to N220. Government officials claimed that the irrigation schemes in the country were capable of producing 300,000 tons of cereals and vegetables annually; but in 1981–2 they produced only 40,000 tons (Watts, 1983: 500). The RBDAs were managed by technocrats and 'planistrators', while the peasantry were simply expected to conform to their demands (Wallace, 1978/9).

Though the IRDPs were more peasant-oriented than the RBDAs, there was the same disinterest in peasant participation in policy formulation and implementation at any level. Under the scheme, which was partly financed with loans from the World Bank, feeder roads, earth dams and service centres for the distribution of subsidized inputs like fertilizer were built in rural areas. Other social infrastructure like bore-holes were also constructed. Some have argued that these IRDPs have had a generally positive impact on the rural areas (Adejo, 1983). Others point out that the Projects do not generate net returns on the investment, thereby casting a shadow over their capacity to generate long-term development (Williams, 1989). Others, still, have criticized the performance of the Projects, drawing attention to organizational lapses and policies of resource allocation which were detrimental to the interests of the bulk of the peasantry, because of a pronounced bias in favour of so-called 'progressive farmers' (Wallace, 1980; Ouoje and Baba, 1983).

The Projects have been of some benefit to the peasantry, for example in providing some infrastructure, and by introducing them to new inputs. And as Keynesians would rightly argue, any government expenditure in the rural areas is bound to generate some increased economic activity. But some healthy scepticism needs to be exercised when considering the long-term impact of these Projects, especially the long-term indebtedness of the country to the World Bank. Without doubt, however, the Projects have had a differential impact on the farming community, benefiting some more than others.

In 1979, the Green Revolution became state policy, complementing the RBDAs and the IRDPs. The fledgeling group of aspirant capitalist farmers were given a major boost. The 'newbreed' farmers benefited enormously from generous government packages which gave them access to cheap loans, land, technology and foreign exchange. For example, between 1979 and 1982 the poultry industry alone attracted a subsidy of N99 million under a single scheme (Alkali, 1985). Many senior civil and military officers, both in and out of office, used their access to the state to take advantage of the wide range of facilities committed to the Green Revolution. These bureaucrats-cum-farmers were also joined by many private businessmen.

Some 'newbreed' farmers are only interested in getting Certificates of Occupancy for large tracts of land. The land can then be used for speculative purposes, for example, as collateral for securing loans. Some of those who actually did farm often use inappropriate land-clearing machines, leading to environmental damage (World Bank, 1987). The operations of these capitalist farmers are very import-dependent; in the early 1980s, the poultry industry imported its maize, despite the fact that Nigeria produced this crop in abundance. Their profitability is also heavily dependent on special privileges bestowed by the state, and it is doubtful whether it will persist in the face of government cutbacks on subsidies, rising input costs, rising interest rates and serious problems of labour control. While these capitalist farms may have benefited some of those directly involved, they have failed to solve the problems of Nigerian agriculture.

Even if the newbreed farmers were to be successful, the resultant impact might be the development of 'functional dualism', in which the capitalist sector produces commodities with semi-proletarian peasant labour, while the peasant sector produces use-values, petty commodities from family labour and cheap wage labour for the capitalist farms. Such an outcome could lead to the collapse of the resource base controlled by the peasantry and this might, as in South Africa and parts of Latin America, lead to serious ecological and demographic pressures in the countryside, as the peasantry struggle to maximize their ability to eke out a living from a diminishing resource base (de Janvry, 1981; Williams, 1988). In Malawi, for example, a capitalist large-farm strategy has already immiserized the bulk of the peasantry, and led to a pattern of growth that is not robust and whose sustainability is problematic (Lele, 1989).

By 1985, the impulse towards large-scale capitalist farming was given a boost by the constraints imposed on the economy by the current economic crisis. Industrial firms took to farming, in efforts to secure a measure of backward integration. Others simply wanted to be seen to be responding positively to government initiatives, in the hope that that would give them access to scarce foreign exchange (Andrae and Beckman, 1987). Though recourse to plantation farming could secure the access of some firms to much-needed raw materials, the cost of production is high, and the pattern cannot be generalized for the whole of the agricultural sector. As in the case of large-scale private capitalist farms, there were social costs to be borne by the peasantry, who were often displaced to make way for plantations.[2]

The Agrarian Question in contemporary Nigeria, and current efforts to tackle it through the Structural Adjustment Programme (SAP), should, therefore, be seen as the result of the failures of policies since the 1970s.

II. Manifestations of the Agrarian Question in Nigeria

In its original conception, the Agrarian Question was a political question which confronted the parties of the Second International in Europe towards the end of the nineteenth century. These parties were contesting for power in societies with large peasant populations, a situation which confronted them with awkward questions, such as whether or not the peasantry was disappearing, and whether these parties should support peasant property. Thus in this period:

> The agrarian question was composed of a set of questions which the Social Democratic parties faced: how to win the electoral support of the peasantry, which section of the rural population should the party try to appeal to and on what basis? (Hussain and Tribe, 1983: 18)

From these origins, the Agrarian Question gradually expanded to acquire other related meanings. With Kautsky and Lenin, the focus shifted to the examination of the development of capitalism in agriculture: why does the form and pace of capitalist development differ in industry and agriculture? Why does the capitalist mode of production, despite its predominance, co-exist with pre-capitalist modes, and what is the impact of such a co-existence? With Lenin, however, the reference point was not Western Europe, but the relative backwardness of Tsarist Russia (Byres, 1986).

After the Russian Revolution, the term expanded yet again to include notions about the role of the peasantry in socialist society, in accumulation for industrialization, and the role of the kulaks within rural society. By the 1950s, the focus of the Agrarian Question shifted to reflect questions concerning the role of the peasantry in national liberation movements, in social revolutions and in agrarian struggles that are not connected to wider political struggles (Byres, 1986). In the contemporary African context, however, the meaning of the Agrarian Question needs to be further expanded to include issues relating to food security and rural immiserization.

In 1966, the Food and Agriculture Organization (FAO) hoped that in the 1970s Nigerian agriculture would provide an adequate and well-balanced food supply for the country, large export earnings, employment for additional millions and the capital resources for economic development, and would initiate the process of agricultural modernization (cit. Kungwai, 1985: 68). But by the mid-1970s, it was obvious that peasant smallholder agriculture was in crisis. The agricultural sector was now seen as an obstacle to development (Berry, 1985: 1). And from the perspective of those who controlled the Nigerian state, the root of the problem was seen as the obsolence of the peasantry. The costly results of that mistaken outlook have been briefly presented above.

From about 1970, therefore, the Agrarian Question has been reflected in Nigeria in the form of a food 'problem'. Whether or not that amounts to a 'crisis', and whether it is a crisis of declining production, is open to question. For example, Raza claims that between 1970 and 1978 Nigeria registered a negative annual increase in cereal grain yield of − 1.4 per cent (Raza, 1983). Similarly, USAID figures for 1970 to 1979 suggest that the index of per capita food production (1961/5 = 100) fell from 95 for 1970, through 87 in 1973, to 84 in 1979 (Watts, 1983: 6). Moreover, Watts claims that per capita food production in 1981 was 18 per cent below that of 1967–70, while the World Bank's projected food deficits for 1984 and 1990 are 6.6 and 10.6 million tons of staple foodstuffs respectively (Watts, 1987a: 71–2).

However, Beckman argues that the major thrust of development within Nigerian agriculture was not a decline in production, but the increased commercialization of the output (Beckman, 1983). Even the World Bank now admits that its estimates for the 1980s were wrong. Food production is now said to have been better than previously thought, and total production probably just kept up with population growth:

> It would appear that Nigeria's producers of sorghum, millet, cassava and yam have been able to provide basic caloric requirements, even as the work force shifts proportionally out of agriculture. The surge in production in the 1984/85 season under the stimulus of drought-induced high prices is a reminder of the potential responsiveness of the food crop farmers. But they have not been able to satisfy the demand from an increasingly urbanized public for wheat and rice and convenient preparations of all starchy foodstuff, tastes that have been greatly enhanced by the very low prices of these imported grains. (World Bank, 1987: 2, 43 and 44)

Thus, a major aspect of the food 'problem' is the creation of new tastes which fuelled a massive food import bill.

But the intensification of demands for imported crops like wheat was only part of a much wider problem militating against the achievement of sustained growth and profitability in local food production. Local food prices were also depressed by cheaper imports based on an over-valued currency. At the same time, rural labour costs rose sharply due to increased urban demands for labour as a consequence of the oil-boom. Increased inflation fed into increased input costs.

A second manifestation of the Agrarian Question in Nigeria is the persistence of rural poverty which is reflected in the poorer quality of life in rural areas relative to urban areas. This situation is illustrated by the high infant mortality rate in rural Nigeria, which, in 1983/4, was 183 deaths per thousand, nearly double the urban infant mortality rate of 92 per thousand (*The Nigerian Household*, 1985: 15). These depressing statistics are reflected in the sense of gloom in parts of rural Kwara State (Atte, 1983). Studies in rural Kano State also revealed a high degree of dissatisfaction with the quality of rural infrastructure (Voh, 1983). World Bank figures indicate that rural *real* wages in southern Nigeria fell from an index of 100 in 1983, to 82.5 in 1985. Similarly, the *real* incomes of rural households in the country fell from an index of 100 in 1980/1, to 78 in 1985/6.[3]

III. State Failure and the Agrarian Question

Central to the resolution of the Agrarian Question in Africa is the nature of the state. It is not a simple technical matter of finding the most appropriate technological and financial packages with which to rescue the agrarian sector; at the heart of the problem are political questions about the allocative efficiency of the state, the control of economic resources and the monopolization of political and economic power (Hart, 1982: 166; Dearlove and White, 1987; Brett, 1987, 1988). These political issues emphasize the crucial role of an efficient state in the resolution of the Agrarian Question. But in many parts of Africa, the role of the state in agrarian development is not only crucial, it is also contradictory (Hart, 1982: 14 and 99).

This contradictoriness is expressed in the centrality of state policy in shaping the direction of agrarian change, and the apparent irrational allocation of developmental and agrarian resources. Addressing the same problem, the World Bank stated:

The central issue in the emerging debate about Africa's agricultural crisis is not about methods of cultivation or the changes which need to be made to them. . . . It is not, in a real sense, about agriculture at all. The essence of the problem lies elsewhere, in an all-pervasive scepticism about the only social mechanism capable of responding to the situation in both the short and the longer run. There is a problem about the state in Africa: it doesn't work. What was once seen as the solution is now the problem. (Cit. Mars, 1986: 16)

From this standpoint, the numerous examples of state 'irrationality' in Africa have raised 'an unresolved question mark' about what can be done with African agriculture (cit. Mars, 1986: 16). An understanding of the workings of the African state is therefore important for the appreciation of the conditions necessary for the resolution of the Agrarian Question.

The crises of the contemporary African state have been subjected to intense analyses. Four broad schools of thought can be identified, each with its own peculiar emphasis on the nature of the problem and the possibilities of a solution.[4] The first position, put forward by Sandbrook, emphasizes the 'neo-patrimonial' nature of African states, dominated by 'patrician' leaders. Personal rule is said to lead to the strengthening of communal ties, ethnic conflicts, corruption and political violence. The spiral of political decay in turn leads to state irrationality and economic deterioration. The answer to the problem is seen as a benevolent personal rule which is able to reorganize the state and restore a measure of rationality to the management of the development process (cf. Sandbrook, 1985).

The second school of thought, evident in Bates's work, emphasizes the monopolization of power by a larger social group: the inheritors of the colonial state. Bates draws attention to the pursuit of narrow self-interest by this political élite, and the disastrous economic consequences of their grip on the post-colonial state (Bates, 1981). Similarly, Dutkiewicz, writing with Shenton, sees the agrarian crisis of Africa as one other dimension of the crises of the state in Africa. They argue that the root of the crises lies in the appropriation and misallocation of resources by the 'ruling group' state. The interests of this ruling group are in stark contradiction to the reproductive needs of the peasantry, leading to a crisis of diminished reproduction in the society as a whole. In future, the 'ruling group' states with some geo-political value may be propped up from the outside; others will have to reorder the state in order to permit capitalist accumulation. The nature of the reordering is not specified. Failure to reorder the state may lead to it becoming the international equivalent of the long-term 'structurally unemployed' (Dutkiewicz and Shenton, 1986). Drawing on the experience of Poland, Dutkiewicz, in an article with Williams, adds that the vicious circles of economic decline and political instability are unlikely to be broken by reforms from 'above' or 'below', leading to the self-perpetuation of the crises (Dutkiewicz and Williams, 1987). The decaying state system in Africa is seen as a 'humpty dumpty' case which cannot be put together again.

The third approach tries to locate the crises of the African state within the context of problems of social organizations. Mars argues that the problem of the African state is not to be located in class or cultural conflicts *per se*, but in theories of organization:

That agenda locates the potential for pathology in the fact of organisation itself, not in the delusions, venality and incompetence of individuals. It is a critique which is ruthless about the potential consequences of wrong organisational choices. (Mars, 1986: 19)

Mars argues that organizations confer great benefits on society, but there are also dangers of 'organisational failure', for it cannot be assumed that the Weberian model of rational bureaucracy can just be transplanted to Africa like 'some startling technological device', and then be expected to function properly in an unproblematic manner. Formal organizations displace some of the ability of individuals to choose and act; organizational values displace individual values, and organizational rationality and knowledge displace individual rationality and knowledge. But these organizations can fail, and also have the capacity to perpetuate failure by creating one problem in order to solve a previous one. Failure can therefore be cumulative. Organizations can maintain themselves, but when failure sets in, then a gradual 'organisational decline' takes place.

The African state is seen by Mars as a chain of linked organizational relationships; between the politicians and the administrators, the administrators and the technocrats, and between them all and the people. The problem of the African state is located in the problems involved in the articulation of the 'critical joints' which link all the parts of the African state together. But these problems are also seen as problems inherent in the twentieth-century state:

> Africa is not the only place with a shrinking, dying political arena, systems of personal rule, large, blundering, pointless bureaucracies, increasing authoritarianism in the face of state failure, inability to cope with the world market and a loss of coherent public purpose. (Mars, 1986: 21)

Klitgaard adopts a similar organizational approach to the problem of state failure in Africa, but he is concerned largely with the impact of the current economic crises on the African state. He argues that the economic crises have led to a situation in which drastic cuts in budget deficits are carried out and massive cuts in real wages imposed. Consequently, public sector wages have fallen too low, and it is increasingly impossible to attract and maintain the needed talent in state bureaucracies:

> As a consequence, the incentives facing public employees erode. This results in brain drain, inefficiency, moonlighting, demoralisation, and corruption. As these phenomena become generalized, government starts to break down. . . . The business of government shifts from development to predation. (Klitgaard, 1989: 448)

Mars suggests the need to reconstitute and democratize the African state, so that the peasantry and other classes can better impress their needs on the state, while Klitgaard argues for better incentives for public servants.

The fourth view emphasizes the comprador nature of the African ruling classes and the states they control. It is a nationalist anti-imperialist critique which argues that the African ruling classes are hirelings of external interests. The corruption and mismanagement observed in African states are therefore seen as an accumulation process in favour of an external bourgeoisie, at the expense of the interests of the nation (Mamdani and Wamba-dia-Wamba, 1987; Beckman, 1988).

Some of these views on state failure in the wider African setting are to be found in the analyses of the Nigerian state. Many titles by Nigerian writers aptly convey the deep disillusionment with the hopeless performance of the Nigerian state (Adeniyi, 1976; Achebe, 1983; Sanda, 1985; Randle, 1985). Similar views have informed the analyses of the particular role of the Nigerian state in the agrarian sector.

Berry, leaning towards the monopolistic theory, argues that exploitation in western Nigeria is not so much through the labour market, as through the monopolization of government office, contracts and licences. Corruption is seen, not as an ethical matter, but as a mechanism of resource allocation and control. The struggle for access leads to constantly shifting alliances which in turn contribute to political instability, the strengthening of ethnic and communal ties and the wastage of resources in the unproductive construction of political monuments and conspicuous consumption by the ruling class. Because of the over-taxation and subsequent neglect of agriculture, cocoa farmers and their sons abandon agriculture for artisanal jobs in the urban centres. The expansion of these trades is not matched by improved productivity because of problems of labour control and the centrality of patronage in the acquisition of custom. A vicious circle of the frantic expansion of non-productive activities is therefore set in motion, ultimately undermining the productive basis of the society (Berry, 1985).

Tiffen, in her earlier study of Gombe, noted that the co-operative movement failed because of political interference. Furthermore, she states that government involvement in economic activity is likely to lead to corruption and the wastage of resources. The operations of market forces are likely to produce better results (Tiffen, 1976).

Watts, expressing aspects of the comprador theory, sees the Nigerian state as a rentier state, fractured, segmented and a blockage to systematic accumulation based on the development of the productive forces. He argues that, while commerce and finance may survive the arbitrariness of patrimonial rule, massive state indiscipline, bureaucratic irrationality and corruption combine to prevent the development of industrial and agrarian capitalism. The entire state structure is seen as weak, presumably because it is dominated by 'drone capitalists' (Watts, 1987a: 68, 1987b).

Most of these analyses accurately describe state failure in Nigeria. However, they fail to reveal salient aspects of the social drama they seek to explain. These aspects have been well summarized by Beckman as a failure to take account of the underlying process of accumulation within the context of state failure, lack of attention to the attendant process of bourgeois class formation, and the absence of any consideration for the role of subordinate classes in the shaping of the nature of the state (cf. Beckman, 1988).

Brett points out, for instance, that the monopolization of power and the 'irrational' management of state resources in Africa might not be unconnected to the building of a material base for the petty-bourgeoisie that took control of many African states at independence. He suggests that political failure may be part of a wider process of primitive accumulation in which gains are made by a few at the expense of the political integrity and economic coherence of the polity as a whole (Brett, 1986). The same argument is forcefully made for Nigeria by Toyo (1985) and by Iyayi (1986).

Studies of Nigeria's agriculture reveal this connection between economic 'irrationality' and primitive accumulation. Palmer-Jones points out that though the irrigation schemes may be wasteful of national resources, they nevertheless operate to the economic and political aggrandizement of powerful segments of the Nigerian ruling class (Palmer-Jones, 1987; Watts, 1983: 498). Even the more peasant-oriented IRDPs have had a differential impact on the peasantry, favouring capitalist farmers and rich peasants at the expense of the bulk of the peasantry (Forrest, 1985). These policies and processes initiated by the state have therefore contributed to the emergence of capitalist farmers from 'above' (cf. Alkali, 1985) and from within the peasantry itself.

The failure to analyse state failure and primitive accumulation in Africa as two sides of the same coin leads to the dismissal of the local bourgeoisie as 'drone capitalists' or compradors, and therefore no serious attention is paid to the implications for the state of the need of the local bourgeoisie to exercise power and hegemony. All too frequently, the local bourgeoisie is only presented as a divided bunch of squabbling ethnic ideologues, prone to corruption, political violence and electoral chicanery.

There is, however, another side to the local bourgeoisie. As Olukoshi aptly demonstrates, they have also been able to engage in commercial, speculative and industrial accumulation to build up a formidable material base, albeit one still subordinated to external influence (Olukoshi, 1986). Hodd also suggests, with the aid of econometric models, that the current international offensive for privatization of state assets in Africa is consistent with the needs of many African ruling classes who have accumulated capital through primitive accumulation, and now hope to reap even greater benefits through the operation of more 'rational' market forces (Hodd, 1988). Beckman suggests that this local bourgeoisie must be taken seriously, if the ramifications of state failure are fully to be understood. Finally, the resistance of subordinate classes to the predatory activities of the state and the ruling class should constitute an aspect of the analyses of the African state, for political reality is not the sole preserve of victors and rulers (Shanin, 1989: 359; Moore, 1989; Mamdani and Wamba-dia-Wamba, 1987).

IV. Beyond the State: The Market and the Agrarian Question

In recognition of the failure of agricultural policies since the 1970s, and in the face of a major economic crisis which started in 1978, but intensified in 1982, the Nigerian state has resorted to a Structural Adjustment Programme (SAP) whose very introduction is cause for contemplation about the Agrarian Question and the market principle in contemporary Nigeria. Can the market be an answer to the problem of state failure? Given the Nigerian situation, can the market be used to allocate resources in a more efficient manner than has hitherto been the case?

In October 1985, the Nigerian government enacted a National Economic Emergency Decree under which the military junta took on powers to reduce wages and salaries, remove subsidies on petroleum, ban the importation of some commodities and suspend non-essential projects. In July 1986, the SAP was introduced. The policy package included the managed floating of the naira, the liberalization of the trading and financial sectors of the economy, deregulation, reduction of bureaucratic control of the economy, removal of subsidies, reform and rationalization of tariffs, demand management, stimulation of production and privatization. It was hoped that these measures would not only restructure the economy, but also stabilize it and provide a framework for growth.

In the agricultural sector, SAP policies aimed to remove problems perceived to be emanating from state intervention. These were seen as high levels of subsidies, high overhead costs on government projects, high levels of food imports, inappropriate product and factors prices and terms of trade that were unfavourable to agriculture. The SAP package therefore included currency devaluation and import restrictions on some agricultural commodities in order to stimulate internal output, reduction of state regulation and increased dependence on market forces. The six commodity boards were disbanded, thereby abolishing state involvement in produce pricing and marketing. The RBDAs were reduced from 18 to 11, government-owned agro-based companies were disbanded and subsidies on inputs slashed (Usoro, 1987).

It is as yet unclear what the full and long-term impact of SAP will be on the agrarian sector. However, from available evidence, it seems that the policy package has led to increases in food production. But this apparent increase has been accompanied by a paradoxically upward spiral in food prices. Hikes in food prices have been of such proportions that the food security and nutritional standards of rural and urban households have been compromised or even threatened. Many Nigerian newspapers recently complained about the 'spectre of famine' which some of them described as a 'most frightening social epidemic', and instances of malnutrition and kwashiorkor amongst children are reported to be on the increase. Even the government, committed as it is to market-regulation of the economy, was obliged to introduce a law threatening food exporters with life imprisonment and the seizure of all their assets (Phillips, 1987; Mustapha, 1989).

The paradox of increased food production and a simultaneous threat to the basic food security of many households can be explained by the structural relationships within the economy. The economic crisis and the continuing foreign exchange shortage have intensified the trading of Nigerian agricultural produce in the parallel markets of neighbouring countries belonging to the convertible CFA Franc zone. For instance, Niger Republic, in the Sahel, is said to be exporting cocoa.[5] In addition, the export of Nigerian staples, such as guineacorn, to Niger has intensified. Increased agricultural productivity, under SAP, does not necessarily translate into improved nutritional standards.[6]

Furthermore, there is no guarantee that the modest increases in production registered under SAP can be sustained on a long-term basis. High input costs have reduced the use of fertilizers in cultivation, and the current increases in production are largely due to more extensive, rather than intensive, methods (Titilola, 1987). Historically, a major structural problem in Nigerian agriculture has been the need for the raising of productivity through the intensification of cultivation. For example, in 1977, chemical fertilizer usage in Nigeria was estimated at only 3.4 kg/per hectare, while the same figures for the rest of Africa and for the world as a whole were 13 kg/per hectare and 69 kg/per hectare respectively (Bienen, 1985: 50). By lowering this level further, the monetarist SAP policies have succeeded in solving the short-term budgetary problem of balancing the books at the expense of the longer-term structural needs of Nigerian agriculture. The net benefits to be derived from such a policy must remain in doubt. Already, production costs for some crops like maize are now so high, due to increased input costs, that they may no longer be profitable (Usoro, 1987).

Another impact of SAP has been to raise the cost of loans due to the deregulation of interest rates. This may have served the useful purpose of making the 'newbreed' farmers bear the full costs of their operations. Already, some ex-Generals are reported to have put their farms up for sale, while others are reported to be in serious financial difficulty. But this might also make it more difficult for small and medium farms to gain access to needed institutional loans and might cripple much-needed long-term investment in agriculture.[7]

The major positive impact of the SAP policies to date has been the increase in cocoa prices paid to farmers. The area under cocoa cultivation is said to have expanded by 30 per cent between 1987 and 1989. Output is argued to have shown an upward trend during the same period (Scott, 1989). Though cocoa prices picked up from N1,000 to about N9,000 (*West Africa*, 13–19 November 1989: 1902), many problems emerged in the new cocoa marketing system. 'Cowboy' traders have gone into cocoa marketing principally with an eye to exporting their capital which had been tied up in the country due to the foreign exchange shortage. Deregulation of cocoa marketing also led, for a while in 1986/7, to the abolition of produce inspection. Consequently, adulterated and under-weight cocoa from Nigeria found its way on to the world market, which consequently considered imposing a boycott on Nigerian cocoa (*West Africa*: 13–19 November 1989: 1902). By contrast, in Ghana, where government controls were only relaxed, and prices raised, cocoa exports were boosted, and smuggling reduced (Van Hear, 1989: 23).

In March 1989, cocoa was being bought in Nigeria for sums equivalent to US$3,773 per tonne, while the world market price was just around US$1,400 per tonne (Van

Hear, 1989: 23). This speculative trading in cocoa has introduced a serious volatility into the market and raises questions about the sustainability of prices sufficiently high to encourage cocoa farmers to maintain the long-term investments needed for the rehabilitation of the cocoa industry. Already, there are signs that the cocoa 'boom' has gone bust:

> Hisses, sighs, abuses, curses – all sum up the angry mood of the Ondo state cocoa farmer. His mood is a sign . . . of a boom gone bust [sic], a tragic reversal in fortunes. Now farm hands are hungry. Farmers are bankrupt. Creditors are unpaid. (Oguntayo, 1990: 43)

Escalating input costs, high labour costs, hyper-inflation and an all-time low price for cocoa on the world market have all contributed to depress real cocoa prices below pre-SAP levels (Oguntayo, 1990: 44). The negative effects of deregulation in the cocoa industry have led to a limited intervention in production and trading by the Ondo State government. Some effort is made at providing subsidized inputs, and an edict has been passed restricting the free movement of cocoa. The government is also actively engaged in attempts by established cocoa traders to fix cocoa prices at 'reasonable' levels.[8] Nigerian economists are claiming that, in the Nigerian context, the reliance on the market may not produce the desired results (Phillips, 1987). This failure is illustrated by the *ad hoc* interventions by governments aimed at redressing some of the worst dimensions of market operations.

It would seem, however, that the impact of SAP on Nigerian agriculture so far is a partial return to the colonial economic arrangement under which concern was for balancing the budget, at the expense of any consideration for development. This outlook is marked by extensive rather than intensive methods of increasing productivity, and might be inappropriate for the needs of a developing country in these modern times. Given the possible impact of biotechnology and genetic engineering on world agriculture through such processes as cloning of high-yielding oil-palms in Malaysia and the tissue-culture production of cocoa in factory farms, and the changing patterns of demand for raw materials, it is doubtful whether such a strategy can adequately meet the demands of the world market, or even the challenges of producing relatively competitively priced wage goods for the Nigerian market (Meagher, 1990).

Thus, contemporary Nigerian agricultural policy is characterized by the contradictory impulses towards marketization, and some measure of continued government intervention. This contradiction might not be unconnected to the fact that the ideology of privatization and marketization is not home-grown; it is basically an imposition by the IMF and the World Bank on an essentially statist army and bureaucracy. While marketization creates problems in the agricultural sector, *ad hoc* interventionist attempts made to correct these problems also create the conditions for continued state failure.

The new bureaucracy set up by the Federal Government to renew the drive towards rural development, the Directorate of Food, Roads and Rural Infrastructure (DFRRI), has been plagued by massive corruption and the misdirection of resources. A report on the activities of DFRRI in Anambra State by a monitoring team discovered that it had been misusing public funds and filing false reports about its activities:

> The team . . . was told by DFRRI officials in Enugu, that 360 communities had been supplied with portable water at a cost of N5.322m. But, after a 10-day tour of the 14 local government areas, the team discovered that 64 of the communities listed as beneficiaries were non-existent, and 153 had no functioning water scheme as claimed. (*West Africa*, 17–23 July 1989: 1187)

Other monitoring teams discovered similar situations in other states.[9] The resultant revelations have forced the Chairman of DFRRI to concede that his organization wastes public funds. He said 'there are those who believe that the measure of their success is the amount of public funds they spend, irrespective of what it was spent on, why, and the results achieved' (Koinyan, 1990: 16). Similarly, the much-talked-about attempt by the Kano State government to promote the cultivation of wheat has led to the wasteful procurement of expensive but inappropriate combine-harvesters and racketeering in subsidized wheat inputs.

Apparently, there is a continuation of state failure, at the same time as the poor are increasingly exposed to the rigours of marketization. Furthermore, the long-term dependence of SAP policies on export-led development might give additional cause for concern. The failure of development in Africa is rightly seen by many as a failure of the import-substitution strategy which squeezed resources from the peasantry but put little of it back to improve rural productivity and welfare. But the strategy of export-led development may also not lead to long-term development. Instead, the economic dislocations caused by SAP, the volatility of the currency, the severe cost-induced infla-tion, the massive constriction in effective demand and the attendant political and social tensions have all contributed to capital flight. As a Nigerian banker put it: 'SAP anticipated that financial good manners will necessarily encourage an influx of foreign investors. Wrong . . . [L]ack of capital inflow has thrown SAP completely off-balance' (Balogun, 1988: 34).

In the same vein, the rosy picture of SAP painted by World Bank economists (Tallroth, 1987) is now under strain. The World Bank chief economist for Africa has conceded that: 'We did not think that the human costs of these programs could be so great, and economic gains so slow in coming' (*Globe and Mail*, Toronto, 22 June 1988, cit. Bienefeld, 1988). Reviewing the experience of liberalization in African food marketing so far, Kydd and Scarborough point out that:

> It is clear that there was a need for change in African food marketing systems. However, having assessed the origins and progress of liberalization, it is apparent that the early enthusiasm for this policy needs to be tempered in the light of experience. Expectations of easy and speedy implementation, and immediate and unambiguously positive effects, were the result of simplistic analysis. (Kydd and Scarborough, 1988: 25)

Even World Bank economists are now said to doubt the wisdom of removing the state completely from cocoa marketing: 'Just leaving it to the private sector may not be good enough' (cit. Van Hear, 1989).

In all probability, the increasing reliance on market-regulation and export-promotion is likely to bring only very short-term relief. After many years of 'structural adjust-ment', many countries are worse off than when they started (cf. Bienefeld, 1988). The IMF 'show-piece', Ghana, is no exception. If Africa is not simply to 'adjust' herself to perpetual underdevelopment, there is still the need for an effective developmental state which addresses the twin issues of economic rationality and political accountability. It must be recognized that 'there is no independent sphere of economic rationality bounded by market exchange and fully explicable through a series of equilibrium equa-tions based upon assumptions of individualistic exchange relations' (Brett, 1987: 37).

V. Beyond the Market: Towards the Complementarity of State and Market

The new monetarist orthodoxy is a challenge to Keynesian economists who tended to emphasize market failure. These Keynesians also assumed that governments in a democratic society would play a benevolent role by intervening in the operations of the market to safeguard the public good. The monetarists, on the other hand, emphasize political failure, the 'wickedness' of governments and the unquestioned efficiency of the market (Dearlove, 1987). State failure in Africa and the dependence of crisis-ridden African states on Western financial assistance have turned these canons of monetarist ideology into the prevailing trend in many African countries. But as this chapter has tried to argue, the logic of the market may not adequately address the developmental needs of African countries.

It is therefore important to emphasize Dearlove's warning that there is a danger in mechanically counterposing the realistic views of the vices of the state with an idealized view of the alleged virtues of the market. The lessons of the Nigerian SAP so far are that, even where states have failed, developmental needs cannot be served by simply turning to the market. SAP policies are predicated on the assumption that the problems in agriculture derive solely from 'internal constraints' on market operations. But this is only one aspect of a much wider issue, as there are other equally important long-term structural dimensions to be considered: first, food self-sufficiency, comparative advantage in crop production or different blends of both; secondly, the desirability of promoting regional specialization; thirdly, the choice between cheap-food policies which lead to food imports or the encouragement of the development of capitalism in agriculture by allowing food prices to rise, thereby providing an incentive for local production; fourthly, the encouragement of land-saving or labour-saving technologies; and finally, the use and reproduction of the peasantry as a source of cheap food (de Janvry, 1981: 158).

All these fundamental and structural dimensions of a national agricultural policy are ignored by the current SAP policy which is based on the implicit assumption that the workings of the market, coupled with the dynamics of comparative advantage, will produce optimum returns to the country. This mistaken viewpoint may only serve the purpose of tying Nigerian development to the needs of external interests, such as those of American grain farmers.[10] Already the US government is threatening a trade embargo against Nigeria for banning wheat imports. When comparative advantages are not natural, but are historically acquired through relative advances in productivity, they tend to preserve the *status quo* in the international division of labour by keeping low-productivity activities in the periphery (de Janvry, 1981: 161). Thus, while comparative advantage may lead to short-term gains, it may also establish durable foundations for the deepening of underdevelopment.

Current trends in world market terms of trade suggest that the long-term dangers of a strategy of comparative advantages are real. For example, in spite of massive increases in coffee prices, it cost Latin American countries 160 bags to buy a tractor in 1960, but by 1977, the same tractor cost 400 bags (de Janvry, 1981: 161). And the World Bank price index for non-fuel commodities registered a fall from 100 in 1979/81 to 91 in 1989 (*West Africa*, 13–19 November 1989: 1902).

What is needed to address the Agrarian Question, therefore, is a comprehensive strategy which considers the roles of *both* the state *and* the market, and which is equally sensitive to the needs of economic rationality, political accountability, long-term stability, *welfare* and *growth*. This implies the transcendence of market fetishism.

To address these issues, and to respond to the continuation of state failure in spite of SAP, it is necessary to reconstitute and democratize the Nigerian state:

> This may involve a move away from Weberian principles of 'rational' bureaucracy. . . . The central focus would be on the question of *restructuring the state*, devising new institutional forms and methods of intervention which may serve to reduce its bureaucratised power and well-established developmental deficiencies. (Dearlove and White, 1987: 3)

Perestroika (economic restructuring) in Africa must be accompanied by *glasnost* (openness and democracy) if any progress is to be possible.

Unfortunately, in Nigeria, when we look beyond official rhetoric, we discover that neither the current military regime, nor its Transitional Programme, is providing the needed impetus towards such a democratization (Mustapha, 1990).

It must, however, be borne in mind that even the successful operation of the fabled market will depend upon the effectiveness of the state in building and maintaining market institutions. It will also be necessary to check any tendencies towards market monopolization, which is as real, and as dysfunctional, as the monopolization of power within the state (Reusse, 1987; Kydd and Scarborough, 1988; Lele and Christiansen, 1988). Furthermore, the operation of comparative advantage which is central to the monetarist case will need some long-term investments, which might mean a systematic departure from current market signals (Bienefeld, 1986). It is this developmental state that will ensure that the unprofitable aspects of rural and agrarian life – infrastructure and inputs in remote areas – are maintained in the face of possible reluctance by capital to take risks (Christiansen, 1989). The IMF-supported market-oriented policies *also* have no hope of success unless the question of state failure, in all its ramifications, is addressed in Nigeria.

Thus the Agrarian Question in Nigeria poses a fundamental challenge concerning the need to restructure and democratize the Nigerian state, such that it will not only confront the problem of short-term economic rationality and the efficient operation of markets, but also incorporate a strategy for long-term *growth, development, welfare, equity* and *accountability*. Not to do so would amount to abdicating its responsibilities in the face of the human predicament confronting the country.

Notes

1. The Farm Settlement Schemes of the 1960s were a complete disaster, but they are not part of the concerns of this study.
2. For example, the case involving the acquisition of peasant lands by a company called *Al-Hilal* in Muri Emirate of Gongola State. Claims and counter-claims over the payment of compensation for the land ultimately led to a major political crisis which saw the dismissal of the Emir of Muri and the removal of the State Governor.
3. World Bank, 1987: 57 and 60. These figures are also based on unreliable statistics collected by the FOS.
4. For a review of three of the schools see Beckman, 1988.
5. For the analysis of the parallel market and its impact on food supplies, see Meagher, 1989.
6. Another reason driving up food prices under SAP is the increased industrial use of food staples, as the drive for local sourcing intensifies. Guineacorn, traditionally a 'food' crop, is now widely used in the brewing industry.
7. In Chile the raising of interest rates by the monetarist 'Chicago boys' forced many smallholders to sell off their farms. (Scott, 1989.)
8. Another recent government intervention stipulates that, as from the end of 1991, only semi-processed

cocoa can be exported. This decision was, however, reversed in late 1990 in the face of spirited opposition by cocoa farmers and traders.
9. Cf. Ibrahim, 1989. And for a criticism of widespread corruption in the general implementation of SAP, see Ayagi, 1988.
10. 'The Williams Report [US government document] . . . elaborates a plan for reorganization of Third World agriculture in the emerging new world structure. The report explicitly recommended that peripheral countries apply their comparative advantage to the production of labor-intensive crops . . . for export and thus earn foreign exchange with which to finance their balance of payments and import cheaper US grain' (de Janvry, 1981: 179).

References

C. Achebe (1983), *The Trouble with Nigeria*. London: Heinemann.
A. Adejo (1983), 'The Impact of Agricultural Development Projects on Quality of Life in Rural Areas', in U. Igbozurike and R. Raza (eds), *Rural Nigeria: Development and Quality of Life*, ARMTI Seminar Series, no. 3. Ilorin.
T. Adeniyi (1976), *The Lunatic: Epitome of our Golden Age*. Ibadan: Deto Deni Productions.
R. Alkali (1985), 'United States Multinationals in Nigeria's Agriculture: A Case Study of Poultry Industry in Kaduna State', M.Sc. thesis. Zaria: Postgraduate School, ABU.
G. Andrae and B. Beckman (1985), *The Wheat Trap*. London: Zed.
—— (1987), *Industry Goes Farming: The Nigerian Raw Material Crisis and the Case of Textiles and Cotton*. Uppsala: Scandinavian Institute of African Studies.
O. Atte (1983), 'From Inside Looking Out: An Emic Perspective of Life Quality in Rural Nigeria, A Case Study from Kwara State, Nigeria', in U. Igbozurike and R. Raza (eds), *Rural Nigeria: Development and Quality of Life*. ARMTI Seminar Series, no. 3. Ilorin.
I. Ayagi (1988), 'Who is SAP for?', *New Nigerian*, 19–21 January.
A. Balogun (1988), 'The Nigerian Economy Today', *Platform*, December.
R. Bates (1981), *Markets and States in Tropical Africa. The Political Basis of Agricultural Policies*. Berkeley: University of California Press.
B. Beckman (1983), 'Public Investment and Agrarian Transformation in Northern Nigeria'. CSER Reprint no. 13. Zaria: ABU.
—— (1988), 'The Post-Colonial States: Crisis and Reconstruction', *IDS Bulletin*, vol. 19, no. 4.
S. Berry (1985), *Fathers Work for Their Sons: Accumulation, Mobility and Class Formation in an Extended Yoruba Community*. Berkeley: University of California Press.
M. Bienefeld (1986), 'Analysing the Politics of African State Policy: Some Thoughts on Robert Bates' Work', *IDS Bulletin*, vol. 17, no. 2.
—— (1988), 'Karl Polanyi's *Lessons of History* and the Present Crisis in the Developing World' (mimeo).
H. Bienen (1985), *Political Conflict and Economic Change in Nigeria*. London: Frank Cass.
E. Brett (1986), 'State Power and Economic Inefficiency: Explaining Political Failure in Africa', *IDS Bulletin*, vol. 17, no. 1.
—— (1987), 'States, Markets and Private Power in the Developing World: Problems and Possibilities', *IDS Bulletin*, vol. 18, no. 3.
—— (1988), 'Introduction', *IDS Bulletin*, vol. 19, no. 4.
T. Byres (1986), 'The Agrarian Question and Differentiation of the Peasantry'. Foreword to A. Rahman, *Peasants and Classes: A Study in Differentiation in Bangladesh*. London: Zed.
R. Christiansen (1989), 'Editor's Introduction', *World Development*, vol. 17, no. 4.
J. Dearlove (1987), 'Economists on the State', *IDS Bulletin*, vol. 18, no. 3.
—— and G. White (1987), 'Editorial Introduction', *IDS Bulletin*, vol. 18, no. 3.
P. Dutkiewicz and R. Shenton (1986), 'Étatisation and the Logic of Diminished Reproducton', *Review of African Political Economy*, no. 37.
P. Dutkiewicz and G. Williams (1987), 'All the King's Horses and All the King's Men couldn't put Humpty-Dumpty Together Again', *IDS Bulletin*, vol. 18, no. 3.
T. Forrest (1985), 'Agricultural Problems in Nigeria: 1900–1978', in *Rural Underdevelopment in Nigeria: 1900–1978*. Department of Political Science Seminar, vol. 2. Zaria: ABU.
K. Hart (1982), *The Political Economy of West African Agriculture*. Cambridge: Cambridge University Press.
M. Hodd (1988), 'The Political Economy of the Liberalising Society: Africa in the 1980s' (mimeo). ASAUK Conference. Cambridge.
A. Hussain and K. Tribe (1983), *Marxism and the Agrarian Question*. 2nd edn. London: Macmillan.
J. Ibrahim (1989), 'Succession Politique et Crispation Sociale au Nigeria' (mimeo). Bordeaux: CEAN.
F. Iyayi (1986), 'The Primitive Accumulation of Capital in a Neo-Colony: The Nigerian Case', *Review of African Political Economy*, no. 35.

A. de Janvry (1981), *The Agrarian Question and Reformism in Latin America*. Baltimore: Johns Hopkins Press.

R. Klitgaard (1989), 'Incentive Myopia', *World Development*, vol. 17, no. 4.

Air Vice Marshal Koinyan (1990), Cited in *The Democrat*, 12 February.

N. Kungwai (1985), 'The Agrarian Crisis in Nigeria Today', in *Rural Underdevelopment in Nigeria: 1900–1978*. Department of Political Science Seminar, vol. 2. Zaria: ABU.

J. Kydd and V. Scarborough (1988), 'Food Market Liberalization in Sub-Saharan Africa: A Survey of the Issues' (mimeo). Brighton.

U. Lele (1989), Public lecture. IDS, University of Sussex. 23 February.

—— and R. Christiansen (1988), 'Marketing, Marketing Boards and Cooperatives', *MAIDA*, October.

M. Mamdani and Wamba-dia-Wamba (1987), 'Social Movements, Social Transformation, Democracy and Development in Africa', *NILS*, nos 32–3.

T. Mars (1986), 'State and Agriculture in Africa: A Case of Means and Ends', *IDS Bulletin*, vol. 17, no. 1.

K. Meagher (1989), 'A Vent for Shortage: The Development of Parallel Trade in Northern Nigeria'. M.Phil. thesis. IDS, University of Sussex.

—— (1990), 'Institutionalising the Bio-Revolution: Implications for Nigerian Smallholders', *Journal of Peasant Studies*, April.

B. Moore Jr (1989), 'Revolutions of the Oppressed: A Case Made', in T. Shanin (ed.), *Peasants and Peasant Societies*, 2nd edn. Oxford: Blackwell.

A. Mustapha (1989), 'Peasantry, State, Market Forces, and the Agrarian Question in Nigeria' (mimeo). Workshop on Nigeria since the Civil War. St Peter's College, Oxford.

—— (1990), 'Peasant Differentiation and Politics in Rural Kano: 1900–1987'. D.Phil. thesis. Oxford University.

The Nigerian Household, 1983/1984 (1985), Lagos: Federal Office of Statistics. December.

A. Oguntayo (1990), 'Riches to Rags', *African Concord*, 5 February.

A. Olukoshi (1986), 'The Multinational Corporation and Industrialisation in Northern Nigeria: A Case Study of Kano, c.1903–1985'. Ph.D. thesis. University of Leeds.

J. Ouoje and J. Baba (1983), 'The Impact of the Ayangba Agricultural Development Project on the Quality of Rural Life', in U. Igbozurike and R. Raza (eds), *Rural Nigeria: Development and Quality of Life*. ARMTI Seminar Series, no. 3. Ilorin.

R. Palmer-Jones (1987), 'Irrigation and the Politics of Agricultural Development in Nigeria', in M. Watts (ed.), *State, Oil and Agriculture in Nigeria*. Berkeley: University of California Press.

A. Phillips (1987), 'A General Overview of the Structural Adjustment Programme', in A. Phillips and E. Ndekwu (eds), *Structural Adjustment Programme in a Developing Economy: The Case of Nigeria*. Ibadan: NISER.

J. Randle (1985), *Who is Fooling Who?* Lagos.

R. Raza (1983), 'Basic Needs Approach to Rural Poverty in Nigeria', in U. Igbozurike and R. Raza (eds), *Rural Nigeria: Development and Quality of Life*. ARMTI Seminar Series, no. 3. Ilorin.

E. Reusse (1987), 'Liberalization and Agricultural Marketing', *Food Policy*, vol. 12, no. 4.

B. Sanda (1985), *The Problem with Nigeria*. Ibadan.

R. Sandbrook (1985), *The Politics of Africa's Economic Stagnation*. Cambridge: Cambridge University Press.

S. Scherr (1989), 'Agriculture in an Export Boom Economy: A Comparative Analysis of Policy and Performance in Indonesia, Mexico and Nigeria', *World Development*, vol. 17, no 4.

C. Scott (1989), Seminar. Queen Elizabeth House, Oxford. 7 March.

T. Shanin (1989), 'Peasantry in Political Action', in T. Shanin (ed.), *Peasants and Peasant Societies*, 2nd edn. Oxford: Blackwell.

R. Shenton (1987), 'Nigerian Agriculture in Historical Perspective: Development and Crisis, 1900–60', in M. Watts (ed.), *State, Oil and Agriculture in Nigeria*. Berkeley: University of California Press.

N. Tallroth (1987), 'Structural Adjustment in Nigeria', *Finance and Development*, September.

M. Tiffen (1976), *The Enterprising Peasant: Economic Development in Gombe Emirate, North Eastern State, Nigeria, 1900–1968*. London: HMSO.

S. Titilola (1987), 'The Impact of the Structural Adjustment Programme . . . on the Agricultural and Rural Economy of Nigeria', in A. Phillips and E. Ndekwu (eds), *Structural Adjustment Programme in a Developing Economy: The Case of Nigeria*. Ibadan: NISER.

E. Toyo (1985), 'Neocolonialism, Primitive Accumulation, and Third World Orientations', *Nigerian Journal of Political Science*, vol. 4, nos 1 and 2.

—— (1986), 'Food and Hunger in a Petroleum Neocolony: A Study of the Food Crisis in Nigeria', in P. Lawrence (ed.), *World Recession and the Food Crisis in Africa*. London: James Currey ROAPE.

E. Usoro (1987), 'Development of the Nigerian Agricultural Sector Within the Framework of the Structural Adjustment Programme', in A. Phillips and E. Ndekwu (eds), *Structural Adjustment Programme in a Developing Economy: The Case of Nigeria*. Ibadan: NISER.

N. Van Hear (1989), 'Nigeria Loses Zest for Reform', *South*, August.

J. Voh (1983), 'Farmers' Levels of Satisfaction with Rural Infrastructure in Selected Communities in Kano State', in U. Igbozurike and R. Raza (eds), *Rural Nigeria: Development and Quality of Life*. ARMTI Seminar Series, no. 3. Ilorin.

T. Wallace (1978/9), 'Planning for Agricultural Development: A Consideration of Some of the Theoretical and Practical Issues Involved', *The Nigerian Journal of Public Affairs*, vol. VIII.

—— (1980), 'Agricultural Projects and Land in Northern Nigeria', *Review of African Political Economy*, no. 17, January–April.

M. Watts (1983), *Silent Violence: Food, Famine and Peasantry in Northern Nigeria*. Berkeley: University of California Press.

—— (1987a), 'Agriculture and Oil-Based Accumulation: Stagnation or Transformation?', in M. Watts (ed.), *State, Oil and Agriculture in Nigeria*. Berkeley: University of California Press.

—— (1987b), 'Introduction', in M. Watts (ed.), *State, Oil and Agriculture in Nigeria*. Berkeley: University of California Press.

G. Williams (1988), 'Land and Freedom' (mimeo). Oxford.

—— (1989), 'The World Bank in Nigeria Revisited', *Review of African Political Economy*, no. 43.

World Bank (1987), *Nigeria: Agricultural Sector Review*. Washington.

JIBRIN IBRAHIM

The Transition
to Civil Rule:
Sapping Democracy

I. Introduction

This chapter is entitled the transition to civil rule rather than the transition to democratic rule because the conditions of the transition programme are leading towards increased authoritarianism.[1] At the economic level, the difficult conditions imposed by the Structural Adjustment Programme (SAP) of the Nigerian state are leading towards increased unemployment, inflation, scarcity and the consequent decline in the standard of living. This problem translates at the political level into increased public contestation on the one hand and massive state repression on the other.

The essential problematic posed for Nigerian democracy relates to the way in which the neo-patrimonial manner which capitalism is developing in the country leads to increased utilization and control of public resources in an undemocratic manner.[2] This means that, presently, democracy is a threat to the bourgeoisie because it threatens their means of accumulation in addition to amplifying intra-bourgeois conflicts thus threatening the very existence of the proverbial goose (the state) that lays the golden eggs (the national cake). For the people, democracy is an important means of acquiring suitable conditions of struggle for improved economic and political standards of living. The most dangerous effect of the on-going adjustment programme and the attached Political Transition Programme (PTP) is the narrowing of the space for popular participation in the struggle to improve economic and political standards of living.

II. Dominating Nigeria and Nigerians

On 2 October 1985, President Ibrahim Babangida called on the Nigerian people formally to debate the merits and/or demerits of taking a loan from the IMF and implementing the linked conditionality of a structural adjustment programme with devaluation as its centre-piece. The President argued that the people should break the deadlock that had existed between the government and the IMF since 1982 and promised that 'all our decisions must be governed by the yearnings and aspirations of the Nigerian people [and] . . . it is the decision of the people that we will carry along to the negotiation table' (*New Nigerian*, 27 September 1985).

A panel was established to monitor the debate and report on the conclusions reached

129

by Nigerians. Within three months, 4,200 contributions had been received, 65 per cent of which rejected both the loan and the attached SAP conditionality (*The Punch*, 6 December 1985). This rapid and clear response resulted from the fact that, since the 1982 Economic Stabilization Act introduced by the Shagari administration, a heated debate had been raging in the country on the measures necessary for tackling the national economic crisis first brought to the notice of the public by the late Obafemi Anolowo, and initially denied but later admitted by the government of the day. Both the Shagari and succeeding Buhari administrations opted for anti-people solutions based on mass retrenchments and massive repression in their bid to tackle the crisis. The discontent generated by their policies created favourable conditions for the *coup d'état* which overthrew the two regimes. This was the reason why Nigerians took Babangida's call for a national debate seriously and gave him a very clear verdict.

In a pertinent and well-reasoned contribution to the debate, Professor Sam Oyovbaire argued that the issue posed was not just one of structural adjustment of the economy and transformation of social relations of production but also a major political debate over 'the exercise and consequences of power' in which the IMF was an instrument to recolonize the country and deepen its 'dependence and subservience in the world capitalist system' (*National Concord*, 2 and 9 November 1985). It would seem that this 'complete subservience' has been established and both the country and its inhabitants are now completely dominated by the political and economic logic imposed by SAP. This logic reserves for the Nigerian state the role of repressing its people so that Washington can impose its SAP.

How else could one explain the fact that although the popular verdict in the IMF debate was a firm rejection of SAP, the government went ahead to implement it anyway? In fact, the government became increasingly unwilling to allow discussion, let alone dissension, on the issue. During the 1989 OAU Summit, for example, Professor Adebayo Adedeji, the ECA Chairman, presented his proposals for an 'African Alternative Framework to Structural Adjustment Programmes' (AAF–SAP). Rather than joining the debate on how Africans could solve their economic problems, the Head of the Nigerian Delegation, Admiral Augustus Aikhomu, declared brusquely that 'the Nigerian government does not believe that there is an alternative to SAP . . . nor is there an Alternative African Framework' (*West Africa*, 14 August 1989: 1332). Since June 1989, when General Babangida started what was to become a ritual declaration that 'there is no alternative to SAP', there has been a concerted effort by the government and its security agencies to prevent any discussion on the issue.

The most glaring example of this anti-debate stance was the police raid in June 1989 to prevent intellectuals, journalists, labour leaders and lawyers committed to civil rights discussing alternatives to SAP. Three of the speakers, Gani Fawehinmi, Tai Solarin and Micheal Imoudu, were detained for some time for daring to discuss their country's future. We shall return to this unwillingness by the state to accept the exercise by its citizens of their civil rights in the section on the 'Gani Fawehinmi Saga' below. On numerous other occasions, however, the security forces stopped public debates and symposia on SAP. On a wider scale, the major objective of the state seems to be to restrict popular participation in the political process so as to be able to impose SAP measures.

III. Shrinking the Political Arena

According to Nelson Kasfir (1976: 227), de-participation is the most striking feature of political change in post-independence Africa. The political arena is shrinking as

African states actively promote de-participation by 'strengthening the central administration' and assuring the 'desuetude of participatory structures'. The PTP of the Babangida administration is a project that is clearly aimed at reducing the Nigerian political arena and consequently restricting democratic and popular participation.

For the first time in Nigerian history, a constitution limits the number of political parties to be registered and in fact reduces their number to two. It should be recalled that even though the tripartite system of the First Republic was relatively exclusionary, especially towards the minorities, there were no limits on the number of parties that could be established. Similarly, during the Second Republic, although only five parties were registered, there were no constitutional restrictions to party formation except those that related to national spread and the absence of discrimination. Past constitutions, therefore, had some room for manœuvre for sociological and ideological minorities who could legally form parties and struggle to maintain and expand their political space. It is this possibility that the state has decided to block by PTP. By imposing a bi-partisan system, the multiplicity of groups, forces, ideologies, interests, parties, etc. that have helped create a culture of democratic struggle in Nigeria could be forced to coalate into two political oligarchies. And the logic determining two political oligarchies also determines one because it is difficult for a sole opposition party, excluded from power and subjected to the carrot and stick tactics of harassment and incorporation, to be able to resist.

If it tries to resist, the bureaucratic machine could always be used as a caveat to refuse to recognize 'trouble makers' as bona fide members of the party. This attempt at restricting the political arena is aimed at breaking the democratic drive embedded in Nigerian civil society. Guy Hermet (1984: 99) has correctly argued that a democratic drive is nourished by contradictory elements – in particular the growth of the desire for popular participation faced with sociological 'suffrage censoring'. The implication of this is that although the objective of the state is to sap the democratic drive by restricting the field of political struggle, the result is often the opposite. Civil society tends to revitalize its resistance and the struggle for civil and democratic rights is heightened. This can be seen clearly in the battles currently raging in the Nigerian mass media, its trade, professional and students' unions and in its judicial process.

IV. Sapping the Mass Media?

The Nigerian mass media have a very long and rich history. The written press in particular developed into a major force in the 1880s and was manned by independent journalists who had been excluded from the colonial system in spite of their high level of education. They established a tradition of combative journalism committed to the improvement of civil and democratic rights in the country and by so doing created a relatively free press. Succeeding political regimes, alarmed by a press they considered too powerful, have always tried to emasculate media organs, although their efforts are rarely completely successful.

In 1903, the Newspapers Ordinance was passed to control the press and in 1909 a Sedition Ordinance was passed to strengthen the first law. Journalists such as Herbert Macaulay were imprisoned several times under these laws. With independence, the anti-press laws were strengthened instead of being relaxed. In 1962, an Official Secrets Act was enacted. (It was under this law that *Newbreed* and *Newswatch* magazines were proscribed in 1978 and 1987 respectively.) The 1903 Ordinance was strengthened with the 1964 Newspapers (Amendment) Act and in 1984 the Public Officers (Protection Against False Accusation) Decree was enacted to establish finally that 'protection of public servants' rather than 'truth' should be the basic principle of journalism. Although the Babangida regime abrogated this last decree, its attitude towards the press has been even more authoritarian than that of its predecessors. Chief of General Staff Aikhomu warned chief executives of Federal- and state-owned media that they 'will henceforth be held responsible for any adverse stories published by their organs. . . . It would be an offence for any of their organs to criticise government policy' (*Reporter*, 11 February 1988).

Even more obnoxious is the elaboration of what has come to be known as the 'Momoh doctrine', enunciated by the former Minister of Information in October 1987. It objects to the reporting in the press of the harassment of journalists because:

> these reports themselves could amount to abuse of forum because there may well have been many other Nigerians in many other areas of calling who were also invited [by security men to be harassed], whose invitation was not reported. (*African Concord*, 16 August 1988)

Since this declaration, scores of journalists have been detained and harassed by security officials. In May 1988, for example, Osazuwa Osagi was detained for one week because of a cartoon he drew for the *National Concord* which depicted the collaboration between the military government and Western powers in imposing the anti-people IMF measures. In June 1988, Nduka Obaigbena was arrested for his story in *Thisweek* on the power play within the government. The examples are endless.

The most dramatic and potentially the most dangerous development under the Babangida regime was the assassination of Dele Giwa, a popular journalist and editor of *Newswatch*, by a parcel bomb in 1986. This is the first case of murder in the 130-year-old history of Nigerian journalism. As Nigerian editors are obliged to print their home addresses on all newspapers, the implications of this permanent threat of the 'final solution' are clear. The level of resistance of the Nigerian mass media has, however, remained high and they continue to expose and criticize the excesses of the regime.

Even the economic crisis has not cowed the number or vigour of Nigeria's media establishments. In 1987, Nigeria had 23 dailies, 39 weeklies, 9 vernacular newspapers, 54 magazines, 29 radio stations and 32 television stations (*West Africa*, 16 February 1987). Since then many more have sprung up in preparation for the political transition process. This huge mass media constitutes a formidable challenge to arbitrary government action.

V. Sapping Trade, Professional and Students' Unions?

The dynamism of trade, professional and students' unions in Nigeria is one of the clearest signs of the democratic drive embedded in its civil society. The ability of trade unions to carry out their basic functions of struggling to improve the material and social conditions of labour is itself an important aspect of the democratic struggle. The trade union movement, in conjunction with progressive movements and organizations, has consistently fought for the rights of the common man. Little wonder then that the Nigerian state has always tried to destroy trade unionism. In 1977–8, for example, there was a massive purge of 'Marxist' elements from the leadership of the trade union movement. The most prominent radical unionists were banned and a new central labour organization, the Nigeria Labour Congress (NLC), was established. During the NLC elections, another generation of radical unionists under the leadership of Hassan Sunmonu emerged. In addition, a common front was created between the NLC, the National Association of Nigerian Students (NANS) and the Academic Staff

Union of Universities (ASUU) to organize popular struggles for improved conditions of life as well as to resist state repression.

This front has been playing a major role in the struggle against SAP. In May 1986, students protesting against an authoritarian university administration and against SAP measures such as spiralling prices and the reduction of social services, introduction of school and hospital fees, mass retrenchments, etc. were fired upon by armed policemen. At least seven students were reported to have been killed. This was followed by mass solidarity demonstrations and protests all over the country, which were also massively repressed. Similar mass demonstrations occurred in April 1988 in which market women and other elements joined demonstrating workers and students in towns such as Jos and Ilorin. Ten people were shot dead in Jos, while in Kano government cereal stores were broken into by hungry people. In May 1989, at least 58 people were killed in two weeks of mass protests against SAP (*West Africa*, 12 June 1989). The response of the state has consistently been to harass or dissolve all organizations that dare to protest against its excesses. ASUU was disaffiliated from the NLC in July 1986 and proscribed in July 1988. The students' organization, NANS, has been operating in illegality for over ten years. Even the NLC was dissolved and handed over to an administrator to be reorganized (read tamed) in 1988.

VI. Sapping Civil Liberties?

Nigeria has a judicial machine that operates in a relatively non-arbitrary manner with some respect for due process, the rule of law and the possibility of protecting civil liberties. This judicial machine has, however, come under increasing pressure to reorient itself to serve uniquely the interests of the state rather than protect the civil liberties of citizens. The principles of the rule of law have themselves been increasingly threatened by the state in recent years and the consequent arbitrariness in fact openly justified. In his speech to the 1989 Conference of the Nigerian Bar Association (NBA), the Chief Justice of the Federation, Mohammed Bello, argued that

> The so-called crisis in the rule of law in Nigeria lies in the resolution of the conflict between traditional constitutionalism and the supremacy of the decrees of the Federal Military Government . . . during a military regime, some elements of constitutionalism have to be sacrificed in the interest of security and public order. (*West Africa*, 11 September 1989)

In his response, Alao Aka-Bashorun, the then President of the NBA, correctly pointed out that, in their attempt to destroy the rule of law, the military were unwilling 'even to abide by their own decrees'.

Decree no. 2 of 1984, which is still in force, allows the Chief of General Staff to detain citizens for extended periods without taking them to court. The decree suspends the important instrument of habeas corpus that citizens could use to compel the state to produce detainees in court. It should be remembered that in April 1961 three 'National Government' leaders, Ahmadu Bello, Micheal Okpara and Tafawa Balewa, met and decided to enact this type of detention law but resistance to their plans was too strong (*African Concord*, 16 August 1988: 16). It has taken the Nigerian state 23 years of 'effort' to be able to impose this repugnant law.

The Nigerian legal system is, however, still in a fairly combative mood. In 1984, the whole legal profession rose against the suspension of due process and systematization of military tribunals to 'persecute' rather than 'prosecute' politicians. They are now trying to resist the authoritarian excesses of the Babangida regime. One of the poles around which the struggle is being organized revolves around the various cases being fought by Gani Fawehinmi.

VII. The Gani Fawehinmi Saga

The assassination of Dele Giwa, editor of *Newswatch* magazine, has popularized an important civil liberties struggle in which Gani Fawehinmi has been playing an important role. At the root of this case was an interrogation and a threat Dele Giwa was said to have received, just before his death, from Colonel Halilu Akilu, the Director of Military Intelligence, and Lieutenant Colonel A.K. Togun, Deputy Director of State Security, over a lead story he was preparing. In spite of the suspicious circumstances that surrounded his death, the Director of Public Prosecutions was unwilling to prosecute the two officers, and a private lawyer, Gani Fawehinmi, decided to take the matter up in court. In a historic judgement delivered on 18 December 1987, the Supreme Court upheld the right of private persons to prosecute criminal cases that have not been taken up by the Public Prosecution Department. While the numerous substantive cases raised by the judgement were still in court, the state and some of its agencies started a veritable campaign of systematic harassment against Fawehinmi.

In June 1988, 496 copies of the book he had written on the case, *The Murder of Dele Giwa: The Right of a Private Prosecutor*, were seized by agents of the State Security Service (SSS). In September 1988, on returning from medical treatment in London, his passport was seized by the SSS. On 1 June 1989, he lost all his five cases against the government in a row and on the same day in Justice Mamman Nasir's Appeal Court. The following day, 2 June 1989, he was sentenced to pay an unprecedented N6 million for the libel of the two security chiefs, Halilu Akilu and Kunle Togun.

Two weeks later, on 17 June 1989, Gani Fawehinmi was arrested, together with 89-year-old veteran labour leader Micheal Imoudu and social critic Tai Solarin, and while the two others were released almost immediately, he was detained for 121 days, up until 15 October 1989, at an obscure prison at Gashua, without reading material or treatment for his hypertension. Public outcry against his detention forced the government to take him to court.

On 15 September 1989, he was arraigned before the Transition to Civil Rule Tribunal and the main charge against him was his opposition to SAP. As the prosecution said:

> That you Chief Gani Fawehinmi in or about the month of March 1989 at Lagos caused to be published in a publication in the form of a special interview in the *New Horizon*, Nigeria's Marxist monthly, vol. 9, no. 3, March 1989: '. . . A system that has worsened the plight of the workers must not be embraced by the workers. For once, the workers should take a new direction socio-economically opposed to the present direction, which has led them to the abyss of discomfort. A system that has denied them the right to free education, employment and good shelter. . . . This government is infested with socio-economic AIDS and it cannot deliver a socio-economic AIDS-free civilian regime'.

The message from the state is very clear: it is a culpable offence for citizens to complain about the dramatic decline in their standard of life or to wish for a better life programme, as is titled one of the government's propaganda stunts.

Although Fawehinmi was released in October 1989 and the anti-SAP charges were subsequently withdrawn, a new chapter had been prepared for him. Three months after his release from Gashua prison, Fawehinmi was sentenced to twelve months by Justice Ligali Ayorinde of the Lagos High Court allegedly for contempt. The sentence was later reversed by a higher court. According to the Judge, seeking to justify his harsh action, there has been a 'scandalous, intimidating campaign deliberately embarked upon by Fawehinmi to lower the integrity of myself and the High Court of Justice'

(*African Guardian*, 15 January 1990: 14). The said contempt was a 17-point affidavit concerning a stay of execution of the N6 million awarded against him. Fawehinmi had asked that the case be transferred away from Ayorinde's Court because he had consistently lost his cases there.

Gani Fawehinmi is, however, a fighter and he refuses to be intimidated. He has actually been a social crusader for a very long time. He first came into public notice in 1969 when he defended Bala Abashe, a factory hand, whose wife, Hannatu, had been 'appropriated' by Andrew Obeya, the then Secretary of the Benue-Plateau government. For daring to embarrass a highly-placed government official by taking him to court, Fawehinmi was detained for seven months. In 1978, he was charged and detained for allegedly assaulting two policemen and 'stealing' a government camera. All that happened, however, was that he and striking NUNS student leaders meeting in his office had been harassed by policemen during the 'Ali must go' crisis. During the Gowon regime, Fawehinmi was said to have 'single handedly handled 55 out of the 65 detention cases' (*African Guardian*, 15 January 1990: 15).

Fawehinmi has not been the only civil rights crusader in Nigeria, even if he is one of the most spectacular. We have already argued that there is a rich tradition of the struggle for human and civil rights in Nigeria. In recent years, the struggle by lawyers and other activists for these rights has been assuming a sharper organizational focus. The Nigerian Bar Association has become more openly assertive of its commitment to the rule of law. In 1985, the National Association of Democratic Lawyers (NADL) was formed and in 1989 a Committee for the Defence of Human Rights (CDHR) under the chairmanship of Dr Beko Ransome-Kuti was created to broaden the struggle for human rights beyond the legal arena.

One of the most significant developments in this regard, however, was the formation in October 1987 of the Civil Liberties Organization (CLO). In its inaugural statement, it emphasized that 'mass violations of human rights in Nigeria occur as a result of deliberate government violations or as a result of government omissions to monitor the efficiency of its agencies, units or laws' (*Newswatch*, 25 September 1989). In May and in December 1988, the CLO published reports on human rights violation in Nigeria as a working document to help in the fight against arbitrariness by the state and its agents. The reports covered the use of banning and proscription orders against associations, dissolution of executive committees of labour unions, deportations of foreigners, suspensions and sackings of government journalists, and the harassment of dissenters. They have taken up the defence of hundreds of persons detained under Decree no. 2 or those detained for long periods while their cases were pending. They also revealed the existence of a penal island – Ita Oko – four hours into the Atlantic, where prisoners were kept surrounded by crocodiles, alligators and sharks.

The protection and deepening of democracy in society requires that civil society enjoys a certain level of relative autonomy *vis-à-vis* the state. In Nigeria, the relative autonomy enjoyed by the mass media, trade, professional and students' unions, as well as the judicial system, has allowed watch dogs against excesses by those in control of state power to operate and thus permitted the protection of minimum levels of civil and democratic rights. This relative autonomy is now subjected to serious assaults by the state, as we have shown above, and although the capacity for resistance has been significantly high, the level of repression under Babangida's PTP matches it. In addition, it is not only the strength of civil society that is being sapped, but the political class and the political process themselves.

VIII. Programme of Successive Political Exclusion: Sapping Democracy

By 3 May 1989, the day President Babangida announced the promulgation of the 'new' constitution and the lifting of the ban on civilian political activities, a large section of public opinion was sceptical about the regime's willingness to withdraw from the political arena. The military government had taken too many decisions on behalf of the people. The proposals of the numerous transition bodies – Constitution Review Committee, Political Bureau, Constituent Assembly, etc. – have been accepted only to the extent that their views have coincided with those of the government. On a number of important questions, they have been given directives on what they can or cannot decide.

The political transition programme is a clear agenda for shrinking not only the number of political actors but also the political arena itself. We have already mentioned that the new constitution formally limits the number of political parties to two. By imposing a bi-partisan system, the multiplicity of groups, forces, ideologies, interests and parties, among other factors that have helped create a democratic culture in Nigeria, could easily be excluded from the official political space. The question posed, however, goes beyond that of political parties and organizations. All existing and potential political forces in the country are being destabilized, or even destroyed, in a very systematic manner. Starting from influential soldiers, old politicians, rich politicians, new politicians to socialists and so-called 'extremists', everybody is being destabilized.

The Military Party

It was former President Shehu Shagari who argued that there were only two political parties in Nigeria, the military and the National Party of Nigeria. Nobody doubts that the Nigerian Army is virtually a political party composed of men who have no antipathies to political power and its perquisites. It is clear today that the faction of the military party that took over power in 1985 has shrunk into a 'one man show', or as a former military officer put it, 'Babangida has been able to prove he is his own junta' (*African Guardian*, 15 January 1990).

Most of the 'strongmen' of the original junta have been thrown out. It started in a tragic manner in March 1986 when one night Nigerians were informed that there had been an attempted *coup d'état* and that ten of the top officers involved had already been executed. Among them was Major-General Mamman Vatsa, a member of the Armed Forces Ruling Council (AFRC) and childhood friend of the President. In October of the same year, Chief of General Staff Commodore Ebitu Ukiwe was unceremoniously sacked by the Head of State. Numerous changes of ministers, governors and military commanders were to follow in the next three years. In February 1989, the Armed Forces Ruling Council itself was dissolved and a new one reconstituted by the President. In December of the same year, he removed General Bali, doyen of the officer corps, from his post of Minister of Defence and Chairman of the Joint Chiefs of Staff. The service chiefs of the Navy, Airforce and Police were similarly removed. In the words of a leading analyst of power politics in Nigeria, 'no previous Nigerian leader has established a firmer grip over the military hierarchy and indeed the country as Babangida has done' (Othman, 1989: 142).

The Political Class

The Nigerian political class has also received a thorough bashing. Initially, the government announced that corrupt and old politicians would be excluded from the Third Republic. By the time the banning order was issued in September 1987, the list had been enlarged to include almost the totality of those who had held political office in all preceding civilian and military regimes. The aim, according to General Babangida, was 'to develop a new political culture and leadership' (*West Africa*, 15 October 1987) while the framework was the two-party system. What was striking about the proposed PTP was that only 'new' political actors with a lot of money could participate in the process.

To determine the two political parties to be registered, the National Electoral Commission (NEC) and the government imposed very expensive and virtually impossible preconditions that only the upper section of the bourgeoisie or old politicians with established networks could have afforded or met. In three months, the parties were to establish well-equipped offices with at least three paid staff in all the 435 local government areas in the country. In addition, they were to supply 25 copies of the names, photographs and personal details of at least 200 members from each local government (making at least 87,000 files) to the NEC. For good measure, prospective parties were to submit their applications with a registration fee of N50,000. In spite of these draconian measures, 13 parties were able to submit their files before the deadline. In a broadcast to the nation on 6 October 1989, the Head of State in a perfect Catch-22 scenario used the argument that the 'impossible' preconditions had not been perfectly adhered to as a justification to refuse to register any of the parties. The political parties, he said, had

> failed to comply with key conditions in the guidelines such as documentation on members, declaration of assets and liabilities of individual members of the national executive committees . . . most of them [parties] had operated underground prior to the lifting of the ban on politics on 3rd May 1989 . . . [and] had deep roots in the party politics of the First and Second Republics. There were very strong indications of the wealthy individuals in the executive committees of the associations that confirm fears that they were being hijacked by money bags.

As if any mass party in the world could give exact and detailed information on its members at any point in time or as if politics could be played without historical connections to previous actors, issues, interests and formations or as if rich citizens could (or should) be prevented from investing wealth to reap power.

Be that as it may, the government decided to dissolve all the 13 parties and create two new ones for the 'ordinary people' – the Social Democratic Party and the National Republican Convention, with the former leaning 'a little to the left of centre' and the latter leaning 'a little to the right of centre'. In addition, the government drew up the manifestos of the two parties, and decided to fund and staff them, before calling on individuals (as opposed to organized groups) to sign up. In other words, the military government has decided to define and apply each 'democratic' step on behalf of the people. Has the age of pro-forma democracy arrived?

Pro-forma Democracy

Odia Ofeimun correctly notes that one of the most significant aspects of the PTP is 'to turn bureaucratisation into a reason of state for the two parties of the Third Republic' (*West Africa*, 18 December 1989). Apart from imposing manifestos and constitutions (with a very artificial and binary distinction between left of centre and right of centre) on the two parties, excessive powers were given to government-appointed Administrative Secretaries to organize their launch. These bureaucrats were supposed to encourage grassroots participatory democracy but were told to exclude 'undue radicals', socialists, anti-SAP agitators as well as ideological and religious extremists, whatever that may mean.[3] Some analysts believed that the grounds were being prepared for the newly elected local government councillors, the first democratically elected councillors in over a decade. In July 1989, however, all the councils were dissolved and replaced by state-appointed bureaucrats. Meanwhile, the Directorate of Social Mobilization has announced that it will provide paramilitary training to 22,500 youth who will form an 'anti-thuggery squad' to ensure that the right people are elected (*Guardian*, 28 August 1989).

IX. Conclusion

Nigeria enjoys one of the most advanced democratic cultures in Africa because of certain specificities in its historical evolution (see Ibrahim, 1989a). In particular, it has developed a civil and a political society, strong enough to block the emergence of a hegemonic bloc that could have turned into an outright dictatorship. The political engineering being implemented under the PTP is, however, eroding that tradition and the stated objectives of the government are sometimes contradictory. For example, while frequently affirming his commitment of transferring power to democratically elected civilians, President Babangida complains about plots of 'civilian coups'. He even went as far as calling on the military to be vigilant against civilians disgracing them out of office, a statement considered by many as inciting the army against the people (*Newswatch*, 19 June 1989).

It is becoming increasingly clear that democracy is never given; it is obtained. In this respect, Nigerian civil society has a rich tradition of struggle for civil and human rights. The mass media, trade and professional unions and the judicial system have evolved as bulwarks against state arbitrariness. This democratic drive is, however, confronted by a strong authoritarian will exhibited by succeeding regimes who need repression to maintain their power and the 'fruits' it provides. Finally, the point should be made that the preservation of democracy is not a simple function of assets and problems, it is also a question of historical will. Nigerians have demonstrated a will to preserve hard-won democratic rights, and if they are trained in the art of provocation, they are also trained in the art of compromise.

Notes

1. For more details on the democracy/authoritarianism problematic in Nigeria, see Bangura, 1989, and Ibrahim, 1986, and 1990.
2. See Ibrahim 1989a, for a more extensive discussion on the negative consequences of neo-patrimonial accumulation on Nigeria's democratic culture.
3. One of the problems of reducing political space and political choice while simultaneously imposing difficult conditions for economic survival is the possibility of 'religious extremism' emerging as the only perceived solution. The bi-partisan framework poses the risk of reducing a multitude of political forces into two antagonistic forces – 'Christian warriors' versus 'Muslim warriors' (Ibrahim, 1989b).

References

Y. Bangura (1989b), 'Authoritarianism and Democracy in Africa: A Theoretical Discourse'. (Seminar paper). Uppsala: AKUT.

G. Hermet (1984), 'Comment naissent les democraties?', *Esprit*, no. 6, June.

J. Ibrahim (1986), 'The Political Debate and the Struggle for Democracy in Nigeria', *Review of African Political Economy*, no. 37, December.

—— (1988), 'La société contre le bipartisme', *Politique Africaine*, no. 32.

—— (1989a), 'The State, Accumulation and Democratic Forces in Nigeria'. Paper presented to AKUT Conference on 'When Does Democracy Make Sense?'. Uppsala. October.

—— (1989b), 'Some Considerations on Religion and Political Turbulence in Nigeria: Muslims, Christians, "pagans", "fundamentalists" and all that . . .'. Paper presented at Social Movements Seminar, Institute of Social Studies, The Hague. 16 October.

—— (1990), 'Succession Politique et Crispation Sociale au Nigeria: 1987–1988', *Année Africaine* (1987–8). Bordeaux: Pedone.

N. Kasfir (1976), *The Shrinking Political Arena*. Berkeley: University of California Press.

S. Othman (1989), 'Nigeria: Power for Profit-Class, Corporatism, and Factionalism in the Military', in Donal Cruise O'Brien et al. (eds), *Contemporary West African States*. Cambridge: Cambridge University Press.

Index

141

Lightning Source UK Ltd.
Milton Keynes UK
UKHW022157130921
390498UK00005B/474